POOR LITTLE THII

'THEY THAT SHALL ENDURE'

by

BETTY JONES

CONTENTS

Introduction

Acknowledgements

INTRODUCTION

This book was written by my mother, Mary Elizabeth Jones (Betty) born on Friday 13th January 1922. Weighing only 4½ pounds at birth, her grandmother said to her daughter "You'll never rear her; but I shouldn't worry; she's only a poor little thing". Betty lived to be 94 years old; passing away on 30th March 2016.

Betty's story is one of ordinary people – the extraordinary fact being that three generations span 156 years. Her father was 56 years old when she was born; her grandfather was 58 when that son arrived. Betty was 42 when I was born in 1964. Me being her son, Clive Smith, editor and publisher of this book.

The theme of ageing parents is consistent. It is clear that my mother was in awe of her mother. My memories of moving house include the transferring of antique furniture, Wedgewood plates and various ornaments, the origin of which were unknown to me. My job was to dust and polish them – as task I disliked immensely. She also brought vast quantities of letters, diaries and photographs. These were stored in boxes in various attics and only since my mother's death have I started the task of going through them and understanding how many memories she wanted to hold onto.

Betty wrote a letter to The SAGA magazine in 2003 on the subject of older parents.

£50 letter Older parents

My father was born in 1866; his father in 1808 and my son in 1964. I therefore feel that I have a qualification for commenting on "elderly" fathers – and mothers.

My father was a cabinet maker, having served a seven year apprenticeship from 1880 when furniture was made with hand tools. I was born in 1922 of a second wife, father being 56 and mother 39. The years between the wars being economically harsh, and father never having learnt how to use electrical tools, he would sometimes earn only 2/6d a week for fixing a sash cord. My mother took in lodgers and in 1934 turned the front room of our rented terrace house into a shop, selling furniture and carpets. During the war it became a second-hand shop.

I can only remember my father as an old man, though he rode a bicycle well into his seventies and was still working at 83. He would play with me, getting down on his hands and knees to be a horse for me and letting me perch on his knees as he lay in bed, then straighten his legs so that I came down with a bump.

He was a very kindly man, but money was always in short supply. From the age of 23 until I was 35 I saved a quarter of my salary for a home of my own; my mother had saved tiny amounts from 1906 for the same purpose. Father had always been deaf; from 1949 he was blind as well. By 1956 the stairs were very difficult for my severely arthritic mother. There was no bathroom and the lavatory was across the yard. But with the money saved and a small mortgage it was possible to buy a bungalow.

Riches do not necessarily make for happiness, but if there is sufficient money, children of older parents may well benefit. It was, for me at times, a burden and a responsibility, but how much better it was than to be unloved, harshly treated or neglected.

I am happier now than at any time in my life: I would not wish to return to my youth.

BETTY PRESTON, MANCHESTER, BY E-MAIL

She began to write the manuscript in 1977 using her trusty blue Parker fountain pen and it amounts to 148 pages of A4 covering the first 18 chapters. The new technology of an Amstrad word processor was embraced in the 1980's and the last seven chapters were completed by 2003 using a personal computer. Over 100 pages of photographs with descriptions taken from albums dating back to the late 19th Century were collated within the hand written manuscript.

Huge social changes have taken place since the birth of my great grandfather around 1808. From humble upbringings - poverty, limited schooling, caring for parents and siblings, life in domestic service as the only choice for women, the loss of a generation in the Great War, the great depression and the Second World War - to the transformed way of life in what I consider to be "modern" Britain.

Technology has unleashed a wealth of information about our recent past. Books, television programmes and films are numerous. My mother's account is exceptional in that it brings to life the people involved. Individuals, places and dates are precise and uncensored.

This is a true story of real people.

Clive Smith.

January 2020.

ACKNOWLEDGEMENTS

During the 1980's to the 2000's her niece, Eveline Shore (nee Coomer), wrote letters to Betty with information on their shared family ancestry. Pre-internet days, Eveline completed this task by visiting records offices, parish churches and cemeteries.

Eveline Shore (nee Coomer) in 2008

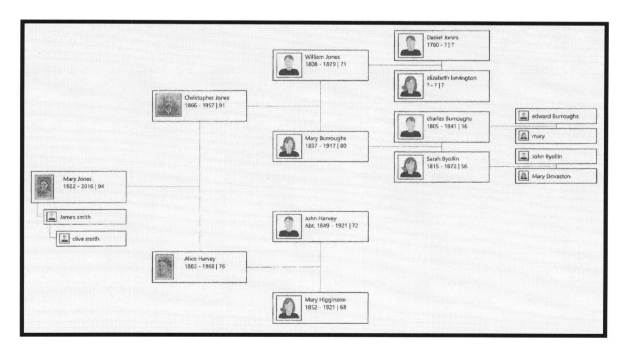

Betty Jones – Family Tree

1: MY FATHER - CHRISTOPHER GEORGE JONES
(7th July 1866 – 28th Nov 1957)

My paternal grandfather, William Robinson Jones, was born in 1808 during Napoleonic times. He married his first wife, Elizabeth Cooper, in 1828, and seventeen children were born to them. Few seem to have survived. The only survivor about whom there is any information was Frederick Daniel Jones, born in 1845. My father was much attached to this stepbrother perhaps because they both shared the same love of music. Frederick is recorded living in three different places; in St. Helens, where he was a church organist; in Corwen, Wales, where he worked for the Inland Revenue - as his copy of 'Elijah' now in my possession proves and in Lewes where for his services he was presented with a marble clock. This stood on our mantlepiece at West Brampton and accompanied us whenever we removed but has now been given to Peter Shore, Eveline Shore's younger son.

Eveline, motivated by her mother's belief that she was descended from Anne Boleyn (which would have been difficult), did some research on my paternal grandmother who was born Mary Burroughs, born 1837, daughter of Charles Burroughs, born in Cockshutt near Ellesmere in Shropshire in 1805 and whose splendid tomb is in the churchyard there. The family home - now a farm - is also there. Charles married a Sarah Byollin (hence the confusion over Boleyn!) and died when only 35. His widow remarried a man called Lloyd and produced a family by him. Eveline suggests that Mary was fostered out and must have had a hard life. She married my grandfather on 7th December 1864 - he being 56 and she 27. The first child of this marriage, Mary Elizabeth, was born 6th February 1865, followed by Christopher George (my father) 7th July 1866, Alfred Edwin (1869 - died aged 3), Frank Burroughs, born 14th January 1870 and Josiah Charles, born 28th October 1872.

William Robinson Jones was a stay maker (corsetiere) in Newcastle under Lyme in the days of whalebone and resided in Merrial Street although the 1861 census indicates that he was then living in the Ironmarket with his first wife, Frederick, aged 16, Martha Ann aged 11, an assistant called John Dobson and a tailor called Thompson and his family. On 30th May 1862 he was presented with a silver snuff box for his services as treasurer to the Ancient Order of Foresters. This is still in my possession.

He died in 1879 when my father was 13 and is buried in St. George's churchyard, Newcastle -under-Lyme, where my parents later joined him.

Of my father's early years, I know very little for he was a very quiet man and also deaf - a great inhibiter of conversation. He confessed to being a very nervous child and told how he was frightened by the sudden sound of a church organ and ran terrified to his mother. He went to school in School Street, Newcastle until he was 14. His elder sister, to whom he was devoted, gained one of the first scholarships to the Orme Girls' School which was established in 1876.

The death of my grandfather must have been a severe blow to Grandma Jones, her daughter and three sons. She was undoubtedly a woman of character and determination, as she needed to be for there was no Social Security for widows and their families. Father was apprenticed to Cabinet Making, a trade of his own choice. It seems that some attempt was made to persuade him to become an upholsterer, for in that trade, for some reason, he might have become a Burgess of Newcastle, but in those days of horse hair and flock he disliked the nasal irritation caused by the dust they made and so refused.

I have the parchment indenture signed by my father, his mother and his future employer, George Mason, on 7th July 1880. It makes fascinating reading. . . ."he shall not contract Matrimony within the said term (7 years) nor play at cards or Dice Tables . . . he shall not haunt Taverns or Playhouses nor absent himself from his said Master's service day or night unlawfully " . . . And all this restraint was rewarded by 2/6d a week - rising to one guinea by the time he was 21.

I imagine that he must have been a most conscientious apprentice. Two things only remain in my mind about his working conditions. During winter the gaslight was turned off at 8am whether they could see or not. And before leaving at night, every tack, nail and screw had to be picked up off the floor and placed ready for work next day. So often am I reminded of this when I see electric lights burning all day long in offices whose huge windows should make it quite unnecessary. I doubt if many nails and screws get picked up now - except for private purposes!

The apprenticeship had run for six years when bereavement hit the family again. This time it was his beloved elder sister who died of one of the commonest Victorian diseases - consumption - when she was only 21. My father and indeed all the family must have felt her death most sharply and now he, being the eldest, was obliged to shoulder the responsibility for his mother and two younger brothers who were apprenticed to tailoring.

My father married his first wife, Florence Maud Hancock (Florrie), in 1895 when he was 29. It was not a success. His dominant mother had found him pliable and obedient until he fell in love. Now she warned him that the girl with whom he was utterly infatuated would not make him happy. It was the one occasion on which he went against his mother's wishes and in many similar circumstances he could have been right. He later recalled that as he stood at the altar he knew he had made a mistake. But then it was too late. It was a long time before the era of *"Four Weddings and a Funeral"*.

Had he been aggressive, even assertive, he might have coped with an incompetent wife. Gradually he realised that bills were unpaid, orders for work were not received and any prosperity that might have come from application to his craft did not materialise. The following year on 5th July a daughter - Eveline - was born, her father's facial features being faithfully reproduced - prominent eyes and large nose. A second girl also came along. But this time Florrie (Florence Maud) had a "white leg" - thrombosis. One dinner time she asked to be moved from the bed to a couch and when he returned home at tea time she was dead. I have often wondered how much he must have reproached himself for having moved her. The baby died and he was left, wifeless, to bring up Eveline.

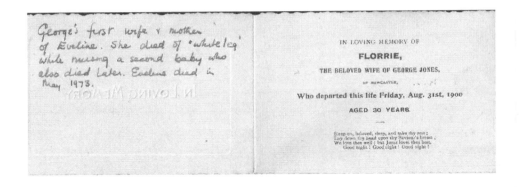

I remember reading *"Cranford"* at school as a set book and marvelling at the genius of Elizabeth Gaskell who could take triviality and transform it into a work of art. How petty were the little doings of the ladies of Cranford, yet by the alchemy of love and compassion they became humorous and even dramatic. This capacity for an understanding compassion was almost totally lacking in me when young and only as I stand back now in old age and through imagination can I attempt detachment and impartiality.

Eveline was three years old when her mother died and of her earliest years I know nothing except the suggestion by her daughter, Eveline (Shore), that there were relatives in Bridgnorth with whom she stayed. Imagination must therefore play a part. One cannot imagine that her mother was a woman of iron resolution and my father was a kindly if stubborn man. He was never intended to be in charge of children being essentially solitary - intensely happy on his own, immersed in his own thoughts and doing his work with all the skill he could muster. He had infinite patience. His solitariness was probably increased by the tendency to deafness, already mentioned, which almost totally isolated him in his later years. It was a curious disability for if you happened to tune in on the right wavelength he could hear you perfectly, but no matter what information you wanted to convey if his mind was elsewhere you could NOT make yourself understood. Consequently, there was very little conversation and indeed I cannot remember ever holding a normal conversation with my father. He had several excellent "sayings" but because of this barrier there could be no real empathy. If he disliked anything I did he would never tell me but always tell my mother to tell me. I clearly remember one occasion when very young; I was in disgrace with my mother, had been rightly punished and was in tears when my father appeared from his workshop. Saddened no doubt by my tears he produced a halfpenny for me. I clearly remember the contempt I felt for someone who rewarded wrong doing.

So what hope was there for Eveline to receive a reasonable, sensible and disciplined upbringing? Guilt ridden by the death of his wife and still remembering the death of his beloved sister he spoilt her by leniency and possibly even lack of supervision. When Eveline was ill as she often was, he would pace up and down outside the house in fear lest she too would die. Grandma Jones must have borne the brunt of his incompetence, but she was by now over 60 and far more interested in the Mormon religion than was reasonable. My father remembered the visitation of thick bearded men with horror. The financial situation was always worse after their departure.

His two brothers, Frank & Josiah were still unmarried and were making a success of tailoring. They were good at business, in contrast to my father who had no business capacity whatever. So, as Eveline was the only grand daughter and only niece, she would have had to be made of very stern stuff in order to avoid being irremediably spoilt. They arranged for her to go to the Orme Girls' School as a paying pupil when she was eleven. But her total lack of application caused her sudden removal after a short time. She could hardly be described as a good business proposition to the uncles who were footing the bill! Later they offered to set her up in business in Newcastle but as she was better at spending money than making it, this opportunity never got off the ground. She never actually earned. Her imagination, however was colossal. She could always write poetry and shared my father's love of music and must have gloried in the idea that she was descended from Anne Boleyn! The Burroughs, already mentioned, were indeed people of some standing in Cockshutt as the splendour of Charles' tomb indicates. They were gentlemen farmers and when on the odd occasion my father wished to vent his rage on my mother he would point out that she "was not dug from the same hole as he was". She was only a gardener's daughter.

During these years of widowhood, my father was a self-employed master cabinet maker. He had an apprentice - indeed many apprentices passed through his hands. He could never understand why the apprentices did not apply themselves with the zeal he expected. One exception was Isaac Todd who was 13 when I was born and whose work bore the marks of excellence expected by my father. In his old age he told me many stories of the work they had done for St. George's Church, Newcastle-under-Lyme. The panels in the organ doors and reredos were made by them. The story of the carver whose artistry was achieved by using his fist instead of a mallet; who carved the tracery of the Lady Chapel, and who died in the workhouse had been related by my father. Isaac died in 1993 and at his funeral I was so touched to hear it mentioned that he had been my father's apprentice.

Apart from his work, his great love was music and he had an exceptionally good bass voice. I was told that he once had the opportunity to become a chorister at Lichfield Cathedral, but his nervousness and false teeth apparently deterred him. In 1911 he was one of a winning quartet in Hanley and received a gold medal which used to hang on his watchchain. I think he knew the great oratorios by heart and was frequently a soloist with local choirs. His copy of "Messiah" is dated 1896. He was a member of the choir that sang in the first performance of Coleridge Taylor's "Death of Minnehaha" - part of the Hiawatha work - conducted by the composer at the Victoria Hall, Hanley. He recalled the gasp that went up from the audience at the sight of a coloured composer and one of the sopranos fainted! He was a chorister at St. George's Church for 40 years. To begin with the choristers were paid, but when the financial reward ceased many left the choir. My father, however, because he loved music more than money, continued to attend and freely gave his services.

Meanwhile his brothers married. Frank married a young woman called Myra Bradshaw, to whom he was utterly devoted, and her early death from consumption was a tragedy from which he never really recovered. Josiah Charles, or Jos, as he was called, married Ada Madeley, by whom he had two daughters, Margaret and Kathleen. My father, too, wished to marry again and for years courted a Miss Deakin who kept a very exclusive drapery shop. She specialised in embroidery and my father framed some of her work. A fine oak fire screen - the embroidery by her and framed by my father I have recently given to Professor Michael Taylor and his wife Adele. Some unkind rumours were afoot - that Miss Deakin kept my father courting her as a blind for a liaison that was secret. "No one," she was reported to have said," would want to marry a man with a daughter like that." No wonder he sang with such feeling, "He was despised and rejected of men."

Eveline, no doubt lonely, utterly undomesticated and living in a world of romance, found a friend in Willie Coomer, a clerk in the Town Clerk's office. One day she complained of feeling poorly; her aunt Ada took her to the doctor and suffered the mortification of being told that her niece was pregnant. Eveline always said that she had no idea that what she had done was likely to have such a result. In those days the disgrace was total. My father bought the wedding ring and the newlyweds lived with him. (This would be during the first World War). It was a most unhappy time for all concerned. Eveline had no concept, indeed no training, for housekeeping. Burnt saucepans were commonplace and bitterest blow of all, Willie always sided with his wife against his father-in-law, although they were living in his home. The child was a boy, Maurice, and Eveline once told me that she did not even know that one fed a baby at the breast.

But happier days were on the way for my father. The homes of the gentry were places where my father was always welcome, and where he could rely on regular employment for furniture making and repairs. In one such house he met my mother, then a cook. So met two people whose different needs brought them together, and who spent nearly 40 years working at a marriage the common denominator of which was a belief in work well performed, a belief in God and a genuine respect for people.

2: MY MOTHER - ALICE HARVEY

(15th Aug 1883 – 11th Aug 1960)

My mother was born on 15th August 1883 at Meaford, near Stone, Staffordshire. She was the fourth of six children born to John and Mary Ann Harvey. There had been seven - one died in infancy. My grandmother used to relate how Lady Forrester, then the Grande Dame of Meaford, once questioned her about the number of children she had. "Six, m'lady," was the reply. "Too many." was the comment, "four are enough." There were no more.

John Harvey & Mary Ann Harvey nee Higginson

My maternal grandparents were married in February 1872. After my mother's death I found a faded envelope containing a broken sliver of gold - the wedding ring my grandmother wore for over 60 years, until her swelling hand required the ring to be removed. When I married Ray Smith I took it with my mother's wedding ring to a jeweller who had both rings made into one.

My grandmother was the only grandparent of whom I have any recollection. She was born in November 1852 at Shallowford, near Stone. Her maiden name was Higginson. She had some siblings, for her nephews and nieces - cousins to my mother - lived in Stafford and were regularly visited. I can remember trying to glean information about her youth and being somewhat frustrated in the attempt - she was 69 when I was born - and by the time she was 80 the worries of the present seemed to predominate over past history. She did say that she attended school only until she was eight and it was a building with benches round the sides. She did commiserate with me when I suffered period pains and said that she too had known similar agonies in her youth.

Mary Ann Harvey nee Higginson

My maternal grandfather died in May 1921, just about the time I must have been conceived. His outstanding physical characteristic was his ginger whiskers! In my mind's eye I can still see the large photo of him - not alas in colour - that hung between the front door and stairs door of the cottage in which they lived. On another wall hung huge portraits of Edward V11 and Queen Alexandra and between them, small but significant - the round plaque and commemorative scroll in memory of Arthur, framed; a constant reminder of the toll the Great War took.

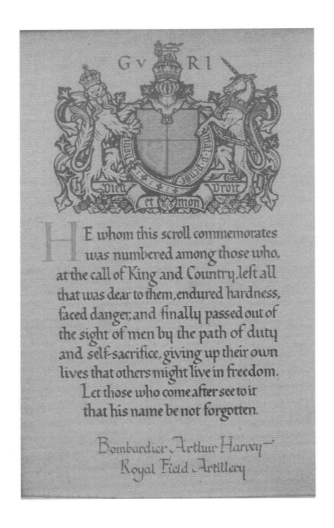

The cottage, proudly bearing the initials of Lady Forrester and the date 1884 still stands. I was told that four cottages originally stood there; my grandparents must have been rehoused when my mother was only a year old. There were two rooms and a larder downstairs and three bedrooms upstairs. Outside was the coalhouse, tool shed and wooden seated loo which was emptied periodically into a cess pit. When I was a child water was fetched from the pump across the yard, but even that was not there in my mother's youth. There was, however a pigsty, whose inhabitants kept the family supplied with pork and bacon. My mother recollected the tears that were shed when the poor pig had to die - but it was an essential death if the family were to survive on 15/- a week - my grandfather's wage as head gardener at Meaford Hall. I was told that Lady Forrester offered grandpa the cottage adjacent to the school but as he insisted on keeping a pig was required to have one further away from the Hall; presumably to prevent offensive odours from wafting in the direction of her residence.

Meaford Cottage – Stone, Staffordshire

Not that that was the only income. My grandmother earned twice that sum in her dual role as midwife and washerwoman. Because I remember her only as an old, complaining woman, it is difficult for me to imagine her walking enormous distances to deliver babies; taking in the fine washing from Meaford Hall and ironing it on the solid mahogany table that I still possess. She always reckoned that the babies who did best were born to women in isolated farms, where they were quiet and could attend to their babies without distraction. Of course the secret of her capacity to be a career woman was that she had two daughters who were able to manage in her absence.

Daughter Annie (born 1875) followed William (1873); then came Henry John (Harry)(1880). How my grandmother doted on her boys! They were the lords of creation; girls were only fit to be hewers of wood and drawers of water. So that Annie could go to school (just across the road) she was obliged to take my mother too when only a year old! My mother was six when another son, Edwin, arrived and eleven when the last one, Arthur was born. These two were virtually reared by my mother, so that their attachment to her was almost maternal. Arthur's birth in 1894 (grandma being 42) was difficult, but her sound constitution brought her through. She reckoned that childbearing in the 40s was an excellent recipe for living to a ripe old age. She lived to be 93.

Alice's four brothers – (L to R) William, Harry, Edwin and Arthur.

My mother's childhood - if she can be said to have had one - was dominated by her brothers. Her elder brothers regarded her as a slave and errand girl. She would walk to Stone across the fields to do the shopping and if she came back without their orders they would send her back again. She showed me the bench where she rested and wept bitter tears. The two younger ones were a different sort of burden. Wherever she went they always had to go and there were times when she resented their presence. If she was asked out for tea she could only go if she took her brothers with her and often this meant that the invitation was withdrawn. She had 'round' shoulders, due, she said to the hours she had spent nursing babies in her youth.

If my mother resented the unfair treatment her mother meted out, she felt respect for her father, who, if stern, was at least fair. I can remember her saying that when bedtime came, her father would raise his eyes from the newspaper, look at their shoes and then at the clock. No word was spoken. They went to bed.

My mother's full time schooling finished when Arthur was born. Thereafter she went half time and this meagre ration ceased when she was 13. The school, a benefaction of Lady Forrester, was also a Sunday School and my mother's attendance must have been very regular to judge by the prizes she received. The nearest church was Christ Church, Stone, where she was confirmed. I still have the little communion book given her at her confirmation in 1900.

It was always a source of regret to her that she had so little education. She would have liked to be a nurse, but that was out of the question. Domestic service was the only possible career. It was the custom then for girls to wear their hair parted down the middle, scraped tightly back and plaited. It seems that my mother once permitted herself the frivolity of a fringe and at the same time a position occurred in Worcestershire which she would dearly have liked - if only to get away from home! It seems that the fringe was unacceptable to the lady concerned - thus the entire direction of her life may have been altered by a fringe!

Her first position was at the Stone house of Mr. and Mrs. Huntbach, who had a large store in Hanley. This was very convenient for the Harvey household as she could thus continue her ministrations at home. Annie, by now was away from home having a post in Yorkshire, where she met her husband, John Cleaver, and raised a large family. Her eldest son, Gerald, emigrated to Australia and by now several generations are living there. It seems that after a few years the Huntbachs moved to Basford and my mother with them. I can remember her telling me that in her teens she was entrusted with carrying large sums of cash from Hanley to Basford - on foot - of course. But I have only a very hazy knowledge of her life between 13 and 23. Sometime in those ten years she began to court Arthur Brough and also began to collect together her 'bottom drawer'.

Harold Huntbach

Often I have wondered about her feelings and desires during those years. On one rare occasion did she mention that while courting Arthur Brough she had met someone with whom she had fallen passionately in love 'the many splendoured thing'. But she would not let Arthur down and put her desires behind her. They were due to be married in September 1906. In the previous July, Arthur, who worked on the railway was fatally crushed during a shunting operation. The wreaths at the funeral contained quantities of sweet peas. She could never bear the sight or scent of these flowers again.

Arthur Brough

So much is made of partnerships and sexual fulfilment today and the glut of films and TV programmes exploiting these themes seems so inescapable that it is difficult for us to imagine a time when there was no pictorial commentary on life except in books (mostly heavily laced with morals) and newspapers. For women, unless they had wealthy fathers to support them, the only way to find one's own home was by marriage. This was essentially a practical step to ensure status, a degree of privacy and an escape from the servitude that 'being in service' could involve. I remember once asking my mother why women got married. I imagined she would say, 'Because they fall in love,' although the reason for the question lay because we had visited a friend of her's whose married life appeared particularly loveless. Her grim reply was, 'To get a home,' and I remember the sense of shock I felt. How very mundane. Yet for my mother a home was of prime importance. She began to save for a home of her own when engaged to Arthur Brough and continued to do so throughout her life. A little was always put by. Yet it took her 50 years, combined with 15 years of my own life to find enough money for a modest bungalow. What effort. Mortgages were not for women. When we did finally buy our bungalow it was in my name; and each time we have moved I can never forget the hard years of work my mother endured to make possible my home. Now my last home belongs to my son and I want him to know just what a debt he owes to a grandmother he never knew.

But I digress. Her expectations of a home and family life were shattered and instead of having a family of her own to care for she became the rock and sheet anchor of her siblings. Her eldest brother (William Harvey) had married and when his wife died of consumption - the scourge of C19 - there were three small children to be cared for; Will, aged 7, Alice, 5 and Marion 3. They were farmed out to relatives, Grandma having Alice with whom she was far easier going than she had been with her own daughters. In my mother's estimation she was spoilt - not least because she was allowed to 'pervit' amongst my mother's belongings, spoiling and destroying them, much to my mother's annoyance. Marion (in the year 2003 is 95) tells horrendous stories of ill treatment. She seems to have lived at Meaford Old Hall and then at Harry Harvey's further along the road (A34) from the cottage. I do not know where Will was lodged.

Having lived her childhood next door to a pub – the Meaford Inn or the George and Dragon - and endured the havoc drink caused in her elder brothers, she was passionately against it. Not that she was tee total. As she grew older she enjoyed a Mackeson, a Baby Cham and a drop of Scotch, but until she reached old age she could never afford it. There was, perhaps, a little brandy kept for medicinal purposes, but I never saw her drink alcohol at all when I was young. She hated the drunken scenes she had witnessed at home and saw the poverty an addiction to it caused. She vowed she would never marry a man who drank, and she kept her vow. But more of that later.

Her eldest brother, William Harvey (Uncle Bill) widowed, took his consolation in drink. After her death I found a letter from a rent collector in Newcastle. He had left the lodging and the unpaid bill. My mother was asked to meet this person to discuss the matter and I can imagine the fury this must have roused in her. She was earning little enough and out of her pittance she was expected not only to contribute to his children, but also, probably, to pay his debts.

Her second brother, Henry John (Harry), had his wife pregnant before marriage and fathered ten children, only four of whom survived - Doris, Eric, Harry and Ethel. Annie, his wife, had an ulcerated leg partly, perhaps because of much childbearing. They lived in a gloomy and poverty stricken cottage along the road from Meaford Cottage yet scarcely ever came to visit their mother unless they wanted money. Harry only had to appear to be given half a crown. Annie's excuse was always her leg and I never saw her at Meaford Cottage.

John and Annie Harvey

Meanwhile (Mother's elder sister) Annie had married John Cleaver. Her life in Yorkshire was by no means a bed of roses. She was driven to fury by her husband's habit of reading the newspaper at table and utterly ignoring her while she waited on him. Each time she was pregnant she prayed devoutly that it would not be twins - by then somewhat late - but her prayers were answered. Her children were Gerald, Hilda, Harold, Marjorie and Nora.

John and Annie Cleaver (nee Harvey) and children

L to R Gerald, Marjorie, Nora, Hilda, Harold

So there were many children for Aunt Alice to find gifts for. Edwin emigrated to Canada before the first World War, having married a local girl. He wrote back that all were equal there - there was no bowing and curtseying and no Sir and Madam to the gentry. Arthur worked at the gas works in Stone, where the manager, a Mr. Hopkinson, befriended him. His wife became a close friend of my mother and when the family moved to Lymington, Hants. they never lost touch. Their son, Edgar and his wife May became my friends and I loved to visit them. May died in 1997 and Edgar in 1999. He had been an organist and choirmaster and for years played at Beaulieu Abbey at Christmas.

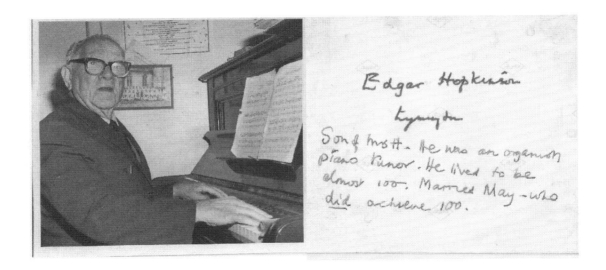

Edgar Hopkinson

Lymington

Son of Mrs H. He was an organist +
piano tuner. He lived to be
almost 100. Married May - who
did achieve 100.

Had she married in 1906, my mother would have left Huntbach's and though she must now remain in service, it seemed a good time to make a move further away from home. Armed with glowing references - an absolute necessity for domestic work - my mother obtained a job at Brampton Tree House in Newcastle, the home of the Coghill family as a domestic servant. Before she left she was cook and earned the princely sum of £20 a year.

Margaret Ford nee Coghill. (b 20th October 1894 – d 4th December 1977). Daughter of Archibald and Jessie Coghill (Descendants of Sir Francis Drake) late of Brampton Tree House.

About her life there I wish I had taken more interest in her reminiscences, for she was a marvellous raconteur. To this day, every February I remember her saying that by the end of the month it was possible to see to get up at 7 o'clock by daylight, and what a difference it must have made in those candle lit days. It still makes a difference now when we merely have to press a switch. The entire staff gathered together for morning and evening prayers and I fear that staff reverence left much to be desired. Whenever Psalm 51 was sung or said she always heard it in Mrs. Coghill's voice," Purge me with hyssop and I shall be clean: wash me and I shall be whiter than snow," but attention to the spiritual climate hopefully engendered was made more difficult by Lizzie Oliver's habit of placing a thimble on her nose when not being watched and then removing it, retaining a suitable look of piety while the rest of the servants strove hard to maintain their composure.

Evening prayers were much more tiresome, especially if it had been your day off, for it was essential to be back by 10pm for the roll call act of devotion. My mother's day off usually involved cycling to Meaford (about 16 miles each way), to help with the chores, one of which was to scrub the schoolroom floor for which my grandmother was paid. I can well imagine her panting up the drive at the last minute, being met by willing hands to enshroud her in her uniform before the stroke of 10pm was completed.

On Sundays the staff occupied an entire pew at St. George's Church - like so many black crows - she would relate. She often vowed that she would never go to church again if she left service, but of course she did. Her faith was stronger than the outward and visible enforcements of life as a domestic servant. There were no Sunday newspapers which to her seemed a pointless exercise. To be truly devout, Monday newspapers should have been banned.

The work was hard and strenuous yet there seems to have been much laughter, dressing up, games and certainly plenty of good food. Her collection of postcards, her autograph book, cuttings from papers and two short diaries I have kept; and these furnish incontrovertible evidence both of her effortless literacy and a full social life.

Domestics at Brampton Tree House - 1919

I had often heard her speak of the time when she and Lizzie Oliver cycled to Rhyl, but until now had not actually read the diary - what a joy missed! This event occurred in July 1912, when she was almost 29 and the account began like this:-

"Lizzie and I started from Brampton Tree House amid a host of good wishes. Our bicycles were decorated with flags on which were written. 'Good Luck'. The day was very cloudy and the prospect of a good holiday anything but promising. We said goodbye to Edie (Edith Oliver) in the Ironmarket and having called for bicycle outfits, we started for Nantwich at 3 o'clock; arrived in town at a quarter to 5. All shops closed, but we were fortunate to find just one place to get tea. We had a pot of nice tea and bread and butter for which we paid 8d. We started for Chester 5.30 and had a lovely ride. The clouds cleared away and the roads were grand. After riding well for 14 miles we got off and rested at a place called 'The Headless Woman' where we had refreshments and a nice chat to a very pleasant woman . . .

As I copy this out - exactly as spelt and punctuated - it seems scarcely possible that this is the diary of a country woman whose full time education ceased at eleven and whose main occupations were rearing children, scrubbing, cleaning, cooking and sewing. This is how it seems now, possibly because of my preoccupation with adult literacy from 1977-87. But judging by the wealth of cards and letters she left, it was not regarded as remarkable then - indeed, illiteracy was scarcely imaginable amongst the people with whom I was brought up. For one thing, they were always writing letters and cards to each other. It seemed that if a friend left even for a night, a card would be sent - almost as if their absence meant a gap in the conversation. This habit of constant correspondence was instilled into me - though now most friends write only once annually and we do have the telephone. I must confess that I found this duty of letter writing less of a joy than my mother did. To her it seemed strange that one could depart from home and not immediately on arrival at the destination pour out on paper all the trivia of the journey; next day the same. It is a queer sensation to read my old letters to her - full of information - and remember that the writing of them was often not done from the spontaneous desire to communicate which she had, but because letters were expected, and I should be told of sleepless nights if I did not comply. My letters show a marked lack of caring - hers were full of interest and concern for those to whom she was writing. The only fault I could find was her inability to paragraph.

She possessed to a remarkable degree a warm and compassionate nature, and loved people. Her diary - from January - April 1916 is so full of visiting and being visited that one wonders when all that hard work was done. I doubt if I could cope with all the comings and goings and still do a full time job.

Here are some extracts from this diary.

'Thurs. 20 January 1916. Went out with Lizzie. Called at Alice May's with nightdresses. Went to see Mr. Oliver. Met Mrs G. and went to church and a walk round the new road.

Saturday, 22nd January. I went home by the 12.30 train for the weekend - a most lovely day. Lizzie (Edwin's wife) and Mary (Edwin's daughter) met me. Edwin came by the 6.15 looking very well. We went into Stone, met Mr. and Mrs. Every - also did some shopping. Got home 10 o'clock and went across to Stathams to sleep. Chatted over the fire.

23rd. Sunday. Helped mother. Edwin and Lizzie took Mary out. In the afternoon we went to the crossing (no tea). Buxtons for tea and afterwards to church and called on Annie (Harry's wife) on the way back.

Monday 24th. Edwin left by 1.09. Went in the town in the afternoon. Called to see Nellie Brough. Lizzie (Oliver) met me at Newcastle 9 0'clock.

3rd March I went to Knights, saw Mrs Knight, also went to see Mrs Allen who had broken her arm. Fetched Miss Elsie from the club.

5th March Went to see Mrs. Allen after church and Lizzie went with me. Found her v. ill. No evening church. Zeppelin raid expected.

6th March Zeppelin raid on Hull. 70 people killed or injured.

9th March Went to see Mrs. Allen and took Agnes. Found her worse, but we enjoyed the walk.

12th March Damp and cold day. Walked to Stoke and had tea with Louis and stayed till 9 o'clock. Called for Lizzie at Gilbert Street.

26th March (Sunday). Lizzie went with me to Dudsons. Saw Mrs.Calverley and Harriet (Hetty Newman). Enjoyed the Sunday v. much.

A slight domestic upset is indicated on 28th March (Tuesday).'Mr. G. gave notice. Mrs. C. would not take it but gave it Violet instead. Everyone very unsettled.

31st March Friday. Went out 6 o'clock. Lovely evening. Went to Thornton Road, Richmond Street and Clifton Street and none of them at home. Walked back and called to see Mrs. Oliver. Met H. Mansfield.

April 7th. Went to Hartshill for some flowers and met Miss Elsie. I think Edwin was crossing over to France.

April 8th. Went to Meaford. Lizzie (Harvey) and Mary came too. All seemed very upset in case Edwin had crossed over.

April 9th Sunday. Went to 8 o'clock service. At 4 o'clock walked with Agnes to Shelton cemetery. Very dusty, but enjoyed the walk immensely. Went with L. to Ada's for tea and afterwards to Trent Vale Church and saw Mr. and Mrs. Hulme who took us for some supper.

19th April. Arthur (Harvey) came up to see me. I was surprised to see him. He looked so well. I walked to Stoke with him and called to see Louie and they were delighted.

22nd Saturday. Most exciting day. Cissie (cousin from Stafford) called with the two boys. Then Arthur came and brought Lucy (his fiancee) and they stayed tea and we all went to the Grand. Ran into Dudsons. Walked all the way back.

There was a most intriguing comment on 21 Sunday. 'Stafford!! never no more.' Whatever happened?

27th Saturday. Went to Stoke market. Owen's for tea. Mr. and Mrs. C. returned. Went to Hanley. Tom and Mary at the pictures. Called to see Mrs. Dudson. Saw Tom and Mary as I came away.

31st Wednesday. Mary Dudson had a daughter.

4th May Sunday. Pouring wet all day. Went to church 11am. Salts for tea and afterwards to see Mary Dudson. Enjoyed Sunday V. much.'

The diary finishes on 12th July. 'Lizzie and Mary came to see me. Went to Stoke with them and afterwards to Salts who asked me to go to Morecambe with them. Decided to go to Morecambe so wrote letters and told mother and Lizzie. A very wet night.'

The Morecambe holiday was to be epitomised in her autograph book with a drawing entitled, "When Alice dived at Morecambe Bay, She filled all the visitors with dismay"!

She kept accounts and apart from the obvious price changes that have occurred during the 20th Century - "Trip round Anglesey - 5s.6d, strawberries, 2d, meat, 1s.3d, bed and board (Chester) 3s.11/2" etc., how often she gave money away - "mother 1s.0d, father 6d." Arthur, Bill and other relations appeared to be given regular donations. She also bought material and made blouses and pinafores for her nieces. I wonder if and what they ever gave her back.

From her diary it seems that she was paid on the first of every month, unless it was a Sunday. The poor wages that domestic servants were paid is legendary and no further comment is required here about that, but in fairness it should be said that in a sense it was an honour to work in a good household, for it was an education in the correct ways of doing things, and although servants were at the beck and call of employers, yet the employers themselves (the good ones) felt bound to behave themselves in a seemly manner and give a good example. The Coghill family were widely known for the benefactions they made. Some were spectacular like the building of St. Paul's Church, Newcastle, which so impoverished them that Brampton Tree House had to be sold - I do not remember it at all - and the Coghills removed to a more modest residence in Basford. But there must be thousands of small, now forgotten gifts they gave, apart from their time. One such was an additional 10s. each month for my mother's nephew and nieces - Will, Alice and Marion. In a sense this money kept my mother at Coghill's, because if she left she would lose it and ten shillings a month in those days would have been a noticeable loss.

When the war came in 1914, my mother had been at Brampton Tree House for eleven years. As can be seen from a letter, she was much esteemed and appreciated. Like all the millions of people in the country, she could never have dreamed what a war that would be. She was probably better placed than most, for one really cannot imagine a shortage of food at Brampton Tree House. But in other respects she shared fully in the sorrows and deprivations of war. Harry, Edwin and

Arthur all joined up. William was on the railway and possibly not fit enough. Postcards, newspaper cuttings and letters bear witness to the numbers of young men known to herself and her friends who went to war. She was constantly writing, sending parcels and visiting those in hospital.

Then Edwin, in 1917, and Arthur in 1918 were killed in France. To lose Arthur was almost like losing her own son. She carried the burden of the correspondence for her parents and supported Edwin's wife too. The letters of consolation flooded in. Arthur's death was one of millions, yet even to this day I remember Arthur on 11th November, for here was a boy of much promise, so lively, full of laughter. So much more accomplished than any of the others, and only 23. My mother told the story of how one Sunday in August 1918 my grandmother suddenly felt life drain out of her as she was preparing a meal. She sat down, unable to do any more. Later they learned that it was at that moment that Arthur had died. My grandfather survived him by less than three years, never recovering from Arthur's death.

Harry came back from the war having been gassed and received a disability pension. I believe he was a painter by trade but I do not recollect him being employed.

Mother's great friend, Lizzie Oliver had married Ted Brammer, a sergeant. After four days honeymoon, he went to France where he died of pneumonia. Thereafter she received a pension of 30/- a week, on which with the utmost economy, she survived.

We are told that sadness may endure for a night, but joy cometh in the morning, and after the horror of 1914-18 was over it seems that by 1919, George Jones, Cabinet Maker, of 6, West Brampton, had fallen in love with my mother. On August 16th 1919 they were married in St. George's Church by the Revd. Arthur Sinker. Father was 53 and mother 36.

3: MARRIAGE OF GEORGE JONES AND ALICE HARVEY

16TH AUGUST 1919

Wedding – George & Alice Jones

Love. Such a short word with such a variety of interpretations. My father was a romantic and I am sure he loved this bright, happy woman that was my mother. And she? I think she felt great compassion for this man to whom life had administered such blows, and he, no doubt, was able to comfort her in her great sorrow, having gone through so much himself. To my mother, love meant serving; it would only show itself in practical ways. It meant seeing that he was cared for, fed regularly and generally looked after. The fact that he lived to be 91 is in itself a tribute to my mother's capacity for caring. But she could not share with him his love of music - true - she liked popular songs, but oratorios left her quite unmoved. She could appreciate the work he did as a cabinet maker, but to her it was much more important that goods were sold, or work paid for, so that they could be solvent. My father, in an unkind mood would say that her only taste was in her mouth! The indisputable fact about such a marriage in 1919 was that it gave my mother a home of her own so that she need not spend the rest of her life in service (though in a sense that is exactly what she did - in service to my father). Even at 36, there was the possibility of her having a child of her own.

Today, of course, it is accepted that a woman can have her own home in her own right and have children without marriage. But the problem is not solved. Money still has to be earned (though there are now state handouts), children need to be cared for and may miss the presence of a father.

The Great War of 1914-18 left a generation of women husbandless in an age when unmarried women were regarded almost as failures, 'on the shelf'. Men were at a premium, and because the desire for husband, home and family was inculcated into women, as well as the biological urge, many women had to drop their standards if they were to marry. Indeed, I was once told that it was better to marry anyone than remain unmarried!

So my mother married for what must have been a variety of reasons and who shall say which had priority. Certainly she did not marry for gain, for position, for show. The large house and its spacious grounds were exchanged for a small terraced house with a backyard, no garden and a horizon of roofs. It shared a narrow entry with two other houses, one of which was a grocer's shop. Behind the back yard, where the entry bent towards the back gate of our other neighbour was my father's two storeyed workshop - the bottom for storage and the top for work. A bell connected it to the house so that if he was wanted he could be summoned. My mother said that the house was double fronted at the back, for both kitchen and scullery looked on to the backyard, which saw the sun only in the morning, for by 2pm no shaft of sunlight could penetrate; whereas the front room and front bedroom windows received the full blast of the setting sun and these rooms were unbearably hot during a heat wave. There were 3 bedrooms; one above the front room, one above the kitchen and the smallest one above the scullery; this was my room when I was very young – lodgers occupied the room over the kitchen and my parents slept in the front room – though when I was ill I was put into their bed.

The living room was always called the kitchen, perhaps because the fire grate was a kitchen fire grate with an oven to one side and a boiler on the other. Water was poured in at the top and a brass tap released it. It was very convenient when as a small child I was bathed by this fire. Each Friday my mother was up at 6am to clean soot out of the flues and blacklead the grate. The smoke emanating from thousands of similar grates made window cleaning each week a necessity. Washing placed on criss-cross lines across the yard had to be watched for smuts or a high wind which could carry sheets on to the smutty tiles of the outhouse or coalhouse. Washing could never be left out at night, for the early morning fires would surely deposit their soot on it.

Not only did she find the change in her surroundings considerable, she acquired a new set of relations. Hitherto she had found friends among the gentry, among the servants of the gentry and among country folk. She had learnt to prefer the ways of the gentry, had copied their behaviour and was highly critical of what she regarded as self induced poverty, usually caused, in her own family at least, by drink. She believed that by care and frugality one could save and so lift oneself from poverty into a better position. Tremendous care was taken so that one did not appear to be poor, and the devices that were used remind me again, inescapably of Cranford. One such (and I did not fully comprehend this for many years) concerned the giving and receiving of Christmas presents. It was just not possible to give all the things one would like to the multitude of friends who surrounded her. Where she could she made and gave Christmas cakes and possibly garments she had made. Another source of presents was the Annual Sale of Work held by St. George's Mothers' Union. But her own inner circle gave each other presents which were totally useless or else far too fine to be used. These were then stored away and presented to other friends next Christmas. In fact my mother rejoiced far more over a beautiful present that she could pass on than something she could use. She was still doing it in her seventies. I remember one Christmas when my Godmother asked me what to get mother for Christmas and I asked for a tea cosy, which duly arrived. My mother was outraged. "Why didn't you ask for linen tea cloths so that I could pass them on?"

However, with marriage came her introduction to relatives whose life and style was different. On the one hand were father's brothers whose business capacity had led them into the ranks of the nouveau riche; and on the other hand there were Eveline and Willie.

To begin with. I think my mother was perfectly prepared to accept Jos and Ada because they had 'got on', and they were pleasant people. I only vaguely remember Jos, who died when I was seven. He was far more outgoing and jovial than either my father or Frank. But Eveline and Willie were far less acceptable. Of all the people with whom my mother was acquainted and certainly amongst all her relations, it was they to whom she felt the greatest antipathy - not that she ever showed it. Possibly her greatest quality was her capacity to conceal her true feelings. She would entertain the most impossible bore without them having the slightest idea that she had privately weighed them in the balances and found them wanting! But Eveline and Willie required special effort. When she promised to marry my father she made only one condition: if Eveline came in through one door - she would go out through the other! The implication being, of course, that Eveline's intentions were to remain permanently in the house. Mercifully, she was never put to the test, but for a person so charitably inclined to all mankind to make such a declaration speaks volumes. She used to say she had never met anyone who had a good word to say about her step-daughter. I can see her now considering this pronouncement as if scarcely believing it to be possible - surely someone must have said one kind thing. But no - she could not remember one. And I can clearly remember that the worst thing that I could be told was that I was just like Eveline. This was the ultimate in failure and inadequacy. In my mother's eyes Eveline was an idle slut. She had had opportunities to make something of her life and had let each one slip by. She neglected her husband, children and home. She read novels when she should have been working. She had never earned a penny in her life. She had made my father miserable. She was extravagant and wasteful. In short she portrayed the opposite of all the qualities that my mother admired. Being aware of my mother's feelings, but lacking her tact, I once refused to play with Eveline's children and was soundly smacked, most unjustly in my view. Each Christmas Day, if not at Meaford, my father and I walked down to Trent Vale to the little cottage they lived in and I can remember most vividly seeing chairs with the springs showing and an appearance of poverty totally foreign to me. When they visited us, as they did from time to time, the children's clothes were held together by safety pins. The hallmark of a good wife, according to my mother was the smart appearance of her husband and poor Willie's collars were never either clean or starched.

So it can truly be said that this countrywoman knew and could cope with an almost complete cross section of society. She treated everyone as they expected to be treated, and our house, having the doubtful distinction of being centrally placed and therefore convenient for tea and coffee, was never free from morning to night of visitors requiring counsel, comfort, advice, encouragement, sympathy and affection. I remember one day counting fifteen callers - from 9am to 11pm, and visits lasted anything from half an hour to two or three hours.

In May, 1921, my maternal grandfather died. My grandmother was up next morning at 5am to do the washing. And when my father died, my mother also washed. It must be an instinctive desire to complete the cleansing.

At about the same time, Frank Jones had taken to himself a wife - Elsie Walters, and they lived at the top of Florence Street. It was this affair that revealed her in-laws in a light which was to my mother totally unacceptable.

Frank was by this time manager of Marsden's, a very superior men's outfitter's shop in the High Street, next door to the Savoy Cinema and Oxens the Chemist. He was an excellent tailor, conscientious and scrupulously honest. One of the women who worked with him in the shop fell in love with him and it seemed that he returned her affection. It would probably have been a most suitable match, for they both knew the business of tailoring and she might well have been a great support for him. She had one drawback - she was not 'smart' (in the appearance sense, not the American sense of being clever). I never met her, but I understand that she was a laughing, happy woman, not unlike my mother.

Now whether Frank, of his own volition, decided that he needed a smart wife who would entertain and give him a social life, or whether he was swayed by Ada and Jos, I do not know. Perhaps they thought that a smart young wife would turn this silent, almost taciturn man into a happy extravert. Considering that he was by now middle aged and would go for weeks with scarcely a word to his housekeeper, their optimism seems unfounded.

However, being also a proud little man (he was quite small and had one blue and one brown eye), he must have dwelt lovingly on the esteem that such a match would give him. Ada was promised a coffee set if she could procure him a suitable wife.

Now Elsie Walters, like millions of others, had lost her fiancé in the war, and Ada went to work on her, telling her of this rich widower that she could procure for her; Frank's appetite was whetted by descriptions of this charming, well bred, genteel, smart young lady who would make the desert of his life blossom as a rose. Ada received her coffee set. The young woman at Marsden's attempted suicide and Frank and Elsie were married in April 1921.

I often wonder how long it was before they realized the enormity of the disaster they had perpetrated. Instead of the gay social round borne upon an ever full reservoir of cash, Elsie found herself married to an incredibly quiet, business like, proud man, totally involved in his business and not given to throwing money around. Anything less like a sugar daddy could scarcely be imagined. Frank found that he had married a woman of small intellect, for ever complaining, resentful of the time he spent at the shop and lacking the breeding he desired. Also she had no money at all except a £5 note given to her as a wedding present. This fact was mentioned with great relish by my mother who was, of course, regarded as a poor relation. "At least I had a sewing machine when I got married," she would say.

As Elsie and my mother were at first near neighbours they saw quite a lot of each other. While the newly weds were on honeymoon, my mother cleaned their house through, (and when she cleaned anything, it shone). Immediately they returned, Elsie unpacked their presents and the entire house was strewn with straw and packing! Not an action calculated to win the affection of her new sister-in-law. Mother had to endure the moans and groans of Elsie; her threats, when pregnant, of putting her head in the gas oven, and all the pettiness her mind revealed.

At the time of my grandfather's death my mother was just a month pregnant, though he would never have known it. So at last she was to have her own baby instead of looking after those of other people. She certainly was ready to embark upon parenthood, having a vast experience which had given her very definite views about how children should be reared. Her nephews, nieces and Eveline and family provided her with all too clear evidence of how children should not be reared. By contrast, she saw how the Coghill and Huntbach children were reared and this was her pattern. The fact that the gentry had ample money and many servants to help probably never occurred to her. She was not easily beaten. She was 38 and my father 55.

Of course the child would be a boy. There could be no question of another Eveline. The memory of Arthur the beautiful lingered and this was the name chosen. He would be trained as a cabinet maker to help father in the workshop. Very few people were told of the impending event. It was not done to broadcast such things. Aunts Ada and Elsie found the whole procedure intensely amusing. It seems that my mother had confided her condition to Ada, binding her to secrecy, whereupon she went straight up to Elsie, told her, and both had a good laugh about the temerity of Alice and George producing an infant at their age. What fools they were! Apparently at eight months pregnant my mother was invited to go to a pantomime, but declined as she felt she could not sit so long. Her friend had, until then, no idea of her pregnancy.

It was a cold, snowy January in 1922. My grandmother came over to be in charge. During the months of pregnancy, the child had been referred to as 'Moses'. He was due on 11th January, but it was not until 1.30 am on Friday, 13th January that the precious burden was delivered. My father, totally unable to cope with the strain, took to his bed and required to be nursed. The doctor feared that the child might not be delivered alive and decided on a forceps delivery. My grandmother was disgusted by all the fuss. She was even more disgusted when the four-and-a-half-pound baby was shown to her. A girl. Another girl. "When I think of all the great bouncing boys I have delivered and this is all you can produce," she complained. "You'll never rear her; but I shouldn't worry; she's only a poor little thing".

The anticlimax, after the long months of pregnancy, must have been a great disappointment to my mother. For one thing, no name had been thought of for a girl. So for six weeks the weighty business of finding a name went on. Name after name was rejected for this or that reason. Patricia was Irish (troubles in Ireland made any Irish name unpopular); Edna Mary or Enid Mary - with Jones added - would make 13 letters and the child was unlucky enough to be born a girl on Friday the 13th. Finally was father was obliged to register the birth, the registry office being just down Croft Street which ran opposite our house. (Sainsbury and its car park are now there). He returned with the certificate. "I have called her Mary Elizabeth after my elder sister. I hope this child may be as good as she was." My mother was unimpressed. "I'm not going to call her Mary - Mary Jones is too common, and if she's called Elizabeth it will be Lizzie, so I shall call her Betty." And so it was and has been ever since.

Shortly after this, Eveline and Willie succeeded in destroying completely any charitable thoughts or actions my mother might have held for them. Willie's work in the Town Clerk's Office included finance on a small scale. According to my mother, Eveline was much concerned that he favoured another lady in this office. If it was so, it must have been a passing fancy, for they remained perfectly united for over 50 years. However, whether it was in order to finance his extravagant wife, or court someone else on the side, Willie began to borrow from the till. Eventually, I was told, a deficit of £200 was discovered which was a huge sum in those days, and I now doubt that it could have been so much. Unless the money was returned proceedings would be taken against him, and by then he had two children, Maurice and Eveline. My mother well remembered the day when Willie appeared and asked to speak to "Mr. Jones". He never called him father. On that day father was laying lino in a house at Hartshill. It was a job he detested, but work was work. So she directed him thither, full of curiosity about what this unprecedented visit might mean. When father returned home he was completely shaken out of his natural calm and described how Willie had followed him all round the room as he worked, begging, pleading with him to let him have the money and save him from disgrace.

Father's first reaction was to consider what he could sell to raise the money, but the house was rented and if he sold every bit of furniture, the money could not be raised. My mother was adamant. "They wouldn't care if they turned you out on to the street, you and your wife and baby". I wish I could reproduce her graphic description of the event. The thought of us all being thrown out on to the street was not an endearing one. I often wonder if they realised how poor my father really was. Did they imagine that he had secret stores of wealth, or did they perhaps think that Frank or Jos would come to the rescue? I shall never know. Perhaps because my mother never appeared to be poor they were deceived. Certainly I always had the impression that they thought we had money to spare - but I know only too well that we had not; that some weeks my father would earn 2/6d for mending a sashcord and that was all. My mother supplemented the income by going out to care for people such as the Coghills and Nurse Hollinshead, who relied on her continually. She washed, baked and sewed for them. I can remember when I was perhaps 7 or 8 being put to bed after tea with books to read, so that father did not have the responsibility of seeing to me and so that she could spend the evening working for other people. It may seem strange, but I never resented it and I was always happy when reading.

Looking back, I am still intrigued about how Willie managed to pay the money back; did Frank or Jos help? If it had not been paid back there would surely have been a court case but I never heard of it. He was, of course, dismissed and became a mould maker at Wedgwoods.

So the year 1922 came to an end. I was placed in a wooden cradle and later in a cot in my parents' bedroom. On one occasion I stood up in it and drew large circles on the wallpaper. I remember the fury and never did it again.

Betty Jones aged 18 months. 1923.

4: CHILDHOOD MEMORIES (1923 – 1932)

My recollections of early childhood are dominated by my mother. Her knowledge of me seemed god like. She believed that parents should control children as soon as they were born, or they would soon boss their parents. She told the story about when I was 18 months old and she was having a party (it would be her 40th birthday); I refused to go to sleep, wanting I imagine, to join in the festivities downstairs. According to her, she went upstairs to quieten me down 15 times until I gave in and settled. I was not allowed to win. Wherever I went or whatever I did she knew about it. I realise now that because she had so many friends there was a positive spy system reporting back. It never occurred to me to disobey her.

Immediately opposite our house was Ryecroft School and when we were upstairs making the beds I would see and envy the children at play in the yard and longed to join them, believing this to be what school was! We slept on feather beds which needed shaking up each day and then smoothing down. I was not very good at this and mother was not impressed with the bed's lumpy appearance. "Oh," she would say, "I'm not going to sleep on Spion Kop." It never occurred to me to ask what she meant – I vaguely thought she meant "Spy and Cop" a sort of police operation bearing no relation at all to a lumpy bed. It was not until I was in the sixth form at school when the South African war was on the syllabus that it dawned upon me what she meant. Opposite Ryecroft on the south side of the school was Shoreditch, a slum, and demolished before I was 12. The site then became a car park. Because I was so frequently ill I was forbidden to go there in case I caught some disease. I can remember being pressed by companions to go and play there and steadfastly refusing to do so. But diseases came despite my obedience; mumps at four; whooping cough at five, diphtheria at seven and measles at eight afflicted me.

When I did go to school at four and a half, I was in Miss Watt's Class. She appeared to me to be an old lady who was kind and gave children sweets. I remember wishing that I had an unusual name so that I could spell it aloud for her. Everyone knew how to spell Jones. Occasionally mother would take me to tea with the Ford family – Margaret Jessie (Madge) Coghill had married Ronald Ford and their elder son John was born a month after me. I remember feeling indignant when told to sound my aitches as John Ford did – I did sound them and needed no instruction! I was told to return home at playtime, not realising that the school should be informed. It was my mother's word that was law!

Ronald and Margaret Ford

Sir John Ford KCMG (b 1922 – d 2018).

As well as being a sick child - I had a tonsillectomy at 3, followed by a severe infection of the throat and ears and can still remember the pain in my ears and the "poppy heads" being put on them - I was also a clumsy child. When I took the course for teaching handicapped children I realised with sudden clarity that I had had minimal cerebral dysfunction, probably because I was a small forceps baby. Such a condition was unheard of then. I could fall over nothing, could not walk on walls, tie my shoelaces or handle a knife without cutting myself. My mother, capability personified, must have been sorely tried by such a clumsy daughter and I was constantly in trouble, so much so that I must have doubted her affection for me.

I remember leaving school one afternoon when still in the Infants and seeing my mother at our front door, dashed across the road. A lorry driver stepped on his brakes and missed me by inches. Whereupon I witnessed the amazing spectacle of my mother, seated on the sofa, crying. This show of emotion surprised me greatly. I was scolded, of course, but my chief recollection was the discovery that my mother cared. And care she did. Throughout all my illnesses, she always came to my calls and never spared herself. I was the most precious thing she had; but that did not mean spoiling me.

Betty Jones – Age 5

Each Sunday we went to St. George's Church where father sang in the choir. I can remember him going to choir practice on a Friday evening and appearing in cassock and surplice, the last of the choirmen to walk up the aisle on Sundays. He often sang solo parts in anthems. When the church celebrated its centenary in 1928 a new North Porch was built and a special photograph of the choir was taken outside it. Before this, Canon Arthur Sinker, who had baptized me, had left for a living in Bermondsey and was succeeded by the Revd. Harold Birch - a gentle, kindly man, but no preacher. I often wondered how he felt at Harvest Thanksgiving when Canon Sinker returned to preach and chairs had to be placed down the side aisles to accommodate the hugely swollen congregation, knowing that the following Sunday there would be more empty pews than people.

My early childhood, indeed, most of my life, was dominated by money shortage. I cannot say poverty because my mother was such an excellent manager that we were always adequately fed, clothed and kept scrupulously clean. She could tell on a Sunday what we were to eat on each day of that week, certainly as far as Thursday. She managed to give little tea parties which she enjoyed doing. On these occasions the great delicacies were potted meat and blackberry jelly. I was sent down to Stathams butchers in Liverpool Road for a quarter of a pound of potted meat which cost 4d. Mother then boiled it and put it in a dish topped with melted butter. I remember on one occasion hearing her complimented on the quality of her potted meat and being asked how she made it. She then proceeded to give the recipe for the entire preparation of potted meat and to my eternal shame I spoiled it for her by revealing the truth of where the potted meat really came from. A most tactless child.

Life was a constant struggle to keep up appearances. Of the three houses that shared the entry, the Joneses had by far the most difficult task. Our house was the smallest and least pretentious. The Goodalls, who adjoined us on one side, approached their back gate at the end of the entry, father's workshop being at right angles to it. Thus we scarcely ever saw them. Their house was at least double fronted, boasted a bathroom and had a fairly large yard with a bit of garden. On the other side of the entry, their back yard easily visible over two low walls, the Meadons owned a grocer's shop which was at least profitable enough for them to retire later to Enderley Street. Their prices, however, compared unfavourably with stores like the Maypole, Home & Colonial and Hubanks, yet it was necessary to give them a reasonable grocery order each week to maintain good relations. Thus I would be dispatched to scour the town for the lowest priced Empire butter - usually 1/- a pound instead of 1/2d for Danish next door. Unfortunately on one occasion I innocently gave accounts of my shopping expeditions to the neighbours, resulting in a distinct cooling of the hitherto cordial atmosphere. The Meadons were better known also because of the young people who stayed there. One was Violet Hickman, their niece, who was glad of my mother to listen to her troubles. It was through us that she met her husband, Isaac Todd, who was apprenticed to my father and they carried on their courtship at the bottom of the entry when only 13.

Isaac Todd & Violet Hickman

Much better known to me was Thomas Thompson, their nephew's son. He was only 18 months older than me and like Violet, had to work hard for his lodgings. His mother was a French woman, married during the first World War, and Thomas came to England speaking only French. I remember seeing his mother once and have often wondered why the boy was deposited at 4, West Brampton where he learned all about life the hard way and must have had an intensely lonely childhood. He married Eva, who was a good wife, and fathered 3 sons, all of whom he could be proud.

The Goodalls I scarcely knew apart from Leslie, a hairdresser who cut off my golden curls when I was four as a preparation for school. The reason was purely practical; it is far easier to toothcomb head lice out of short than long hair. Each day my mother held a small round tray at my neck with one hand and meticulously toothcombed my hair for unwelcome residents with the other.

Another childhood friend was Carol Danbury who lived at the corner of Broad St. and Florence St. Her house had not only a back yard with a tiny strip of garden, it opened into a larger yard from which several houses in Broad St. had back entrances. There we could play all manner of games, hoop rolling, skipping and hide and seek. Carol's birthday was in July and a great luxury was ice cream, bought from an ice cream cart. If only I could have been born in July instead of January when there was no ice cream!

I think the desire for adventure was ingrained in me. My mother said that I would have run away with the bin men if they would have taken me. I remember one day the good Dr. Lyth called to ask if he could take me out in his car. It may have been the first time I had had a ride in a car, for such a luxury was beyond the pockets of our friends and acquaintances. The patients he visited were gypsies living in a caravan. On the way back, he stopped for petrol and commented how much easier feeding would be if we could just fill up like a car. How I longed for a bicycle! Father made a scooter with iron wheels but this made such a noise up and down the entry that it was soon given to Cousin Peter. I think I was five when I asked for a Fairy Cycle, but was told I was too small for it. The following year I was too big. The truth was that they couldn't afford it and in any case I was too clumsy to be safe on one.

I left Ryecroft School when I was seven and was transferred to The National School, also called St. Giles' and St. George's Church School, which was thought more appropriate by my Anglican parents and was situated behind the Queen's Gardens. Miss Lane was the headmistress and my first class teacher was Miss Dorothy Tittensor who lived in Florence St. with her parents. Dorothy's mother, Mrs. Tittensor was a familiar visitor at our house. I think sometimes my mother found her heavy going, but Mrs. T. loved my mother and felt very genuine appreciation for all the comfort and cheer she gave her. Dorothy organized little displays – one of Scottish dancing was shown at the Municipal Hall, and I remember wearing a kilt for this. During my second or third year we listened to a visiting speaker on the subject of Chaucer and were invited to write about it. I had the privilege of writing my account in a special book, for to my amazement I won a prize for my contribution – a specimen book called *Realms of Gold* which I read over and over again. It contained a description of life in Japan and the story of Maggie and the gypsies from *Mill on the Floss*. I was a compulsive reader, probably because of those long spells in bed when there was nothing else to do. I also loved poetry and can still remember some of the poems we learnt. We were told that our bedroom windows should always be open at night, but my mother was less than enthusiastic about this for the air that entered was heavily laced with smuts – making work. One day we were told how seeds grew into plants and trees. I solemnly took a damson stone out of a pot of jam, planted it in a square foot of earth outside the back door and was distressed to find that no damson tree emerged.

St Giles & St Georges School - 1931

Armistice Day, 11th November, was rigorously observed. Just before the Municipal Hall clock struck eleven we stood in our gangways in the total silence shared by the rest of the country for the full two minutes following the last chime. Empire Day, 24th May, was celebrated joyfully with a Maypole in the school yard and special songs were sung.

My friends here were the twins, Jean and Betty Elkes who lived in Cross Heath where St. Michael's Church now stands. I walked alongside the old canal to get there. They kept pets - I remember a tortoise – and loved dressing dolls, whereas I had not been much interested in dolls after I was three or four. I loved things on wheels, and of course, books. Small wonder that Jean had six children and loved babies.

At the age of nine I prepared for the scholarship exam. which involved homework mostly taken from Evans Scholarship Papers and included arithmetic and grammar. That year (1931) the then Prince of Wales came to open a newly built part of North Staffs Infirmary and I joined great crowds in Hartshill to greet him. On the way home I ran across a side road just as a car was reversing, and was knocked down. The next thing I knew I was in an unfamiliar house where I lay. I was taken home; the doctor was summoned and concussion diagnosed. For weeks afterwards my poor brain was full of numbers. They plagued me night and day and would not go away. For two years after that I was terrified to cross a road and I remember being dragged across the road on a visit to Birmingham.

However, in February 1932, I once more ran across the road to Ryecroft School for the Scholarship Exam, having fallen down the stairs first. I had little hope of succeeding in passing the Maths paper, so the English paper was my only hope. I have always remembered the comprehension passage about a boy who lived on a hill and saw a house on the opposite hill which had golden windows in the setting sun. Fascinated, he rose early one morning to investigate, but alas, the windows were of ordinary glass. Then turning round, he looked back at his own home and to his amazement saw that its windows were golden, bathed in the radiance of the morning sun. One of the composition questions was to write a story with a given title. Here, I fear, I cheated. I remembered reading a story that fitted the title and proceeded reproduce it, having considered it unlikely that the examiners would have encountered it. Was it this act of plagiarism that secured for me a Free Place at the Orme Girls' School? It never occurred to me that using someone else's story telling capacity was wrong: I was just using information that I had acquired. It is possible that but for this I might have failed the exam, left school at 14 and found a job somewhere in Newcastle. Would I have attended night school like Tom Dudson? (See chapter 6). I hope so. Fortunately, there was Meaford where blissful days were spent.

5: MEAFORD & DIPHTHERIA (1925-1929)

By the 1920s William Harvey (Uncle Bill) had married again and he, his wife Helen and my grandmother lived in Meaford at Meaford Cottage. My mother visited as frequently as she could, generally to busy herself with tasks that my grandma left for her. By the time I was 3 she would sometimes leave me there and so began my great love of the place.

Uncle Bill was, like his father, a gardener at Meaford Hall where John Jervis, Earl St. Vincent was born. He had once worked on the railway where he had lost the fingers of one hand in an accident. But he knew how to garden. Half way down the large garden at Meaford Cottage were raspberry canes on one side and gooseberry bushes on the other. Beyond were potatoes, cabbages and beans. There were flowers around the borders and cream roses spreading across the house wall that faced the garden. How I loved to eat the raspberries and was never forbidden. In the yard that received all the sunshine one could wish for were two huge water butts, the water being used for all washing purposes. My grandmother's face was almost without a wrinkle; she attributed its youthful glow to the beneficial qualities of rainwater. Near the pig sty (and I do remember a pig being in it) was the water pump and when the water froze I had to go round to the George and Dragon (then owned by Ted and Sybil Straw) and fetch water for drinking and cooking. I would help with vegetable preparation, but most of the time I was free to wander in the wood behind the cottage where hens pecked away and washing decorated the bushes. My father made a swing for me, hanging from the bough of a tree. Behind the wood, where now the A34 runs, was a field bounded by the River Trent. This I was forbidden to go near. Although still a young river it was intensely polluted from its journey through the Potteries and there was no life in it; but the chief reason for the ban was the fear that I might drown. I never did go near the river until I was quite grown up.

Harry Harvey and Ted Straw (Landlord of George & Dragon) at Meaford.

A bluebell wood bordered the field on two sides. In May I would gather armfuls of these lovely flowers and in the autumn go in search of blackberries. When fascinated by the geography of tropical forests, I imagined myself in one of these as I explored the wood, but I had to wait until I was 69 before experiencing the real tropical forest of the Amazon. I never saw a single wild animal. I can remember lying in the field watching the clouds make patterns and listening to a thrush singing. I loved Meaford and I loved my Uncle Bill who would play with me, and when he threatened to smack my bottom, I presented it to him!

There were always cats at Meaford, frequently having kittens, which was a great mystery to me. "Where do they get the kittens from?" I would ask and was told that they found them in the wood. Whereupon I would search for days for kittens, fruitlessly!

Almost every Christmas Day we went to Meaford. After Father Christmas had abundantly blessed me at home - and mother's friends and relatives provided a great bounty of gifts - there was always a Christmas Tree at

Meaford and more presents for me. Christmas, and my own birthday in January made December and January a most wonderful time.

There must have been much tension, totally unobserved by me, in that cottage. My grandmother and Aunt Helen did not agree. Whenever I returned home grandma would plaintively say in what we called her 'singing voice' that she might not be there when I went again. I once told my mother that I preferred Aunt Helen, but that was regarded as disloyalty. Aunt Helen was very good to me and far more sensible.

Things changed at Meaford in 1929 when Uncle Bill died suddenly of a heart attack at the age of 56. Aunt Helen and Grandma could never have lived together. So as soon as possible Helen went up to Meaford Hall to cook for the Colonel and Miss Parker Jervis.

Meaford Hall

Some pressure was put on my mother to have Grandma to live with us. She refused. She already had an elderly husband and knew she could not cope with her mother as well. So Grandma had a series of lodgers – some better than others - and she moaned over them all.

I still went to Meaford and now I also went to Meaford Hall to visit Aunt Helen. This was wonderful. I walked up through the fields to the stable gate and across the stable yard into the servants' quarters. Turning right into a long passage I entered the Housekeeper's room and met Mrs. Lindsay, a dear lady. It was only later that I learned that 'Mrs.' was a courtesy title for housekeepers. I became familiar with the kitchens – beautiful kitchens with great oven ranges and in the scullery huge plate racks. Whenever I went Aunt Helen made drop scones on a griddle over a fire. At the head of the table in the housekeeper's room sat Mrs. Lindsay, while Mr. Madison, the butler sat at the end. Aunt Helen, Elsie Haymes, the parlour maid and I sat in between. Mr. Madison lived at the cottage adjacent to the school and it had been rumoured that his ghost has been seen there.

I remember going to Aunt Helen's bedroom and seeing her undo her lovely long brown plaits. She would take me to Tom Webb's cottage where she was given eggs. Most of all I loved it when the Jervises were away. Then I would go into all the house and play on the grand piano in the Marble Hall. In the 1930s Colonel Parker-Jervis died and because the death duties were so crippling Miss Parker-Jervis eventually had to move to a house in Barlaston. She was still at Meaford Hall in 1939 and on one occasion, while she was away, I found albums of letters – one from Disraeli to Lady Forrester declining an invitation. How I longed to possess it. But I did not remove it and have often wondered what happened to those letters.

One Friday afternoon in June 1929 I came home from school with a very sore throat and can remember feeling very poorly indeed. However, whatever it was cleared up and the following weekend I was dispatched to Meaford. I was usually taken by bus as far as Stoke and put on the Stafford bus which would conveniently and obligingly stop outside the cottage where I was greeted by Grandma and Aunt Helen. The journey took three quarters of an hour - the same as it took for my father to cycle there - which he did till he was almost 70. I used to think how clever the bus driver was to find his way there! During the Saturday I noticed that for some reason my legs refused to run - they resembled jelly and could not be propelled. Aunt Helen tried to jolly me into effort and holding my hand pulled me and my reluctant legs across the field - but to no effect. I was dispatched back home on the Sunday afternoon - not actually feeling ill, I'd felt far worse the previous weekend - but unaccountably languid and sore throated.

My sorely tried parents were extremely weary of my constant spells of illness. Each time the doctor had to be consulted it cost 5/- and although the good Dr. Lyth always found work for father to do it seemed that he was forever working off doctor's bills. This time - perhaps affected by an unsympathetic note from Meaford - father rebelled. "Other people's children get better without the doctor being sent for all the time. I won't bother him this time." So, as usual, I was put to bed in my parents' bed in the front room and the hot evening sun poured in. I didn't really feel ill, just tired and with no appetite. By the Wednesday as there was no improvement, father relented and the doctor was sent for. He examined my throat, found nothing untoward and said I could have anything I wanted to eat or drink. I didn't want anything. He came again on the Friday, took one look at my throat and ran downstairs to my mother with unusual haste. Then my mother came in, sat down on the ottoman by the window and told me I was very poorly and must go to hospital. An ambulance was coming for me. What was it? Diphtheria. She wept. She didn't want me to go but I must be a brave girl as in hospital they would make me better. How little I knew that she never expected to see me alive again. The disease was far advanced and very little hope was given.

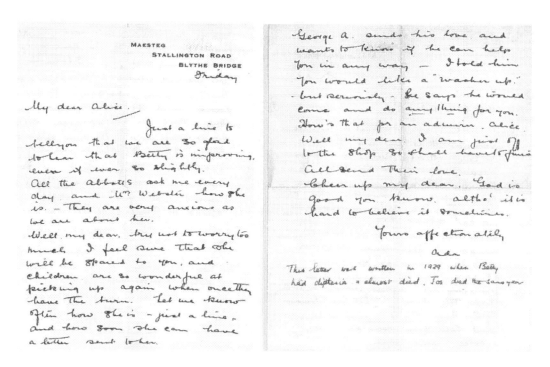

Letter from Aunt Ada to Alice ref Betty's illness.

The people at the Isolation Hospital, conveniently situated adjacent to the cemetery, were expecting a boy - and in the corner of a boys' ward I was put, surrounded and shrouded by a steam tent so that the atmosphere was constantly damp. There was no pillow. That evening I remembered that it was time to say my prayers and I actually knelt up in the middle of that bed to say the prayers I repeated every night. But it was the last time for weeks that I knelt. I was given only warm milk to drink and one day I remember there were a few pieces of shredded wheat in the milk and each day I hoped there would be another such inclusion, but to no avail.

I was in that isolation hospital for six weeks. After the first week I was moved into the girls' ward and given a pillow. A pillow a week was a great achievement. There were, of course, no visitors, but now and then I was told to look through the window where outside on a hill in the cemetery my parents stood, as near to me as they were allowed to get. It was no real comfort. Gradually I was made to walk and finally on 24th August I was taken home. For the first time in my life I was spoilt and I revelled in it. People would actually fetch for me things I wanted. Despite the attempt at walking in hospital it was a long time before I could really walk and I had a push chair. But at least I was alive. The hospital staff said that this was chiefly due to my unquestioned obedience. I wonder what they would have said if they had seen me kneeling up in bed on that first night?

It was decided that we should have a holiday and right from the very beginning Aunt Ada had proclaimed her willingness to pay for it. So to St. Annes-on-Sea we went. We always took lodgings some distance from the sea because they were cheaper. My mother bought in such food as we required and the landlady cooked it. For this facility, the train fare and any small purchases that might be made, the cost was £5 for the week. Yet this money took some saving so that a holiday was only affordable every two years. This time it was going to be different; but alas, Aunt Ada's fine promises came to nothing and father footed the bill as usual. In January 1979 I was in St. Anne's for a literacy course and was amazed to see those familiar sands covered in snow and the sea frozen. The old band stand, now vandalized, still stood and I was reminded of the day that father stood inside it and sang, "Onaway, awake, beloved," from Hiawatha's Wedding Feast; his powerful voice attracting the attention and astonishment of bystanders and the acute embarrassment of my mother.

George & Alice Jones on holiday. 1950's.

6: UNCLE JOS JONES AND FAMILY.

It was also during 1929 that Uncle Jos died. He was only 56 and died of cancer of the bowel. Ada was known to rail on Grandpa and Grandma Jones for having 22 children because in her opinion Jos, being the youngest was the weakest! It was an extra ordinary deduction to make considering that the first 17 were by the first wife. Father's diagnosis was different; Jos's tailor's shop in Longton had its back adjacent to the indoor market and was not apparently well supplied with sanitary arrangements. Father was of the opinion that his brother was so busy making money that he ignored the calls of nature. Recent discoveries seem to support the theory that constipation may be a contributary factor in bowel cancer.

Jos Jones.

Jos was buried in Fulford cemetery leaving Ada acutely aware of her widowhood. She declared that no one wanted you when you hadn't a husband to accompany you. However she set to work to maintain the shop and worked long hours, leaving the lovely Blythe Bridge house - and Kathleen. She was the younger daughter, four years older than me. According to Ada, when she was a few weeks old, doctors had laid her on a marble slab in an attempt to investigate a strange mark in her back. Since then her head had grown and she was slightly paralysed down the right side. It was not until I visited an SSN (Special Needs) school in the 1970s that too my amazement I saw a replica of Kath. "What," I asked, "is the matter with that child?" "Hydrocephalus", was the reply. So finally I knew. But Jos and Ada only knew that they had produced a freak - a freak that at all costs had to be hidden from their business acquaintances. There were no special schools and Kath went to an elementary school where she was taught to read and write. I suppose she must have left at 14 and from then on she spent day after day alone in the house unless the kindness of neighbours intervened. But whenever visitors were entertained Kath was confined to the kitchen so that many were unaware of her existence.

Alas, I too was far from compassionate towards Kath. When Jos and Ada wanted to go out in their car on Sundays Kath would be dumped on our doorstep, heavy, slow and unresponsive. I had a toy gramophone which I loved to play and was inconsolable because Kath had sat heavily on a pile of records. She loved my mother, who was one of the few people who showed kindness and affection to this much neglected child. I can remember their neighbour, George Abbott, visiting my mother in a state of great distress about the 'goings on' at Maestag. I don't remember what caused his distress, but finally he kept saying, 'They that shall endure to the end . . .'

If Jos and Ada were ashamed and embarrassed by Kath, (and their attitude was typical of all such afflicted parents at the time), their pride and joy in their elder daughter, Margaret, were displayed for all to see. She was beautiful; she had blue eyes, golden auburn hair and a very sweet nature. Privately, I believe that Ada had reservations about her elder daughter. She once confided to my mother that she could see too much of Eveline in her. Which may be why her main ambition seemed to be to find a wealthy husband for Margaret.

Margaret Jones

How I envied her! I was a plain, solitary, bespectacled child, while Margaret went to dances and seemed to be continuously courted by eligible young men. Several of them I vaguely remember especially one - Leslie - who joined in with a children's tea party I was playing at in the outhouse when I suppose I was 6 or 7. in 1937 when I was 15, she finally married Fred Peake, son of the owner of a bus company and the Theatre Royal, Hanley. They came to live in Sneyd Avenue, Newcastle, close by the golf links. The merry round continued - parties, dinners, social events etc. while Kath remained solitary at Blythe Bridge.

Then one dark evening in January 1939, when Ada was returning home from the shop in Longton, she missed her footing when boarding a bus and was dragged along the road. She never recovered. Margaret, pregnant with her first child, had to cope not only with her mother's death but with the inescapable fact that she would now have to look after Kathleen. The child was born, so I was told, "without a bone in its body". It did not survive.

For some years they lived at Sneyd Avenue and whenever Kath went shopping in Newcastle she would call at our house and was made welcome. I shall never know what sufferings she endured, what loneliness, and I now wish that I could have understood better. She died in her thirties, a sad, unwanted woman, only useful as a domestic help, shopper and baby sitter. Yet Margaret must have had compassion for Kath - and she, too, in her turn suffered.

'They that shall endure . . ' how that phrase rang in my head! We saw very little of Margaret and Fred for years. They had two daughters, Valerie and Jackie - and another stillborn son. The daughters did well. Valerie became a teacher who married a very successful, hardworking market gardener, Bernard Hargrave in 1964 and bred beagles, competing in dog shows with them. Their son Philip and wife Julie had a son in December 2000. Jackie went into banking, married Paul Shields and had two daughters, Julia and Caroline.

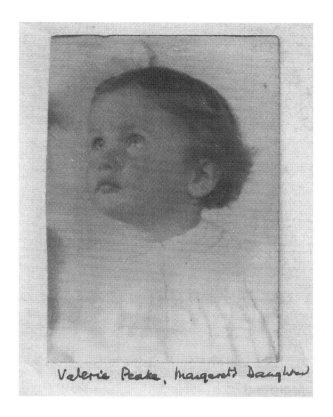

Valerie Peake, Margaret's Daughter

I shall always remember when my son Clive Smith was born (March 1964), how Margaret visited me in hospital with flowers. Her delight that I had a son was so warm and genuine. We went to Valerie's wedding later that year. Then Margaret, the beautiful, fortunate Margaret developed cancer and died at 59. Within a year her husband had remarried and within another 18 months, just before Christmas, he died suddenly, intestate. The wrangling that ensued between widow and daughters was not edifying. I then learnt that Margaret had been unhappy for years and when she died all she possessed was a sheepskin coat and some jewellery. The new wife took the coat and the daughters the jewellery. The wrangle over money continued for years. Poor Margaret! What hell her life must have been. Her daughters loved her and had no time for their father. So finally, truth was out. And I have endured to the end and seen it all.

Fred Peake (Margaret Jones husband) with his second wife Vera.

7: FAMILY FRIENDS AND ACQUAINTANCES (C1900-1956)

To my birthday parties always came the Newmans - and we always went to theirs. The Newmans were my mother's friends and birthdays were great opportunities to get together. Auntie Hetty was a small, smiling Yorkshire woman who with her sister Mary, had married Staffordshire men.

Arthur and Hettie Newman – 10th July 1919.

The friendship may have originated at Brampton Tree House, where one Tom Dudson was a coachman and later a chauffeur. According to my mother he had proposed marriage to her, but she had refused him. He went on holiday to Yorkshire and met Mary Calverley who promptly fell in love with him and threatened suicide if he would not marry her. Perhaps unwisely he did marry her. Soon he realised that Mary was unable to accompany him to any function without showing him up - and he was an intelligent, ambitious man, determined to get on in the world. The story goes that he once took her to a dinner party where Mary, surveying the array of cutlery at each place setting, asked loudly, with a Yorkshire accent what all the knives and forks were for! Tom soon discovered that she knew what to do with knives, for, as he left her at home from then on, he would return to be greeted with a carving knife used as a missile.

The knives he managed to avoid, but a more deadly enemy claimed him - tuberculosis, leaving Mary with a small son to rear, another Tom, and a replica of his father. A daughter too was born, Doris Winifred, but she died in May 1917 when only 11 months old. I have a letter written by Mary to my mother after Arthur's death, not only beautifully written but showing much affection. There is also a postcard containing an epistle in tiny writing.

Tom Dudson the second remembered my mother coming to bath him; apparently Mary was unable to persuade him to submit to ablutions and Tom developed a genuine and lasting affection for Alice. He told me that he remembered his father and my mother taking him to Trentham Gardens and being given a peach to eat. Young Tom inherited his father's intelligence as well as his looks, but Mary would not let him sit for a scholarship and insisted that he left school to work at 14. Whereupon he attended night school classes and finally received a B.Sc. degree at Exeter University. He later became Vice Principal at Portsmouth Polytechnic.

Tom Dudson Jnr.

As I always had enormous problems with maths, Tom attempted to help in this field. True, I did pass School Certificate in maths, but with great difficulty. I remember one of Tom's contributions - I learnt how to multiply by 11 - add e.g. 2 and 3 together and place the answer between, thus 253. Would that there had been such tricks for the rest!

Tom's diligence and brilliance quite overshadowed his cousins, Hetty and Arthur Newman's sons, Kenneth and Donald, who both had a grammar school education but lacked his ambition. It was these boys who were my contemporaries, Kenneth being only two months younger than me and able to benefit from my mother's abundant milk supply when a baby, despite which he had rickets. Donald was 18 months younger and yelled almost continuously until he was over 2. All were musical. Aunty Hetty was a good pianist and would accompany Arthur, a tenor, and my father in a variety of songs at party times. These included, *'Thy Sentinel am I', 'O Ruddier than the Cherry', 'Father O'Flynn',* and

'The Wolf'. I later gave the book containing these to Gordon Stewart who was then organist at Manchester Cathedral. All of us learnt to play the piano and had to perform as well as sing. Donald was a long time learning to sing but eventually he produced his party piece, *'Dear Little Shamrock'*. We played party games -*'I spy'*, *Blind Man's Bluff'*, and *'Musical Chairs'*. Later on there was skittles and later still table tennis at which they were adept. When we reached our teens we began to have ballroom dancing lessons with a Mrs. Fetzer who lived in Basford and had a large room and a gramophone. There we learnt to waltz, foxtrot, quickstep and Palais glide. I enjoyed dancing but never became expert nor was I able to go to dances. How I envied cousin Margaret, her escorts and dances. I think my mother was aware by now of my solitariness and was anxious to rectify it; but I was a solitary child.

As well as supplementing the income by sewing, making cakes for people, looking after people who were ill, my mother also had lodgers. I only vaguely remember two young men she once housed, but when I was seven, one of the Miss Hardies' from across the road asked her to have a young lady from Surrey - Vera Walker, who was to work at the Labour Exchange in Barracks Road. She was a very particular person, keen on wholemeal bread and watercress. After a meal would stand in front of the fire reading a book. Her eating habits fascinated me so much that I must, quite unconsciously have watched her eating. Whereupon one day she complained to my mother that she objected to my scrutiny and I was told to keep my eyes on my own plate. I can remember sitting at table with my eyes cast downwards, not daring to lift them to my right! Miss Walker gave my mother a cut glass vase when she left which I still possess. (Edit – given away to charity by her son Clive, some years later).

When I was nine my mother was involved in dramatic events with a family who lived in Brunswick Street, a Mr. and Mrs. Knight, who had pretensions of gentility, and their three daughters. The middle daughter, Lily, who had married George Mayer, a joiner, had produced two daughters, Jean and Margaret, and lived in Birmingham. It was not quite the marriage they approved of, but Lily seemed happy enough. The eldest daughter, Jessie, became a highly respected dressmaker - so good that the local gentry became her clients and her skills commanded high prices. Amongst these was a Mrs. Edmondson. Upon her death, her husband courted Jessie, now in her forties, and there was a great deal of local excitement about the forthcoming marriage. It was undoubtedly a love match - Jessie, having for so long supported her family was at last to have some support for herself and would be moving to Whimple, Devon, where her husband had a most beautiful home - Southbrook.

(L-R) Ethel, Lily & Jessie Knight

But the rejoicing was short lived. Within a fortnight of the wedding Mrs. Knight died, to be followed a fortnight later by her husband; within six weeks, the youngest daughter, Ethel, had lost sister, father and mother.

The dimensions of the tragedy were first made apparent to me by the fact that I went round to the Knights for my lunch instead of going home. My mother was spending most of her time there. Apart from general help and counselling, her main preoccupation was to keep Ethel alive; for Ethel, a pale, thin, gaunt woman in her forties wanted to die. She took to her bed and refused all food. So challenged, my mother prepared unbelievable delicacies to tempt that intractable palate. All were sent down untasted. Neighbours vied with each other to break her fast.

Someone must have eventually succeeded for Ethel continued to live. The problem now was where she was to live. She obviously could not be left to live alone. Mr. Edmondson, quite rightly, was adamant that she should not share his house. So once the contents and the house were sold, Ethel came to live with us.

She was unique in my experience - I can picture her now, her thin white oily face, brown hair and eyes veiled by thick framed spectacles, which appeared never to have been cleaned, gazing across the table at me. We probably ate exceptionally well at this time for the purpose of tempting Ethel, but to each item of food she made the same reply, "No, thank you." It was a phrase she uttered so continuously that it became memorable, especially as she appeared to have no other conversation whatsoever. For some strange reason, my father liked Ethel. Perhaps her very silence and helplessness made him feel protective. In some ways she was like a child who has never grown up. Overshadowed from youth by an elder clever sister and an ebullient middle one, she must have grown up with a sense of inadequacy. I was told that when young she had wanted to work at Enderley Mills, a cotton mill in Enderley Street, but as this common toil was deemed to be beneath the Knights' idea of ladylike employment, the dream was never realised and she simply became an assistant of Jessie. Poor Ethel. She had no personality, no interest in life and no purpose in living. She clung like a leech to anyone who could lend her support and drained them accordingly.

She did not stay with us long. Mrs. Ethel Morrey from Onneley had worked for the Knights, scrubbing and cleaning for them. She was a mild, pleasant woman who suffered much from an overbearing husband - Herbert Morrey, a timber merchant. They had two sons, a ten year gap between them. The elder, Sam, left home after a violent row with his father with half a crown in his pocket, and eventually built up Porthill Dairy, among many other business interests. The younger, Joe, continued the family business. It was to the house of Joe and Jessie Morrey at Madeley, that Ethel went to live for several years.

Meanwhile, our acquaintances multiplied; they included the Mayers, the Morreys, the Edmondsons, and various other friends of the Knights. There was a Miss Timmis, the head teacher of a Primary School in Chesterton, who had a lovely bungalow and garden in Chesterton and occasionally invited us for tea; there were the Bowers family from Audley. William Bowers was a headmaster at Halmerend. And there were the Bakers - although father had known Mr. Baker for many years; they were both cabinet makers.

A great occasion it was when mother was invited to spend a holiday at Whimple in Devon. She enjoyed herself enormously and for weeks was ecstatic about the wonderful way she had been looked after. Jessie and her husband did at least have a few years happiness. But alas, all too soon, Mr. Edmondson died. Although the estate of £82,000 was left to Jessie, I often wondered if she ever recovered from her loss. Scarcely had her husband been buried when Ethel departed post haste for Devon and attached herself to Jessie once more. This parasitic attachment must have drained Jessie. Ethel insisted on sleeping with her, her clammy arms round her. She constantly had sick headaches which kept her in bed for days. Eventually Jessie succumbed with cancer. She certainly had suffered enough stress, if indeed cancer can partly be caused by stress. Ethel was once more alone.

Southbrook, Whimple,Devon.

Back again to North Staffordshire she came and again the Morreys accommodated her. It was Jessie Morrey who was to bear the brunt of life with Ethel. Doubtless she was paid, for Ethel inherited about £30,000 from Jessie, the bulk of which on her death went to the nieces. But whatever the payment, life with Ethel must have required much fortitude. It was rumoured that she wore a money belt at all times. Upon hearing that her feet were painful, they discovered that she was endeavouring to wear out her sister's shoes - sizes too small for her. Each Christmas we received a postal order for 15/-. Out of this my mother was directed to buy a holly wreath for the grave in St. George's Churchyard - the stone cross now fallen - costing 7/6d. We then each received 2/6d for Christmas. We could not refrain from the comment that it was 7/6d for the dead and 2/6d for the living! Eventually, when 66 years old, she did manage to die and so the tragic history of the Knights came to an end.

There is a footnote. Ethel's death would be in 1956 when we moved to a bungalow in Cross Heath. To our amazement she left my mother £200 in her will. This enabled me to buy my first car which was a boon to my parents as well as me. I therefore have much to thank Ethel for.

Willie Bowers, Alice Jones & Ethel Knight.

8: Grammar School Days (1932-39)

It was not an outright scholarship, which would have included free books, but a Free Place, provided I passed an Oral Exam. at the Orme Girls' School. It was here that I first heard of Demosthenes, the great Greek orator who practiced speaking with pebbles in his mouth. The story appealed to me. I liked to hear of people determined to win.

I remember being given a watch as a reward for getting a Free Place. It was probably the most valuable thing I had ever possessed. Unfortunately I forgot to take it off when having a swimming lesson at Newcastle Baths. I was terrified when I realised it had stopped and because I anticipated extreme wrath at home, hid it away so that when the truth eventually emerged, rust had made it impossible for it to be mended.

The terror that this incident evoked was to be repeated many times during my school days. Perhaps I found it difficult to settle in my new surroundings. My parents received a half term report - an indication that my work was well below the expected standard. I was continually made aware of Eveline's lack of diligence and the fear that I might follow in her footsteps. Every evening I was put in the front room do my homework and there was no release until bedtime. Once I tried to practice some gymnastic exercises, only to be told that that was all that Eveline was good at.

I can understand my parents' concern, for they could ill afford even the most minimal expenses involved in my education. Aunt Ada reminded mother that her niece, Barbara, was given 10/- a week to spend as pocket money at the Orme Girls' School. How would mother manage? My mother replied that if she had 10/- a week to give me she wouldn't! With typical ingenuity she applied for free books and financial help with my uniform. The outfitters were Henry White who had the monopoly and whose prices were high. So my mother saw Sydney Myott, explained he problem to him and bought all my uniform from Myott's. Unfortunately it was not quite the same, and unkind school fellows were quick to spot it. Even worse was when the time came to order books. All the paid pupils ordered theirs on white forms while the scholarship girls revealed their penury by writing theirs on pink forms. My parents' anxiety was increased by the knowledge that the allowance granted for books was subject to good reports. Hence the distress over a half term report.

Scholarship Girls 1932 – Betty top right

At this time my godmother, Elsie Coghill, had moved to Sidmouth Lodge where she was faithfully attended by a lady called Sally. For some reason my mother disliked her and found it difficult to receive communion when Sally appeared at church. I scarcely saw her except on the rare occasions when I visited Sidmouth Lodge. One day my godmother (who visited us every Friday after the house had been thoroughly cleaned) appeared with a complaint. I had passed Sally by without speaking to her. Did I think I was superior now that I was at the Grammar School? Of course, I had never recognized nor noticed her, but I was required to go to Sidmouth Lodge and present a fulsome apology.

When I was 12 St. George's Vicar departed for Beccles and for the next 25 years the parish was entrusted to the care of the Revd. Horace Henry Wellings whose stern features, deeply furrowed, replaced the gentle, kindly features of Mr. Birch. But Mr. Wellings was an excellent preacher. Indeed, it was said, perhaps unkindly, that he would have made a better schoolmaster. He became noted for his comment about "Four Wheeler Christians" who only came to church to be baptized, married and buried. Certainly I listened intently to his sermons and learned much about the Christian faith. With hindsight we were probably wrong to assume that he was more concerned with his social peers who seemed to run the parish than ordinary folk. He visited us very rarely; I remember on one occasion he entered our living room, brusquely pushed the cat off a chair before sitting on it and patiently bore father's instructions about ascertaining the depth of the grave in the churchyard in the event of his death.

Ever since, as a small child, I had read "Line upon Line", a book containing bible stories, religion had fascinated me and by the time I was a teenager I longed to have someone to talk to who could answer the questions that burdened my mind. I attended confirmation classes when I was 15 where the catechism was discussed and part of it learned by heart. It was the custom that the final meeting was a personal interview with the vicar. Now, I thought, is my chance to ask all my questions. To my horror we were asked to go in pairs. How could I unburden my mind in front of a third party? So my questions were never asked nor answered. My godmother presented me with two devotional books with extracts to be read daily written by saintly characters. One was "Character and Conduct" and one "Being and Doing". I enjoyed reading books by Florence Barclay but perhaps the book that had most influence on me was "The Greatest Thing in the World" by Henry Drummond. I still don't know the answers to the questions that bothered me in my teens. Nor does anyone else.

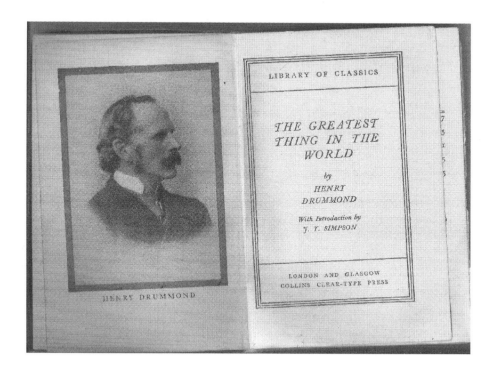

The words, 'inattentive, thoughtless, slow, laying a poor foundation' peppered my first reports. Of course, maths was bound to be hopeless, but German was a new and frightening subject. I never seemed able to understand the basic rules of grammar or be able to apply them. I suspect I did spend a lot of time day dreaming. I suspect also that one of the reasons for my poor results was that I had become short sighted - a condition diagnosed when I was twelve. It must have been impossible for me to see the blackboard properly, but no mention of this ever appeared on my reports. How I hated having to wear glasses which did nothing to enhance my appearance. At the Orme Girls' School I was slow to make friends. Most of the girls were wealthy by comparison and lived all over North Staffordshire so one only saw them at school. I felt that the scholarship girls were much brighter than me. In any case my whole life consisted either of school work, running errands for my mother or learning to play the piano. I had no hobbies. When I was 13 Dorothy Tittensor sold her bicycle to me for 15s. and from then on I would explore the surrounding neighbourhood on Saturday afternoons - Keele and Madeley, Barlaston Downs and Trentham.

Dorothy Tittensor

I dreaded the post which brought my end of term reports and would stay in bed as long as possible in the hope that the first burst of fury had died down. Yet I worked. My mother saw to it that I worked. Idleness was the second worse crime - the first, of course, being having a baby out of wedlock. When the front room became a shop I was transferred to my bedroom to work and in the winter, my mother would go to the trouble of lighting a fire there until the installation of a gas fire relieved her of that chore. Of all her labours for me I was, I think, almost totally unaware. Her idea was that if I could succeed in becoming educated and thereby lifting myself from manual work it would be better than learning how to run a house - especially as I showed no talent at all for household management. True, I ran errands, cleaned windows, brass stair rods and cutlery, prepared fruit and vegetables such as potatoes, runner beans and peas, but I never did the washing or cooked. I never learned dressmaking, though I learned to darn and embroider at the primary school. It was a thousand pities that my habitual clumsiness and lack of domesticity discouraged my mother from teaching me from her vast store of knowledge. I suppose I was so slow that she had not the time to watch me muddle through, make disasters and waste food. Sometimes she was so incensed with me that she declared that if she had had another child it would have been more like her. There were times when I longed for a brother or sister - but had her prediction come true I would probably have hated such a sibling. As it was I was taunted by remarks about other people's children who were able to accomplish things totally impossible to me.

At the back of my mother's mind was the idea that domestic work was somehow inferior. Father's relations looked down on her because she had been a domestic servant. She never tired of insisting that they might look down on her but they should never look down on her child. Nor did they. Yet she stoutly defended domestics and was intensely annoyed when Ada and Elsie dared to compare their one servant to her. She had worked for a very different class of people and knew herself to be superior to both her sisters in law. As indeed she was. She believed in education and regretted that she had had so little. Perhaps she really was disillusioned about marriage, for marriage was often a form of servitude, and certainly there was no point in it unless one's position was thereby enhanced. I doubt if it ever occurred to her that if I were to make a 'good' marriage I would need rather more domestic skills than I possessed.

From the age of 11 I was always in love with some unattainable man. The first was a radio voice - Uncle Eric (Fogg) of Children's Hour. My passion for him was the most intense thing I knew. Through this obsession my love of music developed and grew. I thirsted for Mozart and Beethoven, read the lives of great composers and longed - how I longed - to become a musician. My piano lessons were given by a Mrs. Madeley in Ashfields New Road, 1/3d a time. I passed several easy exams. but however hard I practised - and I did practise for hours - I had neither the ability nor the skill to become a performer. At College I had lessons from Dr. John Lowe and ventured into the easy Beethoven Sonatas. I remember Dr. Lowe saying that he wished he could remove my inhibitions. Alas, they remained with me.

I wanted so much to succeed! I wanted to be exceptionally good at something. In my happiest daydreams I was a great concert pianist or later, an M.P. Alas, my capabilities in no way matched my dreams and no amount of hard work could make them come true. I spent much time thinking and reading – particularly travel and exploration books, John Buchan and Conan Doyle were among my favourite authors. During library periods in school I came across *The Unforgotten Prisoner* by R.C. Hutchinson and fascinated by the story and style continued to reads his books, one of which, *The Fire and the Wood* I chose when eventually I received a prize for Reading and Recitation. The atmosphere generated in *Testament*, a story about Russia at the end of World War 1, is so authentic that, nearly a century later, one can recognize the same attitudes. Above all I loved *Interim*, a slight volume written during World War 2. I acquired quite a collection of desultory general knowledge. I could express myself in writing and in the 6th form was taught to write history essays by one of the best teachers the Orme Girls' School ever produced - Miss E.M. Cowe. I loved drama, enjoyed acting and even won that prize for reading and recitation. I did shine at Scripture - so much of my childhood had been spent reading Bible stories - and I managed to get a credit in that subject in School Certificate having received no tuition in it. But my reports damned me with faint praise - if any. Although never at the bottom of the form, no way could I ever reach the top.

Miss E.M. Cowe

I disliked school rules. We had to move everywhere in silent single file on the left, mounting tread worn steps one at a time or risk being sent back to go up again in the correct manner. Little did I think that the time would come, as it has, when I could have barely got up them one at a time! I hated games and P.E where I could fall off a bar that everyone else could balance on successfully. By the time I had run the extent of the hockey pitch brandishing a stick I had used up all my available energy. Later I played tennis but, lacking hand eye coordination, I frequently missed the ball.

In retrospect I believe that we received a very good education, particularly in the arts field. We did a little science, but then it was regarded as unsuitable for young ladies. If we were regarded as having academic leanings we received very little domestic teaching. I do remember learning how to make Shepherd's Pie and endeavouring to make a pair of pants which became several sizes too large. But we were given an excellent introduction to Shakespeare's plays beginning with A Midsummer Night's Dream and ending with Othello, Anthony and Cleopatra, Julius Caesar and Coriolanus. A rather more impressive collection than that enjoyed by Ronald Preston (my second husband) who did Henry IV part one several times and whose Shakespearean quotations came entirely from that play! We learned much poetry and were given a thorough introduction to the major poets. Indeed, one of the set questions in the School Certificate paper was to write out from memory one of five possible speeches from Henry V.

I attained four credits in School Certificate (one fewer than required for matriculation), the credit in German being almost entirely due to the generosity of Dorothy Tittensor's sister, Florence, who had returned home. Each week during my fourth and fifth years I walked up Florence Street for a German lesson. She must have shown great patience with me and later, after she had married Darrell Robertson, she invited me to stay with them in Axbridge, Somerset, where for the first time I read *Wind in the Willows*. The credit which I was most proud of was in Scripture, for I received no tuition at all in this subject, being the only one to attempt it.

Florence Robertson (nee Tittensor)

Subsequently the problem of my career arose. Without a dead language I could not go to a University, much as I longed to do so. My mother visited the headmistress, Miss Sprunt, ready to be guided by any words of wisdom that might fall. Miss Sprunt decreed that I should become a teacher which would involve two years at a Training College. I rather think my mother was taken aback as my reports certainly did not reveal such promise, but without hesitation, I imagine, accepted that if I were capable of becoming a teacher any further sacrifices that were required would be made and Miss Sprunt was assured of her cooperation.

The sixth form was far more bearable. There were now privileges and duties. There was no more maths - only subjects that I could do - though one year's French and one year's Latin were not in this category. My failure in the realm of languages was crucial and probably affected my life more than any one single thing. My failure in German in Form IIIa decided my future fate. The successful girls took Greek in Form IV and so were already thought of as university material. Because I had no dead language to School Certificate standard I was barred from university entrance and the wide variety of careers that might have resulted. At the age of 17 I took Higher School Certificate in English, History, (main) and German and Geography (subsidiary). I had an extra year in the Upper Sixth and according to Miss Cowe this was virtually as good as a first year at university. I enjoyed the work, particularly history.

I was accepted by Homerton College, Cambridge, for teacher training. This was regarded as the most prestigious of all the teacher training colleges. I remember going to Birmingham for the interview by Miss Skillicorn, then the Principal. Another girl preceded me for the interview and was there for 20 minutes. When my turn came I was interviewed for barely three or four minutes and I thought I had been rejected. However, I was told later that Miss Skillicorn prided herself on being able to recognise a good potential teacher immediately.

I was delighted to leave school and wore a happy smile during the whole of my last day there. I never wanted to return. I looked forward to college with enormous anticipation - two whole years away from home - two whole years in the lovely city of Cambridge.

9: THE SHOP (1934-56)

After Ethel Knight had departed we had our last lodger, Fred Fozard. He was a chemist at Oxens and quite the most bearable lodger we had had. My mother looked after him as though he were her son, and to his dying day he regarded her as a mother, having lost both his own parents. He was keen on motor bikes and after a time began to court a lady with similar interests, Laura Machin who lived at Biddulph. She was a charming person, very fair and of a most kindly disposition. They bought a house at Cross Heath and required to furnish it.

Now by the time I was 12 in 1934, the depression had reduced our income to an all time low. My father, being self-employed, had no dole to fall back on, no assistance from the state at all. All the furniture he made was by hand. It would take him two or three weeks to make a bookcase, for which he might charge £3.15s. He commented bitterly about undertakers who would charge £7 for a coffin which was put underground, never to be seen again, whereas his work would be visible for years. But he could never have become an undertaker. Mostly he did repairs to furniture & upholstery and even removals. We had a brass plate at the front door - G. Jones Cabinet Maker. When a piece of solid, untreated mahogany came his way he had painted on it "G. JONES CABINET MAKER AND UPHOLSTERER" and placed it above the front room window. He did not like upholstery but I often think that the quantity of paper knives I now possess came from the crevices of chairs he upholstered.

Fred Fozard, realising that when he married the 25/- he paid each week would cease unless there was yet another lodger, came up with a brilliant idea. Why not turn the front room into a shop? He needed furniture for his new home and suggested that mother buy a bedroom suite at cost price from a factory and display it in the front room. He would be buying it anyway, so there could be no loss and if she could sell it to someone else for a modest profit there would be an actual gain and the constant fear of poverty alleviated.

For six weeks my mother slept but little. The thought of losing her front room was not a pleasant one, for there were only two rooms excluding the scullery and we would be reduced to one living room.

What finally decided her was the apparently small matter of a displaced door mat. Each morning when she came downstairs the mat by the front room door was askew. "What an untidy lot I've got," she thought, as she put it straight again. Then one morning it had almost disappeared under the door and had been chewed. Now however untidy we might be we did not chew mats. Could it be a mouse? A mouse trap was duly set and next morning when father came down to investigate he was horrified to find the largest rat he had ever seen with its tail in the trap. Mother was called to the scene and together with the coal tongs they picked up the offending rodent and plunged it into a bucket of water outside, while its tail went round spraying water all over the yard in its death agony. My father took to his bed after this event, so shaken was he. The landlady was acquainted with our plight, the rat catcher invoked and a broken sewer discovered, whence rats found their way from the entry, under the fire grate and into our front room. The way was effectively blocked after several more experiences with rats, but my mother's regard for her front room was never quite the same again.

The clearance of the front room began. The piano went into the living room, the grandfather clock upstairs on to the landing, chairs were sold and the new bedroom suite displayed at a price of £20. She sold that suite five times and so was emboldened to continue her trade with manufacturers, many of whom were in Manchester. She sold beds, tables, chairs, sweepers, carpets and rugs and would order goods as required. Thus, until the war came, she was able to add a sizeable amount to the family income.

Father was highly critical of the factory produced furniture which occasionally arrived damaged and required him to put it right. He fumed at the hardboard that was put in the back instead of wood, and the way the polish was put on. But he could not deny that there was a profit to be made.

Fred and I spent hours producing beautiful price tickets and the front door was permanently open except in very cold weather. My mother was an excellent saleswoman and really enjoyed her new role - unlike father who regarded himself as increasingly neglected. Sometimes on washing days, as mother was engaged in sales, an ominous trickle of hot suds would find its way from the copper in the scullery, along the hall and down the front door steps. At that time we still had the old fashioned copper and the mopping up operation was considerable.

Indeed, because of the weekday pressure of business, my mother finally took to washing on a Sunday, her only free day, when she had always managed a rest in the afternoon. Washing in those days was a complete day's operation and it was impossible to get into the scullery or near the sink for any other purpose. Clothes were soaked all night in the sink, then 'dollied' in a dolly tub in hot water until presumed clean. They were then mangled through a big wooden mangle and the whites boiled, mangled again, put through a blue rinse, mangled again and put out to dry if the weather was fine, otherwise they were put on clothes horses round the living room fire in which case both rooms were full of washing. When all was done, the scullery floor was scrubbed, the yard was washed down and all the steps, house, outhouse and lavatory were whitened. We were lucky if the job was finished by tea time and then there was the ironing.

Many of the shop's customers were people recently re-housed in Hempstalls Lane, which had been Sparch Hollow and a pleasant country walk. Shoreditch had been demolished and replaced by a car park. My mother had little faith that the habits of the re-housed had improved. She noted the dirty legs of children as they came past the house to school in a morning and remarked that they had never been washed the night before. Women would pass our house on the way to the Post Office to get their family allowance and call on their way back to deposit it on some article of furniture or a rug. She would keep these articles until they were paid for as a rule, but occasionally her heart got the better of her and I had to go round as an unofficial debt collector.

Fred was duly married and we never had another lodger. By the time the war began things were really picking up. Countless people found this little shop a blessing, for not only were they able to buy more reasonably than anywhere else in town, they had the bonus of my mother's radiant personality and willingness to go to any lengths to oblige them.

Fred and Laura Fozard (nee Machin).

Ever since Neville Chamberlain had returned from Munich waving a futile piece of paper, it had been obvious that war was coming, but memories of the Great War were still so vivid in the memory that people tried to believe that it couldn't happen again. If it did it was thought that it would begin where the other one finished, with poison gas - hence the gas masks. If only we had foreseen September 3rd 1939 and ordered huge quantities of black out material we could have made a fortune. We were able to provide some, however. The sale of new furniture gradually ceased, especially as father's contempt of Utility furniture became apparent. Second hand articles such as sewing machines and prams were scarce and valuable and it soon became known where they might be obtained.

After the war the trade was mostly in rugs and carpets, also bedding. There was always a good profit to be made on Slumberland beds. We kept in touch with warehouses in Manchester such as J N Philips of Tib Street and A W Keggen for carpets in Swan Street and periodically mother and I would go by train to Manchester and have tea at Woolworths after placing our orders. Commercial travellers also called from time to time. I remember one, Dourne Carter, from Keggens - a most unusual name, and there were several others. There was a most amusing incident during this period. The Goodalls having long been gone, the Lindops lived next door with their daughter and son-in-law, Mr. and Mrs. Williams and their family. Old Mrs.Lindop seemed to spend her days at the front room window observing all the comings and goings at No. 6 and must have been intrigued by the visits of commercial travellers, who seemed to spend an inordinate amount of time chatting to my mother. There had been an occasion when my parents were disturbed in the middle of the night by a policeman in the hall because the front door was not properly shut – it had a tendency to stick. After this, father, just before going to bed each night, would dutifully open the front door and bang it shut. One Monday evening, mother, having had a particularly tiring washing day had gone to bed at 9pm, father following much later, as usual. Next day, Mrs. Williams appeared at the back door and reported that her mother, having heard our front door being banged late each night, was spreading rumours about my mother's nocturnal expeditions, which appeared to be on a nightly basis and therefore far from innocent. And commercial travellers did have rather an unsavoury reputation. I can remember how my mother's fury exploded.

Our last orders from Keggens were carpets for the bungalow to which we removed in 1956 and they served us well, going with us from home to home until we had fitted carpets in Chadderton in 1975.

It would be in 1937 that the Government brought in a scheme by which anyone under the age of 55 could contribute to a pension – to be paid when they were 60 – by buying a sixpenny stamp from the Post Office each week. Mother was 54 and duly applied. Unfortunately the powers that be required proof of age – a birth certificate. This her parents had omitted to provide. In country villages in the 1880s it was probably not an uncommon omission. Correspondence flew back and forth as attempts were made to assure them that she was indeed born on the 15th August 1883. She produced a baptismal certificate, but of course, one can be baptized at any time. One day she made a clearance of unwanted correspondence including several old birthday cards and shortly afterwards a request was made that she produce one as evidence of her age. One only remained, from her mother. This was finally accepted as proof and each week father's apprentice bought a sixpenny stamp for mother's card as well as the stamp he required. It was the best investment she ever made. She knew that in August 1943 there would be a little extra money she would not have to work for. The shop continued until we left West Brampton in 1956.

10: The Outbreak of the Second World War

The year was 1940. We had already been at war with Germany for a year when I departed for Cambridge, yet I could write this story almost without reference to it, which, considering the volume of material which continues to be poured out concerning it, must be almost unique. We had feared war from the moment Hitler became Chancellor on 30th January 1933. I remember listening to the Daily Service which was at 10.15 every morning. If there was any special news it would be broadcast immediately after this and the news that morning was that Hitler had become Chancellor of Germany. From then on it was as though a heavy cloud, gradually getting thicker was engulfing our world. The events of the first World War were still fresh in the minds of all those who had experienced it. It seemed incredible that anyone could bear to contemplate another such slaughter. We wanted peace and watched helplessly as Hitler helped himself to German speaking parts of Europe in the name of lebensraum. Neville Chamberlain believed Hitler to be a gentleman - hence Munich.

On Sunday, 3rd September 1939, father and I listened to that now familiar message at 11am (mother was at Meaford) and immediately we loosened the grid in the yard above the cellar presumably to ensure a means of escape. Next day we were besieged for black out material. Had we had the forethought to stock the entire house with it we could have made a fortune overnight. But alas, our small stock soon went.

We saw soldiers sombrely going to report and my mother remarked on the contrast with the young men who so joyfully volunteered in 1914. We had Poles stationed in Newcastle, one of whom I innocently invited to hear Polish broadcasts. Parental disapproval registered itself so strongly that I never again ventured a similar gesture of hospitality.

The early part of 1940 it was impossible to forget. We watched the appalling drama unfold as the Germans swept across Belgium and Holland and listened to the radio in horror when Paris fell. Local comment was that the French were more concerned that their beautiful capital city should be preserved than they were to fight to the last for their country. Our history lessons were interspersed with matters concerning the war and one day in June I remember Miss Cowe with ashen face saying that she believed that invasion was imminent. We all believed that once France had fallen our invasion would follow and waited daily for it to happen.

Yet in material matters, incredible though it may seem, the war scarcely affected us. The only relative to be called up was Eric Harvey who sadly was killed in December 1942. Later, Fred Fozard was called up and served much of his time in the Far East, returning with two little wooden Burmese Tigers as a gift for us.

We had never had enough money for luxuries and so rationing made little difference. Mother was such an excellent manager that we lived just as well during the war as before it and her mafia of friends ran an exchange mechanism for tea, sugar, eggs, cream etc. Vegetables were available from Meaford. I could only afford one best dress to take to college, so clothes rationing was never a great worry.

There were one or two air raids in the vicinity and to begin with the cellar was resorted to, but as it seemed increasingly clear that Hitler's wrath was unlikely to descend on Newcastle-under-Lyme the cellar was abandoned and a compromise was made by bringing the double bed downstairs - this in an already tiny living room. Eventually this too was restored to its rightful place which must have been a great relief. Of course, I was away from home during the greater part of the war, and so only had brief glances of the activity, though I was kept in constant touch by the long and vivid letters of my mother.

Aunt Betty and Cousin Mary in Canada sent us wonderful parcels of impossible to obtain goods, including my very first pair of nylons. They lasted for ages, and we never forgot their great generosity.

I suppose the blackouts were one of the most unpleasant aspects of living during the war, especially in the winter on nights when there was no moon. I remember on one occasion both mother and I were out - she visiting Betty May while I was helping at a canteen on the Higherland. I collided with a lamp post and she with a gate post and both of us arrived back with black eyes. Father was much amused. It was as though he had struck out at both of us simultaneously. Cycling in the dark was dangerous. Only a narrow dim beam of light was allowed and I remember narrowly avoiding a pram.

But once the Battle of Britain was over, my mind was concentrated on thoughts of life in Homerton College, Cambridge to which I departed in September 1940. The train fare was £1.6s and I had to change trains at Bletchley, little knowing how important that small place was to the war effort. So began life at college.

11: CAMBRIDGE (1940-42)

I was so excited at the thought of going to college that it seldom occurred to me to wonder if I really wanted to be a teacher. But all my life I had been brought up to defer to the wishes of others and therefore whatever they decided must be for the best. Moreover, I knew that it was essential for me to get a secure job as my parents could never have supported me – indeed, it was they who needed my support. Moreover, what I believed I really wanted was a husband, a home and a family of my own and in those days women were required to resign from teaching if they married, so I hoped I would not be required to teach for very long - if I thought about it at all.

At school I had been stretched academically and ideally I would have liked to continue the process. How I would have loved to read Politics, Philosophy and Economics. When *Brideshead Revisited* was televised in 1981 I felt nothing but disgust and indeed, fury at the sight of a young man, surrounded by every opportunity at Oxford to gain academic knowledge and deliberately wasting his time. I had regularly attended Workers Educational Association (WEA) classes in Newcastle Town Hall led by among others R.H.S. Crossman, mostly concerned with the interwar period. Nelly Mould, who later received an OBE for her work as local Secretary of the WEA, lived in Florence Street and encouraged me. At 17 I had a letter printed in The Listener in which I criticised Harold Nicholson's argument for open negotiations. I believed and still believe that many negotiations if they are to succeed, need to be secret.

Open Covenants and Open Negotiations

Though finding myself in complete agreement with the thought and argument of Mr. Harold Nicolson's talk on 'Open Covenants and Open Negotiations', I feel that the conclusion he arrived at is altogether too simple and lucid to be practicable. In contrasting the eventual success of the 1906-7 Russian negotiations, which were 'secret', with the very qualified success of those we are at present involved in, I feel that he omitted to mention several very important points. Those negotiations, which were conducted in so leisurely a fashion, were not a matter of peace and war, neither were the public so well-furnished with means of receiving information. The Opposition were not unduly alarmed about the amount of time taken, nor did they accuse the Government of half-heartedness. If today Mr. Chamberlain calmly announced that there would be no more reports on the present negotiations until they were over, the Opposition simply wouldn't be able to find words to express their horror and indignation. And I very much doubt if Mr. Nicolson would apply his theory if there was a chance of turning the Government out ! Also, it has been increasingly evident that the more involved foreign affairs become, the more they rest upon negotiation.

That any Government has a difficult time steering between the Scylla of Public Opinion and the Charybdis of a foreign Power cannot be doubted. We have only too much mournful evidence of this fact. But I doubt if they would find the seas of secret negotiation any safer.

Newcastle, Staffs.   M. Elizabeth Jones

Letter to the Listener – 1939 aged 17.

I soon began to regard college as a rest period academically after the hard intellectual grind of school. The subjects I opted to take, History, English, Geography and Music, had already been learnt to university standard, apart from Music and the teaching at college was neither as inspiring or compelling as that I had received at school. Of course, the aims were different. Here, presumably, we were to be taught to teach and from the very beginning I knew that this was the one thing I didn't want to do.

During the first year we had to tackle a wide curriculum - biology, art, handcraft - at all of which my achievements were abysmal. The only joy was the piano lessons that I received from Dr. John Lowe and I practised Beethoven's easy sonatas for hours - though only seldom without mistakes.

During the second term - Jan. to Mar. 1941, when the country's morale was at a low ebb, we were required to go on teaching practice and I worked myself up into a state of terror. German Measles intervened and I was spared this initial entry into a classroom filled with children that I had to control and teach. But during the summer term there was no such reprieve and somehow I managed to survive teaching practice at Chesterton.

Of course, there was a good library and I found myself being drawn to books on psychology as well as the prescribed reading about various methods of teaching I was entranced by the works of Dr. A.S. Neill who believed that children should pursue their own interests, decide their own rules and be the sole arbiters of what they learnt. That would have suited me, but it was necessary to admit that academic excellence was unlikely to be achieved that way.

Many of the girls complained of the restrictions imposed on them - we required late passes to be out as late as 11pm - but my social life hitherto had been practically nil and I thought college rules very liberal. My upbringing had not only been very sheltered - my naivety was profound - but human biology and particularly knowledge of the male sex were almost zero. I had never had a boyfriend, apart from Michael Loebenstein, who attended the High School and was younger than me. His stepfather was Harold Marks, another WEA lecturer, and our acquaintance was limited to invitations to the house for tea. Later he was to be in Cambridge and read medicine, but the relationship was always platonic. Indeed, my mother's method of protecting me from male predators was to instil fear into me. Men should be repelled. I still had no idea of the nature of sexual intercourse. Influenced perhaps by romantic films I believed that in marriage one found perfect happiness. Brought up by parents conforming to the socially accepted code of the day, it was necessary to preserve virginity until marriage as no man worth having would contemplate marrying what was regarded as 'damaged goods'. And any potential husband must possess the means to provide for his wife by owning a home for her. I was often told, 'You can always stoop down and pick up nothing'.

So it was not to be wondered at that I looked forward to enjoying a social life at Cambridge but my unsophistication, gaucheness and almost total ignorance of young males were not the best preparation into such a society. I cannot now remember any encounters during my first year, but the Dorothy Cafe was a good place to meet people and I also went to several lectures on topics that interested me - mostly politics and current affairs.

During the long vacation at the end of that first year, I took a job as a waitress at the Regent Cafe in Hanley. I worked from 9am - 8.30pm with a two hour break in the afternoon for 18/6d a week. With tips I usually made £2. It was certainly hard work and at first my legs ached appallingly, but I soon came to enjoy the life there - I actually like waiting on people. I remember Renee Houston came once while playing at the Theatre Royal and gave me a half crown tip. It was wonderful. The only drawback was that my hair stank perpetually of fish and chips.

So armed with £12, which had to last a long time, I returned to college and on 15th October 1941 I met my first love in the Dorothy Cafe. His name was Phillip Rees. He was reading law at Downing College, and came from a little village called Llangadog in Carmarthenshire. His birthday was 10th March. What a strange coincidence that so many years later, my son had the same birthday. He had rooms overlooking Parker's Piece - they are now lawyer's offices - and during the next eight weeks my bicycle was very frequently parked there - even during my month of teaching practice which somehow went splendidly. We went to dances, to the cinema and to cafes. He came to a play we put on at college in which I had a part. I even went to the University Rugby match with him and was unwise enough to display a lack of enthusiasm. These eight weeks were, I think, the happiest of my whole life. I knew I was falling in love and let it happen. Here was the man I wanted above all others. If only I had had any social preparation, or had been the 'nice, quiet girl' my mother had longed for. But I could only be me, and towards the end of the eight weeks I realised that his feelings were changing. He knew that he had to join the army in January and the last I ever heard from him was a Christmas card. I did not realise how common this situation was and is, for young men mature more slowly than women who should be advised of the foolishness of such headlong emotional involvement.

For me it was catastrophe. I longed for him with all my heart, had even learned the Welsh National Anthem and for years I could never hear 'Sauspan Fach', the Rugby song, without a tug on the heart strings. It was not only that I had loved and lost. The inevitability of teaching came nearer day by day. I read the whole of the Book of Job and the Psalms, but even such words of wisdom would not make time stand still.

Meanwhile I worked as hard as I could, writing a thesis on 'Conservatism in the Nineteenth Century' - a subject I was well briefed on because of my idolisation of Disraeli, and when exam time came I managed to get a distinction in history. More remarkably, after a final school practice I was regarded as fit to teach.

My parents were overjoyed to have produced a fully qualified teacher. As a special treat they booked a holiday in Blackpool for all three of us. They meant so very kindly, and it must have been an expense they could ill afford, but it was the last thing on earth I wanted. I didn't want a conventional holiday and resented the old constraints after two years of relative freedom. My father was by then 76 years old and my mother 59.

12: Teaching in South Staffordshire (1942-44)

Had I known what was to follow I might have appreciated the Blackpool holiday more. I had elected to teach in South Staffordshire - the one choice I had. It was either that or to begin teaching at home and the thought of failure on home territory where everyone knew me, and the constraints inevitable once life at home was resumed determined my choice. To ensure a job in the 1930s when unemployment was rife, it was expedient to obtain a Local Authority Loan for college. Thus, the Local Education Authority were bound to find you a job in order for the loan to be repaid. Of course, I needed a loan, as my parents could never have afforded college fees. The onset of war had altered the employment situation drastically. Most of the men teachers who were physically fit had joined the forces and teaching had become a reserved occupation. There was no way out of it unless one was so appallingly bad that one was thrown out.

Thus, after an interview at Stafford I was offered a post at Chase Terrace Senior Boys' School. Chase Terrace lies four miles from Lichfield, four from Cannock and eight from Walsall. The last bus went at 8pm. I found digs in a nice detached house with a childless middle aged couple, Leslie and Dorothy Fenn. They were extremely kind to me; the house was kept spotless and to be in a house with a bathroom was sheer delight. I paid 25/- for 5 days board, went home weekends, giving my mother £1 or £2, paying £2.10s a month back on my loan. My first wage packet contained £13.

I began to teach on 11th August 1942. Because of the war the summer holiday was cut short so that there could be a month's holiday for potato picking in October. The date 11th August became quite significant. I passed my driving test on 11th August 1954 and my mother died on 11th August 1960. But I had other things to think about in 1942.

The headmaster, a Mr. Dennis, had not been college trained and displayed unconcealed contempt for college training. The men remaining on the staff were either past military age or in some way disabled. To assist in this male dominated establishment were sent myself and another girl straight from college, Ivy Berrisford, also from North Staffordshire. We were required to teach classes of 11-year-old mining village boys.

Looking back, I wonder how I survived. I had absolutely no confidence in my ability to teach, I had practically no knowledge of the male animal; I had spent the larger part of my teens acquiring academic knowledge which interested me and the last two years in a university city, where, despite the war, there was a high level of intellectual activity which in a limited way I had shared. And now I was required to teach boys who had not the slightest intention of learning, in whom I was not really interested, while hovering in the background loomed the disapproving spectre of the headmaster. My writing did not suit - I must practise 'real writing'. So I laboriously learnt to write in the approved manner. When teaching a grammar rule I ignored mistakes not appertaining to that rule and was upbraided in front of the class for ignoring obvious mistakes. All the staff were on the platform during assembly. As it drew to a close I experienced near panic every day as I knew I had to brace myself to enter the hated classroom. The highlight of the day was 4pm when I knew I had a whole evening and night before me - until the next 9am. I remember waking in the morning and beginning the descent of my spirits which again reached its nadir at 9am. At 7.50am came a 5-minute religious 'slot'. The favourite hymn seemed to be, 'Take up thy cross,' and grimly, each day I did just that. We didn't know then about the horrors of concentration camps or the sufferings of refugees, nor were the people I knew losing family, friends and homes from enemy action; all I knew was my own wretchedness and that there was no escape.

I think the October break saved my sanity. At least I had a whole month away from the place. This also happened at Christmas when the return to school was delayed by the fortunate breakdown of boilers. The only physical effect I noticed was that my hair began to come out in handfuls. It was never exactly luxuriant, but thereafter it was sparse.

By the end of the Spring term it must have been apparent to all that I was unhappy - and I don't imagine that the headmaster was particularly happy with me. I was offered a transfer to a Junior Mixed School in Norton Canes, two miles away, where Miss Plant was the headmistress. I grabbed it with gratitude.

Staff at Norton Canes School 1941 - 43

It wasn't really that much better. I had a class of 40 - 50 eight-year olds in a room next door to the headmistress, and when pandemonium reigned, as it often did, she would march in, stern faced, and within seconds there was absolute silence. Whereupon she would depart with a pitying look. In order to maintain discipline, the policy was to slap the arms of offenders. This I hated doing but was driven to it by sheer desperation. At one juncture my numbers were swollen to 60 with the advent of evacuees. I had an epileptic child who had frequent fits. My attempts at art consisted of using a book called, 'How to draw'. After I had left I was asked what had happened to my handcraft. I still do not know. I have no memory of it.

One useful thing I did learn - a complete knowledge of multiplication tables taken at random. It was the custom just before lunchtime to have the children line up in the order in which they could answer these random numbers. "Twelve twos," "nine fives", "eight threes" and so on. The children in the line remained delightfully silent for if they spoke they had to go back to their places. Arithmetic had never been my strong point but I never need a calculator for multiplication.

All this time I lived with the Fenns and went to school on my bike. As I cycled from Chasetown the road to the school turned left off the main road to Cannock and how often I longed to go straight on and so home. Going home! This was the only relief and even there, as Sunday dawned, my spirits began to descend, knowing that by night I should once more be in Chasetown and waiting for the dreaded Monday. Getting home and returning were quite major problems except in the summer when I could cycle the 30 miles in three hours. Occasionally I stopped at Meaford on the way. From the road between Cannock and Stafford one could sometimes see the Wrekin and beyond, the Welsh Hills, for which my heart still cried out. If one travelled respectably by bus it was impossible to get home before Saturday lunchtime as there were no buses for the entire journey on Friday evening and the return journey would have had to begin on Sunday morning. Five changes of bus were required on a Saturday, one to Five Ways, another to Cannock. From there a bus to Stafford, one to Stoke and another to Newcastle. The time involved was four hours to travel 30 miles. One could get via Lichfield but this was just as time consuming. So very early during my stay in South Staffs. I devised a scheme for avoiding this tedious business. Having bussed to Cannock, conveniently situated on the A34, I thumbed a lift on a lorry and in an hour was deposited in Newcastle - thus home by 6 or 7pm. The return journey was accomplished on Sunday in the same manner. My mother's friends held up their hands in horror at the thought of what misfortunes might befall as the result of this outrageous behaviour. I hope they were suitably relieved when none did. One of the lorry drivers, Darrell Gilton, was from Bolton. He carried propellers. He was an educated man and we got to know each other quite well and he even took me to the cinema once or twice. Once I left South Staffs. the acquaintance died a natural death, but years later I was amazed to receive a letter from his lady friend telling me that he had died of lung cancer and I visited her in Bolton. I still remember him when I see a car registration number BBN.

On my arrival at home I always looked apprehensively round the back gate, for there was usually parked Dorothy Tittensor's bicycle. Dorothy had removed herself and her mother from Florence Street to the Westlands, regarding it as a more salubrious area where it was not done to hang washing outside. The move, however upmarket, also removed old Mrs. Tittensor from her familiar surroundings, shops and my mother, thus increasing her loneliness. After school, each Friday, Dorothy, having parked the bike, proceeded to do her shopping and her return frequently occurred just as we were sitting down to a meal when all the week's events would be under discussion. As the gate opened our hearts sank though mother with her usual welcoming smile opened the door to greet her. Then followed an hour or so when, cup of tea in hand, Dorothy recounted her week's events while I sat there seething. Dorothy had no idea that she was interrupting a family gathering. When she eventually went mother would say, "I can't understand how she can leave that lonely old woman for so long". Of course, life for Dorothy with her mother can scarcely have been a bed of roses.

When the first long summer holiday came I set off on the bike for Wales, deciding to go through Wales to Aberystwyth. I found lodgings at Mallwyd with an old lady who asked me if 5/- would be too much. She read the Bible in Welsh. I returned via Llandilo, so that I could at least have one look at Llangadog. I even found Phillip's house which I photographed and then sped away unseen. Finally I came to Hereford and Ledbury, intending to spend the night at a Youth Hostel at Much Marcle. There were no signposts - any German invaders were to be denied directions - and I was weary and frustrated. A young sailor also with a bike offered to help and eventually we found it. It was a building separate from the warden's house and I was solemnly handed the key.

One could do no other than invite the young sailor in for a cup of tea. Then began one of the strangest nights that I have ever spent. I was the only youth hosteller present and the young sailor, one Jim Apperley, decided that it was a grand opportunity to get better acquainted. I was still a virgin and had no intention of yielding to a casual acquaintance. He had no intention of departing but as the night wore on it dawned upon him that I was serious and his efforts abated. He promptly fell in love with me. We breakfasted at Ledbury next morning and I doubt if anyone would have believed that so innocent a night could have been spent. From that time on I was inundated with boxes of apples, and Jim wrote and visited whenever he could. He wanted so much to marry me and if I had had any decency I would either have married him or sent him packing. But, alas, it was so very flattering to have so much attention bestowed on me, so I was quite content to be courted though I knew that I could never marry him. I did not love him. For years afterwards I heard from him from time to time and incredibly, 20 years later, just before my marriage he found my phone number and called me.

Despite my hatred of teaching and longing for a husband, home and family, I knew I could not marry the average man to live in an average semi and devote myself to an average life. I wanted to explore, to discover, and as I realise now, marriage would have been a caging experience unless I met someone with the same appetite for adventure. I wanted someone to be my intellectual equal or superior. The idea of the dominant male still prevailed and my secret hope was that I could marry a man with a great career and devote myself to him and his career. And how was I to find such a one within the society I knew?

At the end of 1943 came the sad news that Eric Harvey had been killed between two vehicles - one in gear. His wife Jen was left widowed with a small son, Peter, and an old grandmother to look after. An old grandmother whose mind was concentrated on her bowels. She would wait at the window to attract passers by and entreat them to supply her with Epsom Salts. The resulting thin brown lines soon alerted Jen to her activities and Epsom Salts were banned. Jen had her sister Elsie to stay with her for the rest of the war. I remember going over to Meaford with the wreath for Eric's funeral. I stood waiting for the bus to return home, gripped with the most intense pain in my side. It was pleurisy and the Christmas holidays were spent recovering from it. But eventually it was necessary to return to Chasetown and Norton Canes School.

During 1944 I applied for several jobs, one in Ruislip (the size and precision of the school frightened me) and one in the Lake District, where I was unsuccessful. I spent part of the summer holidays potato picking at Preston Brook where I met Anne Stevenson, who later married and became Anne Booth, eventually going to live in Stalybridge.

During the autumn term I was told of a vacancy at Broadmeadow Girls' School at Chesterton. I did not really want to return home, yet neither did I want to remain at Norton Canes. My decision was influenced by the knowledge that I was really needed at home, both physically and financially, and that real love - agape - meant sacrifice. For it was a sacrifice to be penned in again with elderly parents - my father was 78 that year. The only privacy I had was in my bedroom. There was nowhere to entertain young men except in the living room with parents.

So I applied for the job of teaching English at Broadmeadow Girls' School and was accepted. Home I went in December 1944 to begin teaching there in January 1945.

13: TEACHING IN NORTH STAFFORDSHIRE (1945-48)

As I look back on that January in 1945, I suppose my uppermost feelings were sheer apprehension and fear. True, there were consolations. These children were seniors, so there was some chance of academic attempts if not achievements; and they were girls - a species with which I was more familiar than boys. Moreover - especially with hindsight - the staff were agreeable. Some I remembered from the Orme Girls' School. There were people like Kath Yorke and Eileen Braddock (Baker) who did incredible things with the choir. I can never hear *'Lift thine eyes'* without thinking of them. At this school I learned how to make use of ballads dramatically and found out how much I loved teaching drama. There was a snag. The headmistress, a Miss Poppleton, was the worst I ever encountered. Words like diabolical, unreasonable, unsympathetic and even terror and despair provoking only touch the surface of my feelings about this woman.

If I inscribed the words, '**I did not want to teach,**' over every page of this manuscript it could not be uttered as frequently as I felt this absolute certainty. While at Norton Canes I had cycled to Cannock to do shorthand and typing at night school to try to acquire a skill to fit me for another job. But it was not an easy journey in black out conditions either with or without a bike and I found shorthand very difficult. I thought of learning Latin to try for a degree and even had private lessons and began a correspondence course. But Latin I could not manage. Marriage seemed to be the only way out but how could I exchange a cage that lasted between 9am and 4pm for one that was permanent?

So one learned to put up with Miss Poppleton; her habit of keeping the keys under her surveillance until you appeared, often breathless up the stairs, so that she could note the time of your arrival and make a note of any lack of enthusiasm to appear early; the handing in each Monday of work intended for that week; the sudden descent on a class you were teaching to find yourself ridiculed in front of the children. When you had prepared a piece of drama and it had appeared in that wretched record book for weeks she would suddenly enter, watch with a critical eye, alter all the moves you had made the girls do, and excuse herself by saying that she wouldn't have bothered if it hadn't been good.

Was it any wonder that at the first dance I attended at the Castle Hotel I found a young Fleet Air Arm man who was undoubtedly attracted and began to visit me, together with his friend, Dick Swingler, married to Dorothy whose home was Kettering. Eric Barnett came from Nottingham. Despite my mother's reservations (he had no money, education or prospects), love, after a fashion, blossomed. Looking back, I think it was more like desperation. As the affair wore on (and it became an affair) the thought of actual marriage became increasingly undesirable. My mother's silent opposition could be felt; his mother was not particularly keen. He wanted a home next door but one to her. The family played cards - particularly Solo - like fanatics. I was hopeless at that and practically everything his mother regarded as desirable - running a home, for instance. We did become engaged but I think we both knew that the chances of future happiness were remote. I remember I could not bear the thought of sharing a bedroom with him - though I often longed to share a bed. In the end he broke it off and although my agony was intense it was more a bitterness of failure than a sorrow for lost love. I began to create a shell about me that could not be pierced, so that a dichotomy arose between heart and body; the need for sexual satisfaction had arisen; but to whom could I trust my heart?

The war and my love affair now over, I concentrated as never before on the 'brief hours and weeks' when I could legitimately free myself from my job and my home - namely the holidays. Between 1946 and 1951 I cycled - this being the cheapest method of transport - and also managed to visit Switzerland and Italy. The first trip - in 1946 - was via Ludlow, Hereford, Chepstow, Bristol; down to Cornwall, across the south coast, calling at Lymington to stay with Edgar and May Hopkinson, thence to London and the Proms and so to Kettering where Dick and Dorothy Swingler put me up for the night. In all, the three week trip cost £20.

Somewhere in Cornwall I met a young artist - John Paris from Aldershot. He and his brother Colin were also cycling. We joined forces with much mutual benefit and my friendship with John lasted several years. The following Easter found us cycling up to Scotland through Glencoe and to Fort William I made my one and only attempt at Ben Nevis when we got half way up in the snow. We also had a holiday in Wales, visiting Snowdonia and Machynlleth.

I suppose the idea of marriage did occur, but in a way the friendship was too good. I really couldn't see myself permanently sitting around while my lord and master painted pictures. In any case we were more equal than that. John in his turn while appreciating my practicality resented my timetable instincts, especially when it came to getting meals. (Oh, dear! How that timetable has become unseated! – in old age). So he went his way and married a sweet girl whom I never met until after my mother died. A sorrow for them was that she was unable to bear a child and I believe they eventually adopted one.

One of my marathon trips was to the first Edinburgh Festival in 1947 where I went to see Mozart's *'Marriage of Figaro'* and Alec Guinness in *'Richard II.'* Unforgettable. I did this all alone. I had learnt to cheat when cycling long distances. An empty lorry was a great temptation to a cyclist pushing wearily uphill - so I was able to cover much greater distances than when attempting to do it all by pedal power.

I have always been glad of my Irish trip. Through the radio, I had heard of a remarkable teacher in Ballymena, a Mr. R.L. Russell, who taught his pupils to write poetry in the metre of Hiawatha, produce woodcuts and line blocks, etchings and sketches. I wrote to him, visited him and his daughter, Betty, and received a signed copy of the second impression of his book The Child and his Pencil (1936). I corresponded with Betty Russell for several years after that and was much inspired by her father's methods which I often adopted when teaching poetry. I still have several poems written by the children I taught. It was a wonderful way to expand the use of language and imagination.

The Irish trip had other fascinations. My thoughts on Ireland has been coloured by my maternal grandfather's pronouncement in the 1880s when Gladstone was anxious to get Home Rule for Ireland. My grandfather was opposed to Home Rule, "The Irish keep chickens and pigs in their houses," said he, "If they have no more respect for their homes, how can they govern themselves?" It may not be a logical conclusion but it satisfied my labouring grandfather on his 15/- a week.

I was amazed by the great religious chasm. The Church of Ireland's churches were more like free church chapels in their bareness and simplicity.   St. George's, Newcastle was 'low church'. I remember Ronald once commenting that it was 'basement'. There were no candles and communion was celebrated at the north end of the altar. But if that was 'basement' Northern Ireland churches were below that. I found out that one did not discuss religion.

Having left Ballymena, I joined the coast road, through Cushendall, Ballycastle and Bushmills. I visited the Giant's Causeway with its strange hexagonal rocks. Coleraine, Limavady and Londonderry were visited before crossing the frontier into Donegal. I found that one could smell the villages in Eire long before one arrived and I remembered my maternal grandfather's pronouncement in the 1880s. To my amazement, I discovered the Irish were still keeping their livestock in their houses, for out of them came scuttling chickens – though I saw no pigs - emerge. The houses were still lit by oil lamps and each had its stock of peat standing almost as high as the house. Women were burdened down with labouring – I saw them carrying two buckets of water suspended by a yoke across their shoulders, while the men could be seen idly chatting on street corners. The children in many places ran about barefoot – something I had never seen before. I injudiciously mentioned this to an acquaintance who retorted, "And didn't you enjoy running about barefoot when you were a child?" Of course, I would never have been allowed such an experience. Perhaps less was expected of these children. Amidst all this poverty there stood out, in all its splendour, the church. Like many others before me, I was baffled by the contrast of religious wealth and human poverty.

Having passed through Letterkenny, I stayed at a Youth Hostel in Bundoran. It was there that I was impressed by the efficiency of the Garda. I had a treasured fountain pen, bought with money given when I was 21. I discovered its loss and knew who the thief was. I reported it to the Garda and to my amazement the pen was returned. I now spent time studying villages that lay along the border between Northern Ireland and Eire. During the hostilities of the 70s, 80s and 90s, when these places were the scenes of violence and suspicion, the names of these border posts brought back memories. As one passed through the main road, always one was stopped at the frontier, passport noted, pleasantries exchanged and luggage examined. I even recollect one particularly randy Irish Customs Official, whom, strangely enough, I came across again, years later when in other company. He actually recognized me!

The reason for my fascination for the Irish frontier was very basic. For years, rationing had been part of the inevitable nature of life. It was in force between 1939 and 1953 and we learnt to live with it. When I visited Switzerland in 1948 the shock of being regaled with so much and so great a variety of food, was extraordinary. It took months for me to get over it. In Eire meat was plentiful and unrationed. I therefore determined to buy as much as I could, smuggle it over the border and post it home. To do this undetected it was necessary to find where the border bisected country lanes with little customs activity. There was such a one near Belleek, on the Fermanagh border. I practised a 'dry run', noting my facial expressions when totally innocent in case stopped, and then proceeded to buy as much meat as I could (a) afford and (b) carry before making my guilty crossing. As far as I can remember I was never stopped, and certainly never detected. I often wonder what state the meat was in when it arrived home. But the postal service was good and goods posted one day would arrive the next. I think I made three or four such expeditions and thoroughly enjoyed the whole disgraceful experience.

Gradually I made my way back, probably to Belfast, though I have a clear memory of cycling along the causeway towards Holyhead, so perhaps it might have been Dublin.

Of the years between 1945 and 1948 I have little recollection apart from the holidays. I don't even remember the appalling winter of 1947, which is remembered by all I have met who endured it. All I know is that during term time I trudged wearily to Chesterton each day to school wondering what, if anything, I could do to escape.

14: GLASS STREET SCHOOL – HANLEY (1948-55)

In May, 1948, my agony at Chesterton came to an end. It was brought about by the intervention of one Agnes Doig who had been a mature student at Homerton and had recently been appointed Nursery Schools Organiser in Stoke-on-Trent. She must have found my address and came to visit me. After three years of Miss Poppleton I had no confidence, let alone any pleasure in my capacity as a teacher, and because of this I dreaded applying for another post - which might be worse. After all, the track record since 1942 had not been encouraging. In vain I tried to think what else I could do, but I was trained only as a teacher - which was a salaried and pensionable post - any other job would look like failure especially in the eyes of my parents who had sacrificed for my education and were now becoming increasingly dependent on me.

Agnes, having listened to my dismal account of teaching at Chesterton, suggested that I apply for a job in Hanley. Terror seized me. What if it should be worse? However, an application form was produced and Agnes stood over me while I filled it in, breathing such comforting words as, "When I told them I had found a teacher for them they offered to build a school round you if you would come." Such was the severe shortage of teachers in 1948.

Again the job specified the teaching of English. It seemed to be my fate to teach this despite my preference for History and Geography. This time I was not even interviewed, so glad they were to acquire a teacher. I simply went up to the school - Glass Street, Hanley (now a carpark!) and met the headmistress.

Esther Boulton was - mercifully - a total contrast to Miss Poppleton. Quiet, brown eyed and smiling, she looked less than her forty years. She ruled that rabbit warren of a school with a persuasive rather than a dominating hand. To my amazement she joined her staff for morning and afternoon breaks. Every year she made some article for each member of staff as a Christmas present - crocheted tray cloths, hand towels, dressing table sets and the like. If she had a fault it was to become perfect herself, as all her handwork was. She did not believe in illness and being able to 'work it off' herself had little sympathy with frailer mortals who, like myself, invariably became ill again if there was a premature return. I have never absented myself if it was physically possible to get there and have taught with a soaring temperature. But in the days before antibiotics I always found that dashing straight back as soon as one was out of bed was the surest way to return there.

Of all her qualities and capacities, the one that mattered most to me was that she had a leaning towards maths and science and was prepared to give me carte blanche in the matter of teaching English. Indeed she even once asked me for advice on the spelling of 'break' and 'brake'. I was dumbfounded. So for the first time I could organise the English teaching as I liked and was able to introduce drama into the school. The highlights were a Nativity Play which opened with a flute solo in one of Bach's Brandenburg concertos - supposedly played by a shepherd boy. This play apparently continued ad nauseum after I had left. Another production I remember was *'A Midsummer Night's Dream'* and the whole script became ingrained in my memory.

Such was the shortage of teachers that it was almost impossible to replace specialist people, and being something of an all rounder academically, I found myself teaching History when the History person left and Geography when that post was vacated. There was always the stalwart Ann Ferguson to teach English and I could never emulate her beautiful writing. Finally, Mary Prescott left. She had played the piano for hymns and there was now no one else but me who could do this. So I became the music teacher.

To assist me, inspire me and inform me I attended courses, most of which were not only informative but enjoyable. I joyfully attended these, partly, I confess, because I longed to meet someone whom I could marry. This particular ambition was not fulfilled though on one occasion I must have made one woman happy by persuading her lover to marry her. I also remember the childish pleasure evoked by attending a fair with this man and having 'goes' on roundabouts etc. Such frivolity was rare.

On the Geography course in 1953 I fell in love with Ken Marshall all resplendent in naval uniform - a feeling that was returned, but as usual with me, there was no happy outcome because he had a wife in Todmorden. We did actually meet later somewhere near Manchester during Whitsuntide and saw the famous Whit Walks, before the Coronation, but not unnaturally, his wife, having rumbled the affair, did the most sensible thing. She wrote to me and that was that.

The most memorable course of all was the music course of 1950 at Reading University. As I have said, I had striven with great dedication to play the piano accurately, but without success. I had absolutely no voice for singing, nor could I read music well enough to sing by it - even if anyone could have borne to listen! Armed then with an abiding love of classical music and an almost total inability to perform it, I arrived at Reading and awoke next morning to the strains of trios, quartets, quintets and possibly even sextets being performed by the assembled students. This was the morning chorus each day. Over meals, abstruse musical terms, compositions, composers, performers were as natural as meat and drink to my accomplished colleagues, who were fortunately so wrapped up in their own abilities that by keeping quiet and looking on admiringly I was easily able to conceal my ignorance and inability. We formed a great choir which was to perform Vaughan William's *Job* and *Flos Campi*, Bach's *Ein Feste Burg* and a version of *Fidele* from *Cymbeline*. My only hope was to become a soprano, for at least I could possibly manage the top line, whereas I had little confidence in coping with the contralto part.

Being taught by such people as Bernard Shore, a celebrated viola player, and Cuthbert Bates an HMI from Bath opened a new world for me. Everything we did was explained. We were told how to give the effect required so that Vaughan Williams, whose work had hitherto been totally incomprehensible to me, became alive with meaning. Shall I ever forget an inspired Bernard Shore willing us to reach top A in *Flos Campi*! It was like being in heaven and probably the nearest I shall ever get to it on this earth. Till then, Mozart and Beethoven had been my greatest joy. Now I began to perceive the majesty of Bach.

I had made friends with some accomplished and wealthy people from Bath who were taking part in the *St. Matthew Passion* the following October. The conductor was to be Cuthbert Bates and I was given a warm invitation to attend and stay overnight with them.

Having passed a motor cycle test on a bicycle fitted with a little motor on the back, I had recently acquired an auto cycle - a slow and thirsty vehicle. It never did more than 30 mpg despite frequent investigations. On it I began my journey to Bath which was too far to be accomplished in one day, so I determined to stay at a Youth Hostel en route despite the then ruling that one might not use a Youth Hostel with a motorised vehicle. To avoid rejection, I hid the offending vehicle in some bushes, but alas, all was discovered the following morning and some harsh words were exchanged.

Betty on her Autocycle c 1950

The following day it rained. I can rarely remember clothes I wore at any given time, but I shall never forget that brown and yellow herringbone striped coat which had been recently dry cleaned for the occasion. I must have gone straight to the Abbey, for the performance began at 2.30pm. As the coat dried a strange smell grew in intensity. I shall never know what my neighbours thought though it can scarcely have helped their appreciation of the *St. Matthew Passion.* I just sat there feeling desperately embarrassed and wishing with all my heart that the floor would swallow me up. Fortunately the smell ceased when the coat became dry and the evening performance was not marred by such mundane interference.

As a guest of Olive Groves and a pal of the conductor - for I had got to know Cuthbert Bates quite well at Reading - I was able to attend the party after the performance. Suddenly Cinderella was at the Ball. There were Kathleen Ferrier, Henry Cummins, Eric Greene, Elsie Suddaby, Alfred Hepworth and William Parsons. I was introduced to them all and actually spoke to Kathleen Ferrier and listened to her chatting merrily to the others. Someone had asked me where I had come from, to which I replied, "From Newcastle on an autocycle." The news spread like wildfire and incredulity and admiration registered on people's faces. "From Newcastle? Oh, how wonderful!" I fear I added to my other deceptions by not enlightening them about the existence of Newcastle-under-Lyme.

But all good things must come to an end. I think that Olive Groves finally rumbled me and very quickly dropped me. But I'd had my unforgettable moment on the heights: moreover, I had developed an abiding love for *The St. Matthew Passion* and the works of J.S. Bach.

Before I left Broadmeadow School, Eileen and George Baker invited me with their parents and other friends to a holiday in Lugano, August 1948. I mentioned this to Esther during the summer term at Glass Street, and she was included in our group. I have already mentioned the effect of so much wonderful food, but in all other respects it was a very memorable holiday. Not only did we enjoy the delights of Swiss scenery and air, but we were taken by coach through the Dolomites to Venice where we stayed two nights and were able to enjoy the glories of St. Mark's Cathedral and the Bridge of Sighs. We did not sail on a gondola - and the smell emanating from parts of the canal was not attractive, but we did purchase a little of the Venetian glass. We also visited Sienna and Milan.

Venetian Glass - 1948

Other continental holidays followed. In 1949 Miss F.B.Wells, who had taught Geography at the Orme Girls' School, invited me to go with her for a three week holiday in Italy - an incredibly cheap one. We stayed at Viareggio, described as the Blackpool of Italy. My memory of the hotel where we stayed is chiefly of cold marble, cold coffee and cold water. At 8 am each morning on the dining tables were placed croissants and coffee whose heat diminished rapidly, so that if you were slightly unpunctual you had a cold breakfast. The men had no hot water to shave with. Oily salad was served at all other meals. At 8.30 promptly we attended an Italian class where an attempt was made to teach us the language. By then the sun was as warm and bright as at noon in England. Knowing my incapacity for learning foreign languages but not wishing to appear uninterested, I took to wearing dark glasses so that closed eyes would not be visible. However, there were compensations. One was the trip to Florence which remains unsurpassed in my memory for sheer beauty and elegance. Miss Wells and I were joined by a young man of 18 who has mastered Greek to School Certificate level in six months (thereby putting him in the A brain capacity like Miss Wells). Together they viewed and commented on the scene from the Palazzo Vecchio while my mind was concentrated more on the inviting smell of coffee that rose with us. We also had some interesting lectures - one I particularly remember was about the training of Jesuits.

I fell in love with the Vespa at first sight and was delighted to find it was possible to hire one without any documents showing that one was fit to drive. So with the young Greek scholar riding pillion, I drove to Pisa. Together we rowed on the lake and climbed the leaning tower. He and Miss Wells visited Rome but I refused the invitation - it would have been altogether too cerebral - and being only 27 decided I had plenty of time to visit Rome. But I never have done this. In 1951 I discovered that I could have received Income Tax relief for years for dependent relatives and could certainly apply for the appropriate relief for the past six years. This yielded the fantastic sum of £104 – at a time when my net monthly salary was in the region of £30. I remembered my love affair with the Vespa and bought one.

Betty on Vespa in Pisa

There were school trips abroad, one to Ostend and one to Switzerland with Esther Boulton, but they remain vague in my memory. The trip I remember most clearly was a youth hostelling one for which Esther selected the most deprived girls to give them a taste for the outdoor life. There were 20 girls in our party and 10 boys with a teacher at Ilam YH. Soon ten of our girls paired off with the boys but that left a disgruntled 50%. In vain we showed them the beauties of the country side. All we heard was, "Where's the Fish and Chip shop? Where's the cinema?" The climax came at the end of a sleepless week on Friday. We were taken by coach to Matlock Bath, to see and climb the Heights of Abraham. As we approached a gasp went up from the desolate 50% - "Have we got to climb up there?" So we left them in Matlock Bath - against all the rules regarding school trips and began to climb. Halfway up was a booth selling soft drinks and cider. The schoolmaster offered us some welcome refreshment in the form of cider and we continued to climb. It occurred to me that my legs were becoming rather rubber like, but I put it down to sheer exhaustion. We imbibed again on the return journey and to my horror, I found I could not stand, let alone walk. So I was half carried to the bus by my colleagues, all the children were collected, and we set off. I know that the party visited Chatsworth and had tea at Buxton but I remained somnolent in the coach. Miraculously, none of them connected the cider with my condition "Poor Miss Jones," they said. "She was very tired.".

Betty, recovering from 2½ pints of cider

In both 1948 and 1949 Esther Boulton asked me to help her with a Christian Holiday organisation. The first was at Highcliffe, Hants. and I enjoyed serving early morning tea, helping with meals and serving them to clergy and young people. The senior clergyman was a Methodist, the Revd. J.J. Roe, who had been a missionary and then lived at Arnside. I was an immediate success with all the clergy and basked in the sunshine of their appreciation. The venue in 1949 was Chard in Somerset and this time we had a real live cook - one Ted Pearce. As I was mainly in the kitchen we got to know each other quite well. I learned a lot about cooking and towards the end of the 'holiday' it was obvious that Ted had thoughts of marriage and I began to think that this might do. He had visions of taking on a hotel where between us we could make a good living. I made no promise. At least here was a man who was mature, to whom I could talk and on whose judgment I could rely. But love?

There were three disadvantages: he was 41 and I was 27. And had I not lived with the burden of age disparity linked to poverty? Secondly he had no money - not even a home - as he moved from hotel to hotel. I don't think this would have deterred me as I could envisage considerable pleasure in working together; but thirdly - and I discovered this when I returned home and letters began to arrive - he was practically illiterate. My mother was horrified on all three counts and was soon indulging in her favourite, "I haven't slept a wink," syndrome, indicating that her worry about me was depriving her of sleep.

So, as usual, I finally wrote saying that I could not marry him. Had I really cared I am sure I would not have been deterred, and had I realised how much he cared, my attitude may well have been different. Years later I met Revd. Roe again and was told in no uncertain manner how despicable my conduct had been - to encourage a man to care so much for me and then to refuse to marry him. Little did I know that this was the last proposal I would have for many years.

In 1954 Esther told us that she had accepted a headship in Stockport. It was a most unwelcome piece of information, for she was an excellent headmistress and we wondered who would replace her. I cannot remember the name of her successor, but it was not long before I decided that I was not going to endure another period of misery. I applied for a temporary post teaching History and Geography at Clayton Hall Grammar School and began to teach there in January 1956.

I continued to keep in touch with Esther and often visited her in Stockport. Then, at the age of 59 she married her next door neighbour. They went to live in Hazel Grove and eventually removed to the Isle of Man where I visited them. Esther developed a debilitating disease for which she took steroid treatment. Her husband predeceased her and she lived to be 90.

15: Amateur Dramatics (1948-56)

Educational courses were not the only relief from the job of actually teaching – which had become bearable at Glass Street. Drama continued to be one of the loves of my life, both teaching it and enjoying it as a recreation in amateur dramatics. The latter began while I was still at Broadmeadow Girls' School. Eileen and George Baker joined a tiny group in Silverdale, my chief recollection of which was a performance by George and three other unlikely male little swans in the dance of that name. The music still brings back the hilarious memory. One day I was invited to join another society – The Silverdale Players – that is, if I were good enough. It was obviously a very superior group.

The instigator, producer and inspiration of the society was Hubert Pugh, headmaster of Silverdale St. Luke's Primary School. His appearance was not prepossessing; his face was square; two large blue eyes fringed with sandy lashes compensated for an insignificant nose and mouth. He had a stocky frame below average height. But his voice was melodious and beautiful, and like many Welshmen he was a consummate artist in the use of it. He was a devout though ecumenical Anglican, and a Lay Reader with theological knowledge. He maintained that there had always been an English Church despite the Roman Catholicism of the Middle Ages.

The Society began by producing one act plays, but before long three act plays were attempted; the ones I best remember being *The Bridge of Estaban*, *For Dear Life* and in 1953 *Queen Elizabeth*. I became a regular visitor at School House and learned to love the entire family, Hubert, Barbara his wife, and their two children, John and Gwyneth. I often baby sat for them as well as attending the regular weekly rehearsals. Soon I was taking the lead as I did in the first two mentioned plays and how I loved acting. Visiting the Pughs, rehearsals and performances occupied much of my spare time during the late forties and early fifties.

While still engaged in producing plays in Silverdale, Hubert formed an ecumenical Christian Drama Society in Newcastle, Methodists, Congregationalists, Baptists and Anglicans joined together to produce such delights as *Christmas in the Market Place*, (Henri Gheon), *Noah* (Andre Obey) and *Way of the Cross* (Gheon). The biggest cast was for the initial production, *Gates of Hell* which was shown in the Merrial Street Assembly Rooms. It was a wonderful time and some of the spin offs were the dramatic productions I engaged upon in school.

Of course I became far too emotionally involved with Hubert. I felt that I ought to get away if I could and thought of going to teach in New Zealand, a place that appealed to me, after the success of *For Dear Life* and before father lost his sight. Perhaps they could survive without me for a year, and it was possible to do just one year's teaching there. The problem was the cost: had I volunteered for three years, my passage would have been free, but how could I cold bloodedly leave home for three years? The one year I thought permissible required me to pay the full fare, about £200 which I had taken five years to save and was all the money I had. I knew that one day money would be needed to buy a house and to throw it all away on a single journey seemed foolish. So I did not go though I still tried to get a post abroad and was finally offered one in the Falkland Islands. The thought of all those sheep and what appeared to me to be a rough, uneducated society decided me against it. In retrospect, I think that much as I longed to get away from home, I really didn't want to teach and the fear of failure, or stress beyond that which I could bear, was as much a restraint as any other.

About the mid-1950s Hubert's health began to decline. He had a heart condition and was eventually unable to continue with dramatic activities. He left Silverdale and became headmaster at a Primary School in Bradwell. This became too much and he resigned, the family having moved to Audley. He died in 1960 in the City General Hospital and is buried in Audley churchyard. He was only 45.

St. Luke's Players, Silverdale 1948-53

Bridge
of
Estaban

Clifford   Fred   George Eileen
                  Betty

Betty   Don George. Hubert   Fred Eileen

16: MEN FRIENDS (1953-61)

My relentless search for a suitable husband led me up several blind alleys. The men I fell for were either unavailable or uninterested and the ones who courted me I found to be unacceptable. And there could be no chance of a successful marriage unless I was reasonably sure that there was enough compatibility to ensure it.

I met Neil Buchanan, an Air Force Officer at a dance in the Trentham Gardens ballroom. He was a year or two younger than me and in civilian life a civil engineer. He had a BSc. Degree. At last, one would think, there could be intellectual parity. But to my horror, I realised how very narrowly educated he had been. No doubt he was well versed in civil engineering but he did not even know what a marathon was. And his taste in music was certainly not classical. My mother was of course delighted that at last I had a young man with prospects and she could not understand my reluctance to become excited about it. But it was not merely the narrow nature of his education, it was his immaturity and finally the fact the appearances mattered so desperately to him. I remember he had an AJS motor bike and being out in the country on day, feeling thirsty, I suggested that we call at a pub for a drink and possibly something to eat. But because our clothing was unsuitable, he could not bring himself to do this. And later, when he was at home in Newcastle on Tyne, he was afflicted by boils on the face and refused to have me visit him – though I had been there before – because he could not bear to be seen in that condition. Pleasant though things pleasing to the eye may be, they have never been important to me. What a person thinks or says are far more important. The depths of depression I felt during the walk from the station to Mrs. Platt's house in Abergele may be deduced by the fact that I actually contemplated marriage to Neil.

It was my love affair with the Vespa that eventually determined the course of my life from 1953 to 1961. Perhaps I should have bought a car when I received the Income Tax money, but there was nowhere to garage it and even then car tax and insurance were significant items. Moreover I had only passed a driving test for a motor cycle and I really wanted a Vespa. It could be garaged in the entry. I was able to go to school in Hanley each day without having to run for a bus or peddle up Basford Bank. I was able to travel more widely and in 1953 I travelled up to the Coronation in London, leaving the Vespa parked in St. John's Wood while I made my way to Admiralty Arch and spent the night there, rejoicing with others when newspapers announced at midnight that Edmund Hillary and Sherpa Tensing had climbed Everest. Once the great event was over and crowds rushed towards Buckingham Palace, I made my way in the opposite direction. I walked all the way to St. John's Wood through London Streets entirely devoid of people and vehicles. The Vespa was still there.

Alas, the Vespa was far from reliable. Having just had it serviced, the brakes failed when I was out in the country with a colleague on the pillion and into a hedge we were hurtled. Fortunately, we suffered no serious injuries but the Vespa was less fortunate and was returned to the garage, in Longton, I think, that had just serviced it. Not having had any experience with vehicle insurance, I omitted to inform the insurance company immediately and the garage refused to take responsibility so I was left with a damaged vehicle for which the insurance company refused to pay. There had been other failings before this and I was convinced that there was something basically wrong with the machine from its manufacturing days. The garage told me that if that was how I felt I could take it to Bristol where it was manufactured and see if they would admit responsibility and do the repairs. But how to get it to Bristol?

Among the many people that paid visits to our house was Sam Morrey, elder son of Mrs. Morrey of Onneley who had worked for the Knights. I remember on one occasion when father was ill and we were short of milk, Sam drove to his dairy in Porthill and provided us with some. For as has already been mentioned, Sam had left home after a violent row with his father and with half a crown in his pocket. Being a money spinner, he was now the owner of Porthill Dairy, among other enterprises. He happened to call during the Vespa crisis and listened sympathetically to my tale of woe, then, to my amazement offered to transport myself and Vespa to Bristol. It was altogether too good an offer to refuse.

The Vespa was loaded on to a truck and off we went. There were no motorways and the journey to Bristol took several hours. We found the factory and deposited the Vespa to be collected the next day. Sam suggested a hotel for the night and we booked in. It was the first time in my life that I had stayed in a hotel in England, for such luxury was beyond my pocket. I was more familiar with the interiors of Youth Hostels. Here was an unknown world – one of bathrooms; one of toilets that were not across the yard; one of food prepared by unseen hands and apparently instantly available; one where there was no washing up or errands to run and where one was not constantly interrupted by callers.

I knew myself to be deeply indebted to Sam for making it possible to have the Vespa repaired. But how does one pay a very rich man? The fact was that all alternative arrangements for getting to Bristol cost money – always in short supply – and had therefore been rejected. Had I been less naïve, of course I would have foreseen what the trip to Bristol might cost me. Sam simply seized an opportunity, as do all entrepreneurs, to get what he wanted. On this occasion it was not money. It was me.

The Vespa was duly repaired and collected the next day, but to my horror I was presented with a bill for £83 because I had not informed the insurance company promptly and had it examined by them. My mother and I paid the bill but thereafter the Vespa lost much of its attraction. I vowed I would never buy another one. And I never did.

Having said goodbye to Sam in Bristol, I took the opportunity to travel further south and having savoured the delights of a hotel, determined that I would once more enjoy its incredible comforts. I recklessly paid a guinea for bed and breakfast at a hotel in Shaftesbury and enjoyed once more the luxury of the wealthy. It was glorious.

En route for Lymington, where I stayed with the Hopkinsons, I was afflicted by a plague of flying ants and bitten severely all over my face and neck – retaliation I thought for the illicit night in Bristol. The swellings were enormous and very painful and it was several days before I was in a fit state to travel home.

Sam could not have chosen a better moment. His business required short trips away from home on which his wife had always steadfastly refused to accompany him and – to my shame – I did not require much persuading. Yet I think these occasional trips did help to preserve my sanity. There was always London for the Motor Show and I remember the sheer joy of dancing round a spacious bedroom at the Kensington Palace Hotel and the luxury of a bathroom; a trip to Grimsby where I enjoyed the most enormous Dover Sole I had ever seen. There was a trip to Ireland – by air, of course, and the pleasure of being driven expertly across the lovely Irish countryside. Then there were trips to the Isle of Man where he was establishing Landrace pigs with the intention of retiring to this tax haven. I didn't have to plan anything; they cost me no money and they gave me something to look forward to. Moreover, he was an excellent lover. With him I had no fear of pregnancy – it would have been as much against his interests as mine – and because he was, and knew himself to be so dominant and responsible, he had no reservations about letting me take over the dominant role in lovemaking. It did not require to be under the sheets and in the dark. He was amusing; he could tell wonderful stories; his practical knowledge seemed encyclopaedic. Wherever we went he could explain what we saw, such as the principles by which carriage wheels were attached, or the technique of cutting wheat with a scythe. He was an excellent driver and from him I learned much about this skill.

His influence emboldened me to take driving lessons in 1955. I had 13 driving lessons for the cost of £9 and on 11th August I succeeded in passing my driving test first time. It was a wonderful moment. My parents happened to be staying at Meaford. I remember making a fruit cake which I put in the oven just before going for the test and then, afterwards going off to Meaford to tell the glad tidings. Once I had passed the test I was able to drive Sam's cars and quickly learned that passing a test was not all.

I knew that my association with Sam was wrong and many a time I wished that I had the character to end it. But he was so very dominant. I also feel much shame over the way I treated one of the members of the Newcastle Players – one Philip Walker who courted me and let me drive his car when I was having driving lessons. I should not have encouraged him for I could not have borne life with him. I behaved disgracefully.

It was not until after my mother's death that I felt that I could no longer tolerate the liaison with Sam. He could be ridiculously jealous over nothing and began to talk about going to live in the Isle of Man with me as a sort of housekeeper for him. The idea did not appeal. And then, fortunately, I met Ray and, to his credit, Sam never visited me again.

17: Home Life – 1940's to 1960

Throughout this time, I am now ashamed to recollect, home was a place of frustration and irritation. I could have done much more to bring a little solace to my parents who had done so much for me; had endured the war years and rationing and still had somehow to make a living from the shop. At least my mother did. Father still continued to do the odd job as it occurred, but had ceased to have apprentices. He remained extremely active until 1949 and would deliver any articles by handcart which was kept at the top of the entry by the workshop. The only time he used motorised transport was when he was engaged on a removal. But the mainstay was the shop. After the war second hand goods continued to be sold and also carpets and rugs from A.W. Keggen.

August 15th 1943 must have been a day of rejoicing, though I have no recollection of it, for on that day my mother became a pensioner. Her sixpenny stamp per week for over five years was now bearing fruit and at last she could look forward to a little money she did not have to earn – which, of course, highlighted father's continuing pensionless state at the age of 77. He who had anticipated becoming a resident of the workhouse and had therefore seen no point in providing for the future, now needed the financial support he had so contemptuously failed to provide for himself. The only political remark I ever heard him make was that he didn't believe in giving anything to the state, and he didn't want anything from the state. He was obviously no socialist.

My mother put out her antennae to find out what could be done, and as ever, some of her large circle of friends knew somebody, who knew somebody who was able to get the relevant forms for father to fill in. In due course a means tested old age pension was granted to him, provided he never earned more than the stipulated amount – whatever that was. Every year his books were examined and panic always set in prior to this in case more money had been earned than was permissible. It never had: father continued to receive a pension which, by the time he died in 1957 had reached the princely sum of 26/- a week. He died an hour before the next week's pension was due. There was no will. He had left nothing except an Edwardian bookcase, perhaps made by him, two other bookcases and two wooden trays of his, a Georgian sideboard – a smaller version of one I have seen at Broadlands, home of the Mountbattens. There were also copies of his beloved oratorios.

The fact that, for me, the 1940s seemed to be dominated by emotional turmoil and frustration – so much so that I have no recollection of any but the most outstanding events – is now a regret. I regarded the return home at the end of 1944 as determined by Providence, not by me. I simply longed to get away from home, to explore the world, and most important of all, to find love, marry, have my own home and family and never again be obliged to go out each day to teach.

The reality was so different. I have already described that terraced house, which still returns in my dreams – my home for 35 years. By the 1940s some improvements had been made. A tiled grate had replaced the kitchen range; electricity for light had replaced gas, though there were no power points; a gas boiler had replaced the copper and eventually an Ascot gas water heater was placed over the sink so that instant hot water was available. Thus it was not only possible to wash up easily, but by attaching a piece of tubing from the heater to a bath it was possible to have a bath in the back kitchen without having first to heat the water. Emptying it, was, of course, more laborious. The best time for these ablutions was Sunday afternoon as father always retired to bed and mother dozed in the living room. A large white sink (donated by Fred and Margaret Peake when they moved from Sneyd Avenue) had replaced the back breaking low receptacle which we had endured for years. It was ideally suited to the soaking of clothes the night before the wash took place – and this continued much as I have already described. A gas iron had replaced the flat irons. But the floors still needed to be scrubbed by me – and now that I am arthritic I know why it was always my job.

During the rest of the week the house was inundated with callers. Some of these were customers who chatted in the shop or hallway and some were friends for whom there was perpetual coffee on the stove. There was no peace to attend to any task uninterrupted. My mother would occasionally have a boiled egg for tea. From where she sat at the table she could see over the wall dividing our back yard from the entry and sure enough, the head of our next door neighbour, Mrs. Williams, would emerge on her way for a chat. Nowadays, I think it would have been acceptable to continue eating the egg, but then it was considered impolite, so many an egg went cold.

Most of this coming and going took place while I was at school and provided riveting conversation over the tea table each day. My father, silent and apparently unhearing, took no part in this until the climax of the story was reached when he suddenly tuned in demanding, "Who said that?" or "Who did you say it was?" Whereupon the entire episode had to be repeated. Because of the day time callers he frequently felt himself to be neglected by much female conversation which he neither could, nor wanted to hear and interrupted with loud demands for this and that. Tea times were often disrupted and not only by Mrs. Williams. I remember on one occasion when we had actually managed to finish the meal, Mrs. Tams, who kept a dairy shop in Penkhull St. arrived. "Give Mrs. Tams a cup of tea," was the request. To which I replied, truthfully, "I've just emptied the pot." It was not a popular comment and Mrs. Tams never allowed me to forget it. Mrs. Tams' shop faced a high wall on the other side of the street and during the war, when the Free French arrived in Newcastle, she was scandalised by the way they lined up and used the wall as a urinal.

The sitting accommodation in the living room was severely restricted. My father's arm chair in front of the fire had prime position, and as the years rolled by it was seldom vacant. There was room for another, less comfortable chair with wooden arms for my mother, while I was obliged to occupy a child's arm chair – that fitted me in those days – placed with its back to the left side of the fire. It was a scene not unlike the Three

Bears. More often I sat by the table where I could listen to the radio on the little bureau just underneath the built-in china cabinet.

During the 1940s the sale of Meaford Hall took place – due primarily, I believe, to death duties after Colonel Parker-Jervis' death. Miss Parker-Jervis – Pearlie to those who knew her – had lived there for a short time afterwards, served by Elsie Haymes, the parlour maid, but the sad time came when that beautiful edifice became a builder merchant's yard and Miss Parker-Jervis removed to a house in Barlaston. My parents attended the sale of the furniture and returned home with a beautiful rosewood bookcase inlaid with satinwood that my father had declared had been made by him when he worked for Edwards – cabinet makers in Newcastle. The beading on one door was missing and in vain did he attempt to replace it with similar machine made beading. It wasn't worth setting up a machine for such a trifling order, he was told. So, painstakingly he made it by hand and so good was the replacement that I cannot tell which is which. The bookcase was bought for £14 and as there was nowhere for it to go, a dust sheet covered it for years as it stood in the shop.

Elsie Haymes continued to look after Miss Parker-Jervis and mother was a frequent visitor to her Barlaston home, making curtains and setting the place in order. One day she returned with a blue Wedgwood teapot, sugar bowl and cream jug, a gift which she treasured and placed on the Regency sideboard acquired by my father. Undoubtedly my mother contributed much to making Miss Parker - Jervis comfortable during her declining years and there was genuine affection on both sides.

My mother became more involved with another old lady – a Mrs. Platt of Sidmouth Avenue. This widowed and childless lady determined at the age of 80 that she would remove herself to Abergele. Everyone was horrified at the idea, but she was not deterred. Father was in charge of the removal, having hired a firm of professional removers and no trouble was spared to see that each piece of furniture was properly labelled so that it would go into its rightful place in the new home and carefully handled so that not the slightest damage would befall it. When the great day came, both parents accompanied the precious load to Abergele and before Mrs. Platt arrived the house was cleaned through, carpeted, curtained and furnished, so that all the old lady was required to do was to partake of a meal supplied by my mother in the privacy of her new dining room.

Despite the help of a local woman who was employed mainly to keep the place clean – and it was a large house – Mrs. Platt was clearly unable to cope with the shopping, cooking and day to day running of the house. She had been accustomed to the life of a lady; she had a range of friends, neighbours and acquaintances in Newcastle and as much domestic help as she required. Now she was isolated. Several times a year my parents were requested to go and stay with her to provide, not only company, but domestic help.

My father always regarded these trips with delight; Mrs. Platt paid the rail fare; the station was just at the bottom of the road – as was the beach – and all that father was required to do was to enjoy constitutionals to the beach, the sea air and regular meals provided by his wife. Her reactions were more mixed. As ever, she was glad to be of service and as there was domestic help she was relieved of any heavy work though she was somewhat critical of the way it was done – or not done. So she shopped and cooked, sewed and maybe washed and ironed. And listened to Mrs. Platt. Perhaps this was the most wearing part. This lady, like so many lonely people, was delighted to have an audience and my mother had spent a lifetime learning how to be an audience – though she was equally capable of performing in front of one. Unfortunately, unlike all audiences, being regarded as a servant, she was not permitted to be seated and standing was by then not my mother's strongest point. Like most of her generation who through marriage or inheritance were of independent means, Mrs. Platt believed that there was a great gulf fixed between her class and servants. And in her eyes, my mother was not a companion, but a servant: a very superior servant, no doubt, but still a servant. She had, however, forgotten one essential fact – that servants, however low their wage, are paid. True, the train fare was paid, but after that all food bills were scrupulously divided – down to the last halfpenny; my mother paying for what she and father ate and Mrs. Platt her share. She regarded the accommodation provided, which included heat and lighting as sufficient compensation for my mother's ministrations to her and some of these bordered on nursing, for she moved with great difficulty and had various ailments.

Mercifully, I was not expected to share this bounty except at Christmas. Mrs. Platt could not be expected to be alone at Christmas so my parents were summoned. It was unthinkable that I would not join them, so with the utmost reluctance, I spent two or three Christmases at Abergele, the last one being in 1949. I was almost 28. I remember the walk from the station and the depression that I felt. Was this all that life had to offer? We had the usual present giving and receiving upstairs followed by breakfast in the kitchen, after which the Christmas dinner was prepared. Of this I have no recollection until I was asked to lay three places in the kitchen. In the kitchen? But wasn't it Christmas dinner? To my increasing amazement I saw my mother preparing a tray for Mrs. Platt. Then the incredible truth dawned upon me. Mrs. Platt was to have her Christmas dinner in splendid isolation in the dining room, while we lesser mortals were left to display our inferior manners in the kitchen. I was appalled. It was the last straw for me.

My mother's last straw was longer in coming. It became increasingly evident that what Mrs. Platt desired above all was that my parents would go and live with her as she became increasingly feeble and certainly needed continuous care. This posed a considerable problem – not for my father who would have been overjoyed to spend his remaining years as a gentleman of leisure, even with meals in the kitchen. But my mother, who would be 70 in 1953, having endured the burden of a husband so much older for so long, knew that the addition of another octogenarian would be altogether too much. It was one thing to have married for better or worse, it was another to take on voluntarily the burden of an old lady for whom she had no responsibility and to whom she was basically a servant. But like everything else, there might have been an acceptable price. My mother had her own home, though rented, and far from perfect. If she agreed to leave Newcastle and move to Abergele what would happen when Mrs. Platt died? Nowadays she would probably have been quite content to accept a well equipped council bungalow, but her generation regarded council accommodation as totally unacceptable. Only the feckless ended up in council estates in her view. And hadn't she saved all her adult life for her own home? By now this might have amounted to £500 – sufficient in the 1930s but not by 1949.

Mrs. Platt had no immediate family and there was no doubt that she needed the sort of help my mother could give. Had she been willing to arrange to leave her house – perhaps in trust – to my parents, or money to buy a more modest one, my mother would have stifled her reluctance to remove to Abergele. A minor problem for her would have been that I could not have joined them, however unwillingly, as having no Welsh, I could not have got a teaching job in Wales. It would now seem a reasonable solution for me to have remained at home alone, but such was the thinking at the time that this occurred to no one.

Of course, the suggestion of some such provision in the event of her death could not have been proposed, only hinted at. Having received a letter from Mrs. Platt begging her to go and live with her, my mother said that much as she would like to go, it would be necessary to leave her own home – that it was rented and that a small income was derived from the shop. Moreover there would be no home for me. All Mrs. Platt had to do was to assure her that she would be provided for in the event of her death. But she did not. After all, one did not make generous provisions for servants.

She did not live long after this and had to be transferred to a nursing home where she died, never quite forgiving my mother for her refusal to go and live in Abergele. Her will was eventually published. She left £25,000 – a huge sum then – which went to a niece in Kent whose sons already attended Eton. My mother received an oil painting of a bridge, painted by a Miss Edwards, daughter of a Victorian vicar of St. George's, Newcastle. I already had a picture of a country cottage, painted by the same lady, which came from the Misses Brougham. It hung in my bedroom and was a great solace to me as each day I looked at it and longed for such a cottage by a stream.

I am sure that Mrs. Platt's investments were producing a decreasing amount of interest during the 1940s as she often remarked about this and it would explain her extreme frugality. It was, of course a sin to use one's capital. But she had had the opportunity to do good to someone who could have made her remaining days comfortable and even pleasant – at a cost she could well afford and depriving no one. And she chose not to do it.

Early in 1950 my father, now aged 83, still active and working from time to time in his workshop, fell down the workshop steps, wooden steps leading from the actual workshop where his workbenches, tools and varnishes were to the store place below. He apparently protected his head with his hands and rolled up like ball so that, miraculously, no bones were broken. But about three weeks later, he complained that he could no longer see, though no injury was visible. He went to an ophthalmic specialist who prescribed glasses – the first he had ever had, as hitherto he had been able to read without glasses. I now think that he must have been short sighted for to be able to read without glasses into old age would have been remarkable otherwise.

He waited impatiently for the glasses to restore his sight and great was the expectation when they arrived. They made no difference at all. Further examination revealed that he had a cataract over one eye and a blood clot behind the other as a result of the fall. At his age an operation was considered impossible. Gradually the awful truth dawned. Already very deaf, he was now blind. His isolation was complete. And from that time I think he wanted to die. Not being able to hear, he had always relied on his sight for information and had sedulously read the Evening Sentinel every evening. Any spare bits of paper lying around the house would be scrutinized and one had to be careful to leave nothing lying about that one did not want to be examined.

From then on he sat in his chair and concentrated on his bowels. One knew the condition of these from the gloom that enveloped him. When he had had a successful motion, for a short period the gloom was lifted, only to descend, heavier and heavier as unsuccessful visits to the lavatory multiplied. No wonder my mother declared that if ever she married again it would be a man with no bowels! This obsession continued during the night hours. By this time mother had developed high blood pressure and because her nights had become so disturbed by my father, she took sleeping tablets, prescribed by the doctor. My father developed the ritual of getting up in the middle of the night, going down the stairs and out through the back door to the lavatory across the yard, and my mother, unless sedated, would wake up and wonder whether he would fall down the stairs. As my bedroom was at the back, I, too, was often woken by these nocturnal movements, particularly in the winter when the back yard might be covered with a sheet of ice. Invariably, father would slip and fall. Down the stairs I then ran to pick him up – always unhurt.

From then on Psalm 23 frequently came into my mind as the 'valley of the shadow of death' seemed so relevant. At least I was out all day. My mother continued with the shop and this and her many visitors were her only relief from her almost blind and deaf husband. Occasionally we did organise a weekend away for her, but despite all my efforts to attend to his every need, he declined severely during my mother's absences and it became impossible for us both to leave him for more than a few hours. I often wonder what we could have done to make life more bearable for him. But communication – always difficult – had become well nigh impossible. He was given a hearing aid, but because sounds became distorted he refused to wear it. The problem was that he had been so long not hearing that he preferred not to make the effort required for conversation. I remember on one occasion going to the Municipal Hall – now demolished – for an excellent musical concert which I thought he would have enjoyed and coming home looking forward to relating it to him – only to be met with total incomprehension as the bowel gloom hung over him.

Yet he could rouse himself. I shall never forget Mrs. Warham and her Downs Syndrome son, Michael - by then well into his thirties – who lived at the top of West Brampton. So that she could go out she would bring Michael to our house and my father would play his violin or cello, which gave Michael great pleasure and kept him happy. I can still see the spectacle of two severely handicapped people entertaining each other.

By 1955 I knew that we could not much longer continue to live at 6, West Brampton, nor could I for much longer survive Glass Street School with its new Headmistress. As I watched my mother, in constant pain with arthritis, slowly mount the stairs on all fours, descending backwards in similar manner, and listened for my father's nightly trip downstairs and across the yard, I was in despair. A move had to be made. Since the beginning of the century my mother had been saving for her own home and I too had saved for nearly fifteen years. Surely by now it was possible.

18: CHANGES OF SCHOOL & HOME - 1956

The first thing to do was to buy our house as sitting tenants. When we came to sell it there might be a profit. The landlady was only too pleased to accede to our request and we bought it for £500. There was a house for sale in King Street that took my fancy. It was on a corner and was not too far out of town. Henry Todd, Isaac's brother, a solicitor's clerk, was informed and began negotiations, but soon informed us that the structure was unsound and we would be wise not to proceed. So the search began again. We decided that a bungalow would be more suitable, but it had to be near a bus stop, shops, chemist and Post Office, so that my mother could retain her independence for as long as possible. And on flat land, because even a slight incline had become an impossibility for her.

We searched the Evening Sentinel for suitable property and at the beginning of 1956 we found a bungalow in Whitehouse Road, Cross Heath for sale that appeared to fulfil all the requirements. I remember taking my mother to see it. It was on an eighth of an acre of land and a lovely square lawn stretched at the back. There was a pleasant lounge with a window front and side; two bedrooms, a kitchen, a large pantry and outhouse and a bathroom. It was ideal. We had just decided that this was it when we were told it was already sold. I remember going to school that day wondering if anything would ever go right for us. Then suddenly, on Shrove Tuesday of that year, we were told that the deal had fallen through and for another £50 the bungalow was ours.

It cost £2,050. We drew out all our savings which amounted to about £1, 500, and I was able to get a mortgage for the rest – not an easy thing for a woman to achieve in 1956. The bungalow was in my name, though it was really my mother's. It was she who had saved longest for it and deserved it most. We eventually sold 6, West Brampton for £700 – a profit of £200 – and the mortgage was paid off by 1960.

On Good Friday my mother and I went up to Whitehouse Road to see the owner who was shortly to leave and to survey what was to be our new home. Once the house was empty I ordered the first appliance – a washing machine. It was a little Hoover tub with an electric mangle attached. It stood in the kitchen in solitary splendour. I knew that I couldn't attend to a removal until the school term ended, so there was a space of two or three months when I could go up to the bungalow at weekends, do the washing and have a bath. Gradually we were able to lay carpets and hang curtains, so that by July the removal would be simple affair.

It was as well that it was a slow process because my mother had so much sorting out to do, the little business to close and the actual packing. Each article had to be wrapped in newspaper so that the removal men would only have to transfer things from house to van and vice versa at the other end. Father sat quietly in his chair and a short time before the departure announced that he had done his packing. He had put his little plane in a box and that was it.

I remember my mother sitting one evening with the letters of Edwin and Arthur from World War 1. She thought they must be destroyed and was having a final look at them when a friend called and delayed the operation. The letters never were destroyed and because of them I was able to find the brothers' graves when I took Cousin Mary from Canada to visit her father's and uncle's graves in 1978.

The delay was welcome to me because I was able to enjoy a few peaceful hours during that summer in what was surely a dream house. There were problems. The previous owner had considerately left some carpets, but once the house was cleared I noticed some egg-shaped protuberances under the kitchen carpet. They concerned me because I could foresee father falling over them. But when the carpet was removed wet rot was disclosed. A new floor had to be laid and it was a strange coincidence that it was the father of one of my Glass Street pupils who came to lay a new terrazzo floor. The previous owner paid the cost as there was no doubt of the intention to deceive.

During this time we had a wheelchair for father and I wheeled him up to the bungalow which seemed to please him. I thought I might have made his life more bearable by getting a wheel chair before this. When the day of the removal came, Fred Fozard took him by car to his new home. The sheer pressure of the upheaval of the removal exhausted mother who took to her bed for several days. She was 73 and now I understand what a fearful thing is such an upheaval when one is older. She was, however, not only glad to have no more stairs to climb but also to know that when they died I would not have to make such a clearance.

I was happy beyond belief and although totally ignorant of the art of gardening, applied myself with enthusiasm to the spacious plot of earth that was now mine. Thus employed for two or three hours one day, I realised with amazement that I had not been interrupted to make someone a cup of tea or to fetch something: that I had, in fact, been allowed to get on with what I wanted to do in the daytime. The greatest blessing was perhaps the sun which bathed the house all day and whose setting rays flooded the garden. It was possible to enjoy the sunshine sitting on the lawn in an afternoon, enjoying the sight of flowers and the leaves of the sycamore tree which later amused my little son as he lay in his pram.

Father celebrated his 90th birthday in the same month as the removal and a card arrived from Canada on the very day. He did once walk from the bungalow to the end of the road, but never repeated this feat and rarely sat on the lawn, though I have a photo of him on the garden seat. For some time now his Friday evenings had been enlivened by a visit from Don Rogerson one of the Silverdale players and a miner in the Silverdale Colliery. This faithful friend shaved him each Friday and received supper from my mother by way of reward. Gradually father ceased to be willing either to wash or dress himself: his trousers had to be taken down before he went to the toilet and replaced afterwards. But the nightly visits ceased. Now that he could go there in comfort and safety he never once did so. So liable was he to fall over that we felt unable to leave him for more than an hour or two, so if mother went out, I stayed in and vice versa. I remember taking her to see Betty May who had retired from Broughams to a tiny bungalow, now demolished, in Hempstalls Lane. At the end of an hour we both began to feel uneasy and sure enough, when we returned father was stretched across the floor, but unhurt.

George Jones at Whitehouse Road – aged 90.

All this was taking place during the same eight months that I began teaching Forms 1, 2 and 3 at Clayton Hall Grammar School. At last I could concentrate on the subjects I wanted most to teach – History and Geography – although the teaching of English had been in many ways rewarding and certainly necessary for Secondary Modern Girls. It was, of course, a temporary appointment but I had been assured that another permanent post would be found for me for the following September.

So the Vespa began its journeys to Clayton and immediately I found myself totally happy educating girls who wanted to be taught; teaching subjects that interested me and eventually producing exam. results that were quite exceptional. I remember on my first day with Form 3 – which was my form – making some comment which to my surprise had them giggling appreciatively. It struck me that there would have been no response whatever at Glass Street. It was certainly pleasant to perform in front of an appreciative audience.

During that first term I spent almost as much time in my bedroom preparing and marking work as I had done when a pupil. Every lesson had to be prepared fully, particularly the history of Ancient Greece and Rome, which I had not touched for twenty years. I was rarely more than one lesson ahead; but oh, the joy of responsive pupils with retentive memories, capable of asking intelligent questions. By the end of the first term they were remembering facts that I had already forgotten. The exams. which took place in June or July were proof indeed of my success with these girls and I was congratulated by the headmistress, Miss Farrar, on the results they obtained. (When I related this episode to Ronald his comment was, "Anyone can teach bright pupils." Later I learned that when teaching Theology students, he went at such a rate that it was impossible for most of them to take notes so that only the most gifted were really able to hold the information. They were expected to be original. Any one who simply disgorged the information given had no chance of a First).

But all my devotion, hard work and success were in vain. I had one serious defect. I had no degree and in order to obtain a permanent post at that school this was a necessity. So my little Latin and no Greek continued to be a stumbling block. But at least in those two terms I found that I actually liked teaching, could command the respect and affection of my pupils (who presented me with two *Doctor in the House* books and an array of other things). And I had actually seen some results.

We were comfortably settled at Whitehouse Road when September arrived, all too soon, and with it a new school year and a new school. I had been assigned to Bradwell Sec. Mod. Mixed. It was my first introduction to a senior mixed school and it was an unwelcome change from my two happy terms at Clayton. I soon learnt that discipline was entirely the class teacher's job. The headmaster refused to back one up at all. Soon after I got there I had a student teacher and my heart bled for her. It was a new and fearful world in which she was totally unable to cope. I tremble to think how she would manage today.

I was appointed once more to teach English and while there I produced plays, *The Bishop's Candlesticks* being the one I remember. The following year it was decided that the entry into a secondary school with its constant changes of classroom left the less able children totally bewildered. Perhaps a single class and teacher would give them more security. I offered to teach that class all subjects except PE, Games and Craft, and so had my first introduction to the teaching of (in a sense) handicapped children. I remember using milk bottles to show how three made a pint, 6 made 2 pints and so on. It was a great improvement for them and I too enjoyed not having to move from room to room as well as seeing a definite improvement in their work.

It was also my first introduction to a mixed staff and what I saw of men teachers did not fire me with enthusiasm. Most were certainly less conscientious than the women teachers I had known and one of the men cultivated the habit of telling particularly filthy stories in the staffroom. There was one bright exception – Ron Rigby, the woodwork teacher. He and I immediately struck up a friendship which might have developed further but for the presence of his wife and six children. He remained a good friend, who could be called on at any time to assist in any difficulty. He made me a table lamp. Two boards of pitch pine had travelled with us to Whitehouse Road and from one of these he made a sturdy ironing board which is still in use. We did not become lovers – the presence of six children all of whom appeared to be accidental was not a strong recommendation. But I like to think that sexual morality prevailed.

It was either in the autumn of 1956 or early in 1957 that I bought my first car, a second hand Austin30. It cost £450. As already mentioned, the money came from the £200 left to my mother by Ethel Knight and also the profit from the selling of 6, West Brampton. The Vespa had been sold earlier for I remember cycling to Bradwell when I began teaching there. The car was a major acquisition and I was able to take father and mother on little drives. But there was no garage. A builder called Thornhill lived almost opposite and as there was just room for a narrow garage he provided it and also a coal house adjacent to it at the back, for fires were still coal based. They cost £114.

1956 had been an eventful year. There had been two terms of tolerable teaching at Clayton Hall School; the sale of 6, West Brampton; the purchase of a bungalow and the removal to it during the August holidays. But with September came teaching at Bradwell.

19: DEATH OF MY PARENTS - 1957 TO 1960

Of the events during most of 1957 I have little recollection, but I remember one Sunday when mother, originally intending to walk to St. George's Church, decided instead to call on Betty May in Hempstalls Lane. On her way back she was attacked and knocked down. Her handbag was stolen, containing half a crown, which would have been collection money. I became worried about her non arrival but had no idea where she could be. Eventually a car drew up, and a very shaken mother emerged. The shock had taken away her speech and she could not even shout for help, but the kind souls in the car brought her back. Her right arm never recovered from this experience.

Betty May in Brougham's Garden

On Tuesday 19th November father was having a favourite meal of pig's trotters when he collapsed and was put to bed. The doctor's diagnosis was anaemia. My mother nursed him during the remainder of the week, and each day saw a sharp decline in his vitality. On the Sunday he said to her, "Alice, doesn't it take a long time to die". The strain was beginning to tell on my mother and I requested to be excused school the following week, by which time Nellie Brough, an old friend of mother's, had arrived to help. Indeed she saw to all the cooking and kept us going. The doctor had done all that he could and suggested that father should be given sips of water continuously, day and night. So while Nellie and my mother slept on the bed settee in the lounge, I lay with my father for three nights, providing the necessary liquid which I was told later, prevented him from relapsing into a coma.

Nellie Brough

By the Monday, 25th November it was clear that father's life was ebbing away. The changes in his condition from day to day were dramatic. And I remembered father's instructions to the vicar of St. George's Church about the grave on the north side of the church in which his father and a child lay buried. Only my father and Mr. Humpage, the verger, knew exactly where the grave was. Father had planted a small tree there in 1880 after his father's death and during the intervening years it had grown so enormous that it had to be removed and all that remained were widely dispersed roots. Father had assured the vicar on one of his rare visits that there was room in the grave for him and of an iron rod in the vestry that could be used to ascertain the depth of the grave. And the vicar assured him that when the time came he would see to it all. But of course we were now in the parish of St. Michael and all Angels, Cross Heath. Unfortunately, it never occurred to me that this would make any difference: the grave was in St. George's churchyard and it must be at St. George's Church that the funeral should take place, especially as it had been the only church with which father had been associated. For forty years he had sung in the choir until one day he announced that he was going there no more. Apparently he didn't like the way the vicar spoke to the choirboys. It seemed strange to me that no one seemed to notice that he had left. Certainly no one begged him to return. My mother and I found St. Michael's very congenial. There were no steps even when taking communion where all knelt in a semicircle round the altar and it was only a short, level walk. From 'low church' we moved 'up the steeple' and my sense of the dramatic appreciated the ceremony, so beautifully done by the vicar, Father Stevens and his curate Father Thacker. I had joined the Bible Study group during Lent and got to know several people in the parish – all ordinary people – there appeared to be no social standing here. I finally asked the vicar if he would give my father communion and he was delighted to do so. In our own lounge we received communion. It was the last communion my father ever had.

Instead of sending for Fr. Stevens, I thought it would be only polite to inform the Vicar of St. George's of father's serious condition as I felt that the funeral should take place in that church, the grave being in the churchyard. The Vicar appeared on the doorstep on the Tuesday afternoon and immediately informed me that as we were now in another parish I had no right to ask him to call, especially as he had been told that father had received communion from Fr. Stevens. It was hardly an auspicious start to the visit. He did, however, go in to my father and prayed for him with the utmost consideration. What a strange man!

On the Thursday morning the doctor called again and declared that there was an improvement. I shall never forget the strange look my father gave him. Feeling a slight sense of relief I took Nellie Brough for a ride in the car in the afternoon. About teatime I heard him call out, "Mother," in a loud voice about six times and I rushed to fetch her. But it was not her he was calling to. The evening wore on and mother continued to sit with him past her bedtime. During that evening he ceased to be able to urinate and in panic I called the doctor who was not best pleased to be dragged out. He looked at him. "Poor old man", he said. He gave him tablets to help him to sleep and mother stayed. Meanwhile I phoned Don Rogerson and Ron Rigby, feeling the need of some support, and both came immediately. As we talked in the kitchen, mother came out of the bedroom and asked me to go in as the end was near. We stood around the bed. Father made a movement as if to sit up and as he did so he died. It was 11.30pm. It was what he wished – a peaceful death in his own home.

Ron was able to put me in touch with an undertaker who came that night to lay him out, leaving him on the bed till morning. Both men went home and as the electric blanket was of no further use to father I gratefully put it on my own bed and fell asleep almost immediately – only to wake up in a raging heat. I had forgotten to switch it off!

Next morning the undertakers came to collect the body. As I looked at what had been my father, I knew with absolute certainty that this poor piece of flesh was a mere shell. My father was not there. He had obtained his release. Now began the running about – death certificates, funeral arrangements and Mr. Humpage to see as well as St. George's Vicar. Together Mr. Humpage and I studied the churchyard to find the grave. It was not easy but was finally located. I remember there was some difficulty in getting gravediggers, but finally this was achieved. The digging revealed that there was room for two coffins, so my mother would be able to be buried in the same grave.

The following Sunday was Advent Sunday. The funeral took place on the Monday. When the cross of flowers arrived I wondered what to write on the card. Remembering Messiah, and the shell of my old father, I wrote, *"For this mortal shall put on immortality; and this corruptible, incorruption."* It seemed appropriate.

The vicar conducted the service in a most objective manner. My father might have been a total stranger. Indeed, I have been to funerals where the deceased was a total stranger to the priest and yet some suitable words were spoken. On this occasion the service proceeded without any comment. Mercifully we had the organ and choir as a mark of respect. There was one curious feature. For whatever reason, the vicar refused all payment for his services and I wrote to thank him.

After Nellie Brough had gone home, my mother had the comfort of many letters of condolence. Until that time I had not realised what a comfort are letters to the bereaved, difficult as they are to write. Of course, no one could pretend that it was anything but a merciful release, but my mother missed him, as one is bound to do. They had been married for 38 years. She was now alone for most of the day while I was at school and there were fewer visitors than she had welcomed at 6, West Brampton. It was many years before I realised how much she must have missed the daily comings and goings of friends and acquaintances, for she loved people and missed the news and gossip that had filled her days. She joined a Pensioners' Club but did not really enjoy it – they were not her sort of people! And by now she was so crippled with arthritis that all movement was an effort. As she said – she never knew what it was not to be in pain.

My days at Bradwell were coming to an end. I was offered the post of Head of the English Department at the new school in Chesterton that was to replace Broadmeadow Girls'. In January 1958 I began my duties at the school on a hill. The first job was to organise all the library books into the new library and I became quite familiar with the Dewey system, spending many hours after school arranging the hundreds of books. It was a great relief to be teaching girls, fairly intelligent ones, and once more I was able to produce plays. We did *Merchant of Venice* and another Christmas Nativity play. I was also able to take the pupils on camping holidays at Cotwalton where I met Muriel Howells who became a great friend. Newcastle Education Committee decided to introduce a School Leaving Exam. so that pupils who had no chance of taking

GCSEs could at least leave school with a qualification. I joined the marking panel and discovered the delight of finding the odd pupil who chose to answer unpopular questions. One became very weary of hundreds of the same questions to be marked. Although there were some changes on the staff, many of the teachers I had known at the old building in the 1940s were still there. These included Eileen Baker and Kath Yorke. Music continued to be a strong feature. The headmistress was Miss E.V. Mills.

The following Easter – 1958 – we were able to fulfil one of my mother's ambitions – a coach trip to Edinburgh. She loved it all. We stayed at excellent hotels – one in Edinburgh, one in Perth and one in the Lake District. There were other trips by car. She wanted to see Abergele again – so we went. We were so used to economising that we took sandwiches with us and one of my regrets is that I did not treat her to a meal at the Hotel there. We also went to the Malvern Hills. Then there were trips with Aunt Elsie – both ladies now widowed and never ceasing to make snide remarks to each other during the journeys. We acquired a little dog, Scampie, intended to be company for mother, but more attached to me. We went to visit Cousin Peter and Sybil Jones in Cambridge and were present one Whit Sunday for the service in King's College Chapel where mother noted that the choir's surplices were in need of a wash. In 1959 we took Jen and Arthur Shelley on a trip down to Cornwall and Devon. We had no trouble finding bed and breakfast places until we came to Bodmin Moor. I remember driving across it hoping we could find accommodation at Bodmin, which we eventually did. We all shared a room in Plymouth which caused much hilarity as Arthur accused mother of peeping! We had a splendid tea at Dunster. It was a most enjoyable trip.

Scampie

In May 1960 she had a week's holiday in Weymouth with an OAP organisation and brought me back a knitting bag and a yellow backed hand mirror. There was so much to talk about on her return that we commented what it must be like to be reunited in heaven if there was so much to say after a week's absence.

I had planned a fortnight's holiday in Cornwall for her. It was to have been a perfect holiday. I booked full board for us in a farm bungalow – no stairs – near Camborne, thinking that this was a good central position for day trips in all directions, and I could scarcely wait for school to finish on the Friday. As there was no Motorways to assist us, I decided we would go down on the Friday evening and break our journey at a hotel. It took far longer than I anticipated and to my horror we had been given a bedroom up two flights of stairs. Next day we continued and joined slow queues of vehicles on the other side of Plymouth, so that it was late afternoon when we arrived. It must have been a very wearing journey for her.

We went to church on the Sunday and I drove her to St, Ives and round the sea coast there. It was a lovely day. Next morning she felt unable to get up – a most unusual thing for her – but insisted that I must go out.

She was still in bed when I returned and during the night seemed to have developed a little dry cough. More as a precaution than anything else, I asked the landlady to call a doctor who to our astonishment diagnosed pneumonia. So she stayed in bed, assisted by medication, but insisted that I go out each day as we would have done had she been well. The daughter of the house, aged 13, inflicted herself upon me and as the doctor had said the pneumonia was very slight, I did not worry unduly until the next week when I realised that somehow she would have to be driven home. With the doctor's blessing we had a short trip to Church Cove on the Thursday through Mullion, where we called at a pub and she had a Cherry B. I took a photo of her sitting on the sands at Church Cove.

Alice Jones – final photograph – Thursday 4th August 1960 - Aged 77.

Because of the enormous tailbacks we were sure to encounter in the daytime, we began our journey home on the Friday evening, resolving to travel through the night. I had given her two sleeping tablets and had settled her down as comfortably as possible in the back seat, hoping she would sleep all the way home. But she declared herself to be uncomfortable and insisted on sitting in the passenger seat. Not being very good at night driving, I stopped for a short rest each hour, but by 10 o'clock next morning we were passing through Meaford where she begged me to stop. To my eternal regret I would not, believing it to be far more important to have her at home and in bed. She was never to see Meaford again.

The doctor came on the Monday morning and agreed that the pneumonia was slight, but she was obviously having great difficulty with breathing and became unable to talk at all. For one with such a capacity for conversation this must have been a sad blow. There must have been so much she wanted to tell me and could not. I stayed with her day and night and if I was obliged to go to the chemist, a neighbour would come and watch. Mrs. Ford called one day to my mother's delight. Although she could scarcely speak she indicated that she wanted to know what flowers were out in the garden.

The doctor called on Wednesday afternoon and arranged for her to go to hospital, still saying that the pneumonia was slight, but that I could no longer nurse her as she needed expert medical attention. I followed the ambulance in the car and returned to an empty house – except for Scampie who I took for her evening walk and went to bed. At 11 o'clock the doorbell rang and a policeman told me to go to the hospital at once. She was very ill and I sat by her bedside till 6am when it was obvious that I was not wanted by the morning staff.

Determined to spend the whole of the next day with her, I phoned Fr. Thacker first, and having collected him proceeded to the hospital, where to my amazement I found Arthur and Jen Shelley with a huge bouquet of gladioli from the garden, But my mother was wearing an oxygen mask and knowing that she would want to make her delighted response – as she always did for visitors – I thought she needed every ounce of her strength to fight for her life. And having said prayers, Father Thacker, Jen, Arthur and myself left her. I believed I had done the right thing. I hope so. We went home where Jen insisted on remaking the bed ready for her return. At 12 noon the phone rang. My mother had died.

The date was Thursday, 11th August. I think I probably took Jen and Arthur Shelley home to Meaford, and returned to an empty house apart from Scampie who was now my devoted companion. I could neither eat nor sleep but the doctor kindly arrived and insisted on sleeping tablets. During the next days the hardest thing to bear was the avalanche of birthday cards for my mother that came pouring through the door. On the Saturday, Muriel Watterson, a school colleague, asked me to go for lunch and a glass of sherry gave me an appetite. The funeral, at St. Michael and All Angels, was on the following Tuesday, 16th August, the anniversary of her wedding in 1919. The church was packed with mourners and many tears were shed for she had been greatly loved by all who crossed her path. As I looked at the flowers in the wreath, blue scabious and pink roses, I could almost see the colour of her eyes and complexion. She was buried in St. George's Churchyard with her husband. Flowers covered the ground. I remembered having suggested to her that donations might be made to a charity instead of flowers. "Oh, no," was the reply, "I want flowers".

I now felt myself to be all alone in the world though friends were incredibly kind and for the next six months there was always an invitation out to lunch on Sundays. The Revd. Edgar Preston and his wife had invited us both to visit them during August and I was grateful when they were prepared to have me alone for a few days. It was a most blessed visit.

Revd Edgar A. Preston & Wife.

When school recommenced in September I found it difficult to eat on my own and arranged with the butcher to deliver beef steaks which I cooked with vegetables and then made myself sit down with a tray every evening.

As Christmas approached I dreaded being asked to share it with anyone, however charitable and determined to go to Canada to visit my aunt, cousin and her family. My mother had left £100 in her Post Office Savings Book and for an extra £13 I was able to book a flight to Toronto, having ascertained that they were willing to have me. For the first and only time I travelled First Class from Manchester Airport because all the other seats were full. We touched down at Prestwick and Gander and then were diverted to New York having circled Montreal and been unable to land. We were there several hours and although we had no intention of visiting the USA all our luggage was meticulously searched. It was a very exhausted group of people who finally arrived in Toronto.

Much later, I was told that my relations had viewed my visit with some apprehension for they had been given the impression that I was altogether too good to be true, a judgment derived no doubt from my mother's letters and the fact that I had not married young like Mary and had been well educated. They were most relieved to find that I was extremely human and had normal human failings. I formed a great bond with all the family, though I fear that my aunt was somewhat disappointed that I was obviously not the ideal niece she had imagined. They took me about the area and I walked under a frozen Niagara Falls.

20: Marriage & Motherhood (1961-64)

Soon after the death of my mother, we had had a new Vicar at St. Michael and All Angels; the Revd. David Smith, whose wife, Elsie, formed a friendship with me and introduced me to a lady who was willing to clean for me. In February 1961 Elsie told me that her husband's brother was going to live with them as the aunt with whom he had been living in Birmingham had died. Apparently he was the black sheep of the family and they were most charitably giving him a home.

I had decided that the time had come to improve the bungalow. A new roof was needed and I was sure that by taking out the back porch the cooker could be placed next to the sink instead of having to walk from sink through a door to the cooker. A new window could be placed right across the back instead of the little bay where the sink was. During the summer all this was achieved and was paid for by the legacy left to me by Elsie Coghill, my Godmother. It was a very great improvement and had improved the value of the bungalow. But the kitchen ceiling needed painting. I had already learned the art of wall papering and had thus improved the lounge, but I was not prepared to paint ceilings and I never have. I asked Elsie Smith if she thought that her brother in law would do it and in due course Ray arrived and the ceiling was painted. He had lunch with me and I discovered that he didn't care for puddings.

July 28th was the birthday of Oriel, David and Elsie's adopted daughter and I was invited to tea at the Vicarage. It was quite a jolly affair and afterwards Ray and I washed up and found ourselves discussing cars. He showed quite an interest in my Mini and I invited him to drive it that evening. We found ourselves at a pub on the Leek road and during that evening he talked and talked. It was as though he found that he could unburden himself without reproof. He drove me home and I was impressed that he didn't attempt to kiss me.

During the August holidays I drove to Snowdonia and, with Scampie, climbed Mount Snowdon. It was a most glorious summer day.

Scampy on top of Snowdon
1961

The autumn term at school began in September and in October David Smith presented his congregation with a Mission Week. We were invited to offer hospitality to various speakers and at the Vicarage there were morning meetings where Ray provided coffee. I don't know how successful the Mission Week was, but it did bring Ray and myself together. We were neither of us keen on Mission Weeks.

After our outing on 28th July I had thought that perhaps he might offer to take me out again but three or four weeks elapsed before we had another night out, this time at Barthomley and again it was mutually enjoyable. While we were recovering from the Mission Week we went to the Cock Inn near Baldwin's Gate On our return to the bungalow he suddenly proposed to me. Never was I so surprised. I had begun to think that in time a really good friendship might be formed for we got on very well. But he had never even kissed me. He called the next day – to confirm it, he said. It certainly was a strange courtship – to be taken our three times with weeks in between each outing and then having marriage proposed. Perhaps I should have given the proposal more thought than I did, but I really believed that marriage would work and so consented.

Marriage at the age of 40 is a big step to take, but I was convinced I had made the right decision. I really did care very much for Ray. We were the same age, and he was willing and able to tackle jobs about the house. (I had experienced with my father the problems that arose from a big disparity in age and a total inability to do anything in the house); we had been brought up in the same religion and shared a sense of humour. Moreover he needed to be loved, to have a home and, if possible, a family. I knew from Elsie that he lacked any financial ability. He had been obliged to leave his position as Quartermaster in the Military Police because there were financial discrepancies – partly because at times he failed to insist on payment when he was serving at the bar. He was therefore in debt and this had to be paid off. But it seemed to me that I was fully capable of managing the financial side of life – and better marry a generous man than a mean one. He was not a ladies' man. Indeed, when on our honeymoon we called at a pub in Birmingham and I was introduced as his wife it created a sensation – he had never been known to be seen with a woman! So it seemed likely that he would be faithful.

The wedding day was arranged to coincide with the Spring Half Term – 24th February 1962 – so that we could have a short honeymoon. I was up early that morning and cleaned out the grate before getting ready for the big event. Apparently Ray slept late and had to be woken up. The service took place in St. Michael and All Angels Church, Cross Heath and we were married by David. The Wedding Breakfast was held at the Filleybrooks Hotel in Stone which Jen, my Matron of Honour, had arranged.

James Raymond Smith & Mary Elizabeth Jones – 24th February 1962

After returning home to change, we drove down to Kenilworth for the first night of our honeymoon. We were offered a meal at the hotel which I would gladly have had as several hours had elapsed since the wedding breakfast, but Ray had other ideas. He knew some of his old friends in the Military Police would be in Stratford on Avon and intended to show me off there. As the evening progressed I got hungrier and hungrier and finally managed to be given four little sandwiches for 15/-. It was midnight before we returned to Kenilworth. Next day the ground was covered with snow. After another day in Kenilworth we travelled to Ross on Wye. We took photos at Tewkesbury Abbey and at Tintern Abbey and stayed in a hotel in Ross on Wye with a creaking sign. More snow on the way home made us decide to stay at Meaford for the night. And so the honeymoon came to an end.

Ray was driving buses for the PMT (Potteries Motor Traction) and his shifts varied – sometimes there would be an early morning shift at 3.30am, or a late shift finishing at 10pm, or worst of all a split shift when he would do several hours in a morning, have a break and then resume in the afternoon or evening. When he was on early morning shifts I would wake up with him and fail to get back to sleep again. Thus by afternoon I found my eyes shutting while I was teaching. I dreaded the split shift most of all because he would call at a pub during the break. I knew that alcohol was a problem but had thought that a settled and loving environment would make it less attractive. I found it curious that he favoured lunchtime drinking and would then come home and watch television till bedtime. He rarely went out to a pub during the evening, though on occasion he would remain out till the early hours of the morning. He eventually offered to do maintenance work on the buses instead of driving them. The shifts were then more regular – 6am–2pm or 2pm –10pm. We kept a record of his pay which was about £12 a week. My net salary at this time was £80 a month. Whereas my mother had used her £3.10/- pension to buy food and I had paid all other bills, Ray was unwilling to contribute much to the upkeep of the house, which I found strange considering that he had a free home and all his debts were being paid off.

I remember sitting in the lounge long before I met Ray, thinking how satisfied I was with the alterations I had made during 1961. But Ray was never satisfied with the way things were for long. Soon after we were married he decided that he wanted to turn the front bedroom into the lounge and vice versa. He wanted long curtains for the windows and I spent the Easter holidays making curtains.

I discovered that he was basically a very private person. Only sometimes when he had been drinking would he talk about past episodes – generally about life in the army. Of his emotional life I knew nothing. He never divulged anything – nor did I. It amused me to watch him getting undressed for whereas I had no hang ups about nakedness, he would carefully remove his garments and put on his pyjamas without showing even a glimpse of his genitalia. He said it was army life that had conditioned him. Lovemaking was always under the bedclothes and in the dark. Never in an afternoon.

Our early lives could not have been more different. Whereas I was my mother's only child, reared lovingly but strictly; always conscious of money shortage; my parents surviving to old age, Ray's family history was tragic. His father had been a foreman at a steel works in Rotherham and possessed a car in the 1920s. By his first marriage he had a daughter, Anne, and a son, David. His wife died when the children were young. He remarried and while briefly in Canada, Ray was conceived and was born at Brinsworth, Yorkshire. Two years later his sister Joan was born. Ray remembered his early childhood days when he was the centre of attention and even walking Joan to school. Then in February 1930, his mother, aged 35, died of pneumonia and a fortnight later, his father, aged 47, succumbed to the same disease. Anne was 16, David 14, Ray 7 and Joan 5.

The children were sent to Birmingham to be cared for by relations; the girls went to one home; the boys to another. The father had left money for their care and whatever was left over was to be theirs at 21. Ray, distraught by his mother's loss, began to wet the bed and was scolded severely. He was at a disadvantage from the start for his mother was less well regarded than the first wife. Moreover, both Anne and David were bright academically whereas Ray was not. Anne became a schoolteacher and David an Anglican priest. Joan eventually married an Anglican priest. Meanwhile, until the age of 11 when the aunt died, Ray would be up in the mornings cleaning chitterlings and preparing tripe before going to school.

Upon the death of Aunt Ada, the relations prevailed upon another aunt who was living in Scotland to remove to Birmingham and care for Ray – David by now going to college. It must have been a most profound wrench for Aunt Maggie to leave Scotland. But she and her husband accepted the challenge. They must have felt great sympathy for Ray – so much so that they obviously spoilt him. Thus he had experienced a mother's love, followed by a harsh regime and then, ridiculous leniency. He told me that he liked to go to the cinema on Saturdays and would sulk until they gave him the money. I could have sulked for ever without any money being forthcoming.

He stayed at school till he was 16 when he joined an uncle's coal business, delivering sacks of coal. When the war came in 1939 he decided to join up. He became a signalman. During his time in the army he was in North Africa where he drove an officer around. He also spent some time in Palestine – and favoured the Arabs rather than the Jews. He was very fond of water melons and recounted the story of how they would drive in front of a water melon lorry, stop suddenly, so that some of the water melons fell off and then run back to pick them up. He remembered his 21st birthday while he was abroad: no one remembered him. Of course, it is possible that he was not a good correspondent either.

He really should have remained in the army for he was happy with military life but, like so many others, he couldn't wait to be de-mobbed. He then thought of joining the police force, but was apparently half an inch too short. So he joined the Military Police and spent 12 years in that service, living with his Aunt Maggie in a rented house in Blackheath, Birmingham. But in July, 1960, Aunt Maggie died and during the following year financial discrepancies were discovered appertaining to the Military Police and Ray was dismissed. It was at this point that

David and Elsie offered him a home and he got a job driving buses for the PMT.

That first year of marriage was not easy. I couldn't understand how he could spend hour after hour watching television without any sense of discrimination. I remember one Sunday afternoon suggesting that we both went for a walk with the dog and he refused, so thereafter I generally did all the dog walking alone. He was quite capable of gardening and would mow the lawn but when the sun shone for planting he often did not feel like it, so the rains came and it was neglected. On one occasion, before we were married, he was digging the garden and some dirt lodged in his eye. He refused to be taken to the hospital to have it removed. The consequence was that he lost some sight in that eye and having had perfect vision was obliged to wear glasses. But he loved cooking and when he was on an early turn would often have a meal ready when I came home from school.

I was really looking forward to our first Christmas together, but I discovered that Ray had no idea about the giving and receiving of gifts and it was a surprise to him when on Christmas morning he was given various presents. He apparently had to do some driving – were buses running on Christmas Day then? So I prepared the Christmas Dinner for 2pm. But no Ray appeared. It was evening before he reappeared. Very drunk. Hardly my idea of married bliss.

In November 1962 I became pregnant. I remember we had a real fir tree for Christmas and over the Christmas period I felt increasingly poorly and the wretched needles kept falling. We entertained some friends of his and I could barely cope. Then one Sunday evening in January 1963, as I was walking Scampie I felt something come away. Back home I sat on the toilet and blood poured from me. The next day I went to see the doctor – not my usual doctor – who did not examine me and simply told me that if I didn't stop bleeding in ten days I was to go back. It was school next day and somehow I survived, still bleeding, but had to rest all evening and Ray did look after me. He was always very good when I was ill. This continued till the 10 days had elapsed. I knew my own doctor would be there on the Wednesday morning and in that bitter winter, with ice underfoot, I walked to the surgery. The doctor immediately asked me questions regarding my pregnancy and then examined me. He was obviously shaken at what he discovered. He said that the baby was still there, that I must go straight home to bed and he would send a consultant to further examine me. The consultant came: I was admitted to the City General Hospital where I remained for several days and each day the tests were positive. I couldn't believe it. How could I still be pregnant after all the blood I had lost? Eventually the tests were negative and I was given a Dilation and Curettage (D & C) and sent home. Scarcely there and I began to bleed again. Ray sent for the doctor. I had an infection – child bed fever – and antibiotics were prescribed. Eventually, I recovered after several weeks and went back to school. It was while I was in hospital that Hugh Gaitskill died.

It seemed most unwise to risk another pregnancy immediately and we decided to use the 'Safe Period' technique. So it was with some surprise that I found myself to be pregnant again in June. Ray's sister Joan, husband Tom Winter and four children descended on us from S. Africa, David and Elsie having refused to have them. They eventually went to Leek where Tom, a priest, served, temporarily, at one of the churches there.

During July I took a group of girls to Cotwalton again, which was a pleasant break, and then came the August holidays. To our alarm, we noticed fungi growing around the edges of the front room and had builders in to remove them and lay a new floor. Money, was as ever short, and for a holiday we borrowed a bell tent and set out for a holiday at Burnham on Sea. En route we needed to camp for a night, but Ray was very particular not to put up the tent where there was any chance it could be seen and finally, in the dark, we camped in what appeared to be a deserted field. We had taken two fold up loungers for beds. Exhausted, I lay down, whereupon the lounger collapsed beneath me and I wept. In the morning we discovered that the area occupied by our tent was covered in cow pats. We enjoyed Burnham on Sea and visited Wells and Glastonbury while we were there.

I finished teaching in December and began to prepare for baby's birth in March, I borrowed everything I could and bought a second-hand pram. I argued that the baby would not be aware of his possessions whether lavish or not, and the time would come when he would need money. My diet became restricted to scrambled egg and Benger's Food – nothing else would digest. In February the doctor said, 'The sooner, the better,' But it was not until the evening of 10th March that Clive was delivered – by forceps. He weighed 8lb 14 ozs. He was held up for me to see before I was taken to the 22 bedded ward at the City General, but it was 48 hours before I was allowed to see him again, by which time I had no milk.

I was utterly exhausted. I had not thought it was possible to have so much pain and still live. I could neither speak nor listen though Ray came and was with me part of the time but had gone home before the birth. As I was wheeled out the nurse told me that the Queen had had her baby – Edward. He must have been premature. It was a sleepless night and next day I was bathed and tidied up. Eventually, after baby had been brought to me, it became necessary every three hours to walk down this long ward to fetch nappies and milk. I could scarcely walk because of the stitches! But I had many visitors and lots of flowers. Ray was overjoyed that he had a son – who was clearly recognisable as his.

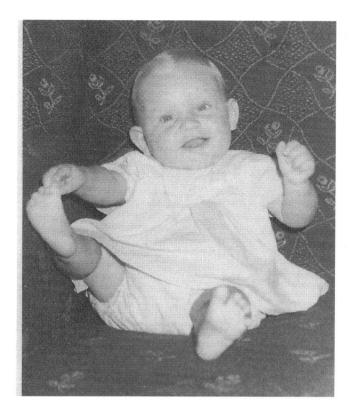

Clive Smith – aged 6 months

I had now to learn, at 42, the endless job of being a mother and I was determined to make a good job of it. Over the next five weeks, during which we had to find the right milk formula because baby found feeding less than pleasant, I think the dominant impression was sheer tiredness. But it was wonderful to me to watch this baby develop each day. I soon found that he didn't cry for nothing; there was always something amiss when he yelled. He was never very interested in food. When he was christened in April and there was so much coming and going, he never slept at all and the bottle would be forgotten as each new arrival appeared. During the afternoons I would lay him on the floor and watch as each day he tried to turn over and eventually succeeded. In June that year we had a holiday at Blue Anchor Bay in Somerset where we rented a chalet. A little of the Video of his babyhood was shot there when he was less than four months old. At six months he was on his feet walking round a playpen and at nine months he walked about the house holding on to my fingers.

During the summer we had visited Ray's Aunt Mary in Matlock. She lived in a two up and two down cottage, six hundred feet above the River Derwent and Artist's Corner, up the third of a mile long St. John's Road. In November 1964 she died. The cottage was to be sold and the money divided between her nephews and nieces. Quite out of the blue, Ray suddenly suggested that we go to live there. Looking back now it seems incredible to me that having been given a home and a son he could suggest moving his wife and nine-month-old child from a comfortable bungalow and friends to a cottage up a steep hill in Derbyshire. But, as I've said, Ray was never satisfied with anything for long. And he seemed to want to get away from his brother and sister in law – not that we saw very much of them.

The matter required some thought. Never very far away from my thoughts was the matter of money. No longer did I have a monthly salary. And I wanted to remain at home to watch our son develop. But Ray's wages, coupled with his propensity for spending money, were never going to allow us to live much above the bread line. I knew that Aunt Mary had used her cottage in the summer to supply visitors with bed and breakfast. It occurred to me that if I could sell the bungalow for £3,000 – the cottage was valued at £2,000 – I could spend the £1,000 profit on refurbishing the cottage to make it into a small Guest House. I already had plenty of crockery, cutlery, towels and bedding and by supplying accommodation for visitors in this tourist area, I could surely make enough money to avoid having to return to teaching – at least while Clive was very young. And, again, looking back, one of my chief concerns was to make Ray happy. He fancied going to live in the country and with Masson Hill, leading to the Heights of Abraham behind us, and woods on all sides, this almost isolated cottage seemed to be the fulfilment of a dream for him. At that time many people were converting barns into houses and then selling them at a considerable profit and it did occur to me that a handsome profit might be made if or when we decided to sell.

There would, of course, be the small matter of finding a job in Matlock. But surely bus drivers were required everywhere, so it was the least of our worries. The sale of the bungalow was achieved simply by putting a For Sale notice in the window. It was bought by a widow who did not quibble about the price. We spent Christmas in the bungalow, being visited by friends – Clive in his play pen, uninterested in actual presents, but having great fun tearing up the paper they were wrapped in.

21: MATLOCK (1965 – 71)

We moved in January 1965 and I remember that Fred and Margaret Peake did a lot to help. I was not able to leave the bungalow as clean as I would have liked because the baby was the first priority. I remember the people next door - Mr. & Mrs. Cope, whose daughter I had taught at Clayton Hall, - were most kind to me during the upheaval. And Gwyneth Pugh went with us to see us settled in. They all probably thought us totally mad – and perhaps we were. To begin with the excitement of the venture kept us going, but one afternoon I remember being in what was to be the dining room watching Clive on the step leading to the kitchen when suddenly he burst into tears and I knew that he wanted to be back home – as I did. I had not realised that I was going to be so isolated and removed from lifelong friends, or that the steep hill would prove so effective a barrier to any social life.

Cliff Cottage renamed Meaford Cottage – Matlock 1964

Artists Corner - Matlock

Ray soon got a job as a clerk at British Aluminium for which he needed the car. I had to allow two hours for any shopping at all in Matlock because of the effort of pushing a pram up the hill. To begin with we had no telephone and it was not funny to have to walk down and up the hill simply to make a phone call. I spent some time thinking about how the cottage could be improved. Like many hillside houses in Derbyshire, it had little depth. Two main rooms were side by side and next to them was what had been a stable where the birds now nested in the rafters. Behind there was scarcely any room and a cliff face inhabited by mice (we later discovered this) overlooked a tiny backyard. I now forget how we found the builders we required, but in due course they began work and transformed the cottage into a four bedroomed house with washbasins in each bedroom, and a lavatory upstairs as well as the one downstairs. An open staircase, positioned facing the front door replaced the one with an entrance door at the back of the dining room, so that access via a landing to all bedrooms was possible. What had been the kitchen became a bathroom downstairs while part of the area that had been a back yard became the kitchen with a pantry off it. All this took the best part of a year, so that Clive was almost two before it was completed. One benefit of the isolation and the total impossibility of a settled life was that I was able to dispense with nappies during the daytime as it didn't really matter where Clive urinated as he ran about during that summer.

While digging outside the men revealed two perfectly paved tunnels, about 18 inches deep below the surface; one leading under the dining room and one under the stable, leading apparently to the cliff at the back of the house. The paving was so perfect that one was tempted to speculate that perhaps it was Roman in origin, for lead mining had been a thriving industry there in Roman times. The stable/garage remained as it was, but the nesting birds disappeared from the rafters as a new floor was laid for a third bedroom and a new roof added. A fourth bedroom was placed above the new kitchen. Clive, now 17 months old, and usually within sight of me, disappeared one day. Mystified, I went outside the front door and looking up, saw to my horror that he had climbed a ladder and was about to get on to the scaffolding at the top of the house. Fortunately one of the men was able to get to him and carry him down.

Once the basic building work was done, the inside had to be made habitable. We bought rolls of wallpaper costing no more than 4/- a roll and while I did the papering, Ray did the painting, laid floor coverings and moved furniture. We became well known at the sale rooms in Matlock as we bought beds and bedding to supplement our store. What had been our own double bed was put into bedroom 1, where there was also room for a single bed or bunk beds; another double bed fitted into bedroom 2, the smallest and warmest room, for the dining room and Raeburn fire grate were just below; the new lavatory lay between this room and the room above the stable/garage, which comfortably could take two or even three single beds. The fourth bedroom above the kitchen took a double bed and as it was the least attractive room became our bedroom when we had guests. On one occasion Ray saw a cabinet with glass doors at the top and underneath drawers and a cupboard. He got it for £3 and was inordinately proud of it. We acquired cutlery through a cereal packet offer; there was no shortage of crockery, tablecloths or towels and the mahogany table (ex Meaford Hall), both leaves up, could seat eight guests at a sitting. Occasionally, if we were busy in the summer, it was necessary to have two sittings for breakfast.

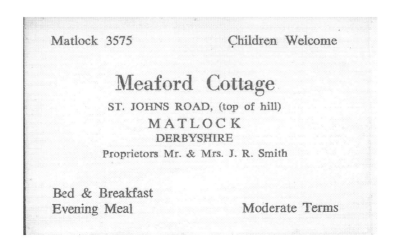

Matlock 3575   Children Welcome

Meaford Cottage
ST. JOHNS ROAD, (top of hill)
MATLOCK
DERBYSHIRE
Proprietors Mr. & Mrs. J. R. Smith

Bed & Breakfast
Evening Meal   Moderate Terms

The immediate problem was to make possible guests aware of our existence. We asked people living at the bottom of St. John's Road if they would allow us to put up a sign. They were not cooperative and I soon learnt that the local people were not open hearted like Potteries people, but tended to be very protective of their property and possessions. You were regarded as an alien until proved a friend. I decided to write to the people at the Town Hall, informing them of our new Guesthouse and received an enthusiastic reply. Our first guests were those recommended by the local Council – an elderly couple from Worcester who had stayed at hotels in the district, but were far from satisfied. I did everything I could to oblige them from early morning tea to Kellogg's grapenuts for breakfast and endeavoured to get what whatever they required. They departed without showing any appreciation, but shortly afterwards a letter arrived from the Town Hall, enclosing a letter from our guests full of glowing appreciation and recommendation. From then on, the Town Hall sent us guests.

Mr. and Mrs. M. Dixon,
212 Malvern Road,
St. John's,
WORCESTER.

Dear Sir/Madam,

Thank you very much indeed for your letter dated 20th August telling me how comfortable you were during your recent stay at Meaford Cottage.

Accommodation is so limited in the Matlock area now, and any "new" Guest House is welcomed, especially so when I receive a recommendation such as yours.

Yours faithfully,

Clerk of the Council.

It was, of course, a seasonal occupation. One could rely on guests at Easter, Whitsuntide and during the August holidays, but this left much of the year dependent on Ray's wages, which were not great and only a proportion went towards the housekeeping. Ray belonged to the generation of men who believed they must always have money in their pocket – in his case for beer at 'The Three Horseshoes'. Not that this indulgence was regular, but one never knew when it would happen. So when Clive was eighteen months old – before we were able to open - there was advertised a job in Matlock teaching Police Cadets English and Geography one day a week. These boys had had a Secondary Modern Education and needed 'O' levels to progress in the Police Force. Mrs. Wardman at the farm further up Masson Hill was willing to look after Clive for the day and he didn't appear to suffer from my absence. And the pay was £8 a day which seemed a fortune at that time. By the end of the Spring term we were able to buy a big frame tent which made possible a holiday. I enjoyed teaching these young men, and was delighted when over 50% of them gained 'O' Levels.

We did have lodgers from time to time. The first one was a young man selling answer phones long before they were such a common feature. He eventually opened a Garden Centre which was very successful. I remember being irritated by his tendency to look down on me. There was a young man who worked for British Rail and there were various assistant vets. A geologist from Yorkshire was with us for many months, rather a particular man, and a committed socialist who sent his children to a private school. There was a Teachers' Training College at Matlock and an advertisement for lodgings appeared. This seemed ideal for the holiday periods would be free of students. I was able to accommodate five at £5 a week each for which only breakfast would be required. For the first year there were girls, all of whom were very pleasant, but the next year we received young men, quite determined to be as awkward as possible. It was, of course, fatal to complain: we were offered no more.

Meanwhile Clive quickly moved from babyhood to being a toddler. Having seen another child about his size walking in the courtyard when he was just one, it dawned upon him that he too could manage unassisted walking and by the time he was eighteen months old he was helping me push to grocery laden pram up the hill. He was never a good sleeper and from 15 months he declined to sleep at all in the daytime which meant that all activity was centred round him. How fortunate are mothers who have an extended family with whom to share the child – fortunate for mothers and children. Every afternoon we would go down the hill and into the park and eventually we bought an old Ford van for £40. It was then possible to drive to Darley Dale Park where he drove round on a toy tractor – and I walked with him almost semi-conscious with tiredness. During the mornings he would play with toy cars, lining them up and rearranging them. Later we had a sand pit which he enjoyed. He showed no interest at all in drawing or painting and seemed to be ambidextrous as he would pick up a pencil with either hand. One day I put a pencil in his right hand to see if he would use it or transfer it to the left hand. He seemed quite happy with using it in the right hand. Every night I read him stories in bed and he prolonged this as long as possible. But he was a slow reader and I searched the library for books about cars, trains, helicopters and aeroplanes to whet his interest. He was three and a half before he could be admitted to a playgroup in Matlock and then only for two hours. By the time he was four he refused to go to the playgroup and at four and a half gaily entered school without a backward glance. But for the first fortnight I slept with him. It seemed that my absence in the daytime had to be made up for at night.

It was the church school right on the other side of Matlock that we chose – and it was a good choice. The A6 lay at the bottom of St. John's Road, but once across it there was a foot path leading straight to the school – about 10 minutes' walk. So, the old Ford van long having failed its MOT, I bought a Lambretta scooter and with Clive perched on the pillion, drove down the hill and walked him to school, thankful for the vehicle to get me up the hill again. It had always concerned me that Clive was an only child and hoped that there could be a brother or sister for him, but despite our efforts, none came. And although we were fairly isolated up a hill the house was seldom empty of visitors, some of whom were children. Mrs. Wardman had a daughter and two sons, the younger of whom was only two or three years older than Clive. We encouraged his friends to visit and parents would drive up the hill with offspring. Clive would sometimes stay after school to play with them.

After the departure of the students in 1969 or 70, I remember hearing about homes needed for children in care and during the autumn months as I looked at the empty beds I wondered if I could do my bit to look after foster children. Ray was all for it. I contacted Social Services and they were only too delighted to find suitable children. The mother of the family they chose had had nine children, five by her husband and four by the lodger. She, the lodger and his children had gone to live in a caravan and the husband had apparently offered to leave if she and the children would return to the home. But she must have been a very poor manager, for soon after she returned home she was obliged to put the children, four boys, in care. We were taken to see them in the Home, and it was suggested that we have them for a weekend to see how it went. Christopher, the eldest was 11, Stephen, 8, Nigel, 6, and Michael 4. I forget for how many weekends we had them before we were asked if we would take them permanently. I remember that the weekends had been hard work – feeding them was no problem although they had voracious appetites and could eat all before them every three hours – but they needed constant supervision. By the time Christmas came I had begun to wonder about the wisdom of receiving them permanently, but it seemed cowardly to withdraw the offer. They arrived for Christmas.

We did everything we could to give them a good Christmas. Their Christmas stockings were filled with good things and we prepared an enormous Christmas Dinner. To our amazement, for the first time, they had no appetites. Then the light dawned. They had eaten every chocolate or sweet in their stockings. During the Christmas holidays a charitable organisation took them all to a pantomime and I well remember the relief of being without them, for they would throw sand in each other's eyes and fight unless constantly watched. On one occasion I picked Michael up to nurse him and found him wet through. He had apparently fallen in the river and no one had thought it necessary to mention it.

Christopher did not stay with us for long and preferred to return to the Home. At first we had two bed wetters, Stephen and Nigel, but Stephen soon ceased to be a problem in that way. Clive took to him, trustingly, but after a month or two, realised that Stephen was destroying his toys – and his faith – and there were occasions when Clive was not well enough to go school and seemed to need his mother all to himself. Nigel continued to wet the bed regularly until August. I remember one occasion when the three boys were sleeping in the room above the stable, and although we had storage heaters in the bedrooms, it was still rather chilly in the middle of the night. I had taken Nigel to the toilet about 10.30 but during the night I went in again to find him wet through. I uncovered him to remove the top sheet and stood for a few minutes looking at him fast asleep. I thought the wetness and lack of warmth would have made him curl up. But it didn't. He lay stretched out just as though he was warm. It was curious to us that whenever we praised the boys – and we tried hard to find occasions for praise – immediately they would do something that they knew would annoy us.

Stephen became a good swimmer and won certificates from school. He was also quite artistic and liked drawing and painting. Nigel was the sensitive one. At one stage we asked the social worker if we could take Nigel to see a psychiatrist, for we were having the utmost difficulty dealing with him. We took him to Chesterfield where we had several sessions with the psychiatrist who was certainly helpful. On one occasion he asked me if I had considered the possibility that my own child was being harmed. Michael, the youngest, was not particularly bright and very stubborn.

I took them down the hill, wheeling the Lambretta, and saw them across the busy A6 to the footpath to school. They were forbidden to cross the road on their return and again I met them and saw them across the road. But one day, when Clive was at home, I was busy making pancakes and a few minutes late going to pick them up. As I began the descent, I met Nigel howling, "Michael's been killed." Down the hill I went and I cannot now remember whether Michael was there or not or who told me what had happened. Apparently the two boys had crossed the road; Michael had been knocked down and his leg broken. He was taken to

Chesterfield Hospital. I immediately phoned the social worker and we all met at the hospital. It was decided not to inform the mother immediately as there did not appear to be any other damage, though the hospital authorities decided to keep him in, in case there were any head injuries.

However, after three days, the social worker decided that mother must be told. When we next went to visit Michael, the whole family was gathered there, mother waxing indignant about Michael being neglected and full of promises to the child that he would be going home. Of course he did not go home, but came back to us with his leg in plaster, frequently getting the plaster wet so that it had to be renewed.

At the beginning of the summer holidays, we took them to Northamptonshire to a camping park with facilities for children. By then, Ray was working for Derbyshire County Council, transporting goods made by handicapped people in a Landrover. We had also bought, for £80, a mobile caravan and with these two vehicles were able to take all the children out for weekends in the Derbyshire country side. I drove there on my Lambretta. There were plenty of things for the children to do, but for the whole fortnight the sun never shone. On one weekend we took them to a secluded spot near Hathershaw and let them loose to explore the area. I remember feeling particularly exhausted. Suddenly, one by one they appeared, covered in paint. They had found a rubbish dump and had proceeded to throw paint cans at each other. We had a busy time trying to remove the paint with petrol.

We frequently explored the Chatsworth area, taking food with us in knapsacks which Ray and I carried. I had become extremely intrigued by their unlimited capacity for food, which is so typical of children in care. They never asked for food but just sat down and gobbled it up four times a day. Clive was never a very good eater so on one occasion Ray and I decided not to offer food until they asked for it, just to see how long it would take them to ask. We walked on and on and eventually were aware of a whispering behind us, but nothing was said to us when we asked what was the matter. Sometime later Stephen muttered that Michael was hungry, and, of course we then produced the sandwiches and drinks. I shall never forget the sight of Michael with mittens on, pushing food into his mouth as fast as he could go.

By the September we were getting desperate. When we mentioned our problems to the social worker we were told how badly it would affect these children if they were moved again, so we soldiered on. She did arrange for someone else to have them for a weekend in October, but before this happened she appeared on the Feast of St. Michael and All Angels. 29th September, and told me to sit down. The mother had found them a home and they were all to return to her. It was an unbelievable moment. We did have the weekend promised while they were still with us and took Clive down to The New Forest in Hampshire, and slept in the caravan. The horse chestnut trees were yielding their conkers and as Clive collected them and strung them together I thought how battle would have commenced had Stephen, Nigel and Michael been there.

We had still a few visitors that year and I can recollect no major problems. Before the students came we had initiated phase two of the refurbishment of the cottage: the stables were converted into a bedroom large enough to accommodate a double and single bed so that Ray, Clive and I could sleep downstairs, leaving the other bedrooms for guests. It was also very convenient when preparing breakfasts in the morning. I found that if I started at 7.30. food would be on the table by 8.30. I made my own marmalade; a variety of fruit juice and cereal were provided with tea or coffee; the full breakfast included egg, bacon, sausages, tomatoes and mushrooms with toast. I once made the calculation that each breakfast cost 2/6d.

Meaford Cottage Matlock + garden.

The latest conversion was estimated to cost £500 and in vain did I apply to the bank for a loan. I was no longer a salaried person and Ray's wages were regarded as insufficient for such a risk. So I went to the Derbyshire Building Society who gladly let me have a mortgage for £500. Again we went to the local Sale Room and for £7 bought a most beautiful mahogany wardrobe with hanging space and many perfectly fitting drawers. We were only able to get it into the 'new' bedroom before it was completed. It would have been impossible once there was a new back door leading through a narrow passage into the kitchen and back into the bedroom. When we came to leave I was sorrowful at having to leave such a beautiful piece of furniture and have often wondered what the new owners did with it.

There was so much happening all at once during the autumn of 1971. Shortly after we learnt about the imminent departure of the boys, a crisis arose with the people who owned Cliffe House, a mansion with eleven bedrooms and four acres of land situated across their courtyard opposite from us. The family who were there when we arrived there had been quite friendly and were followed by a young couple intending to make it a Guest House. They worked hard and we were on excellent terms with them so that if they had more guests than they could cope with they passed them on to us and vice versa. Unfortunately, the husband took a dislike to the work, and the place was sold to a childless couple with four dogs who were able to buy it before selling their own house. Hitherto the courtyard had been used as a general car park for Cliffe House, a small weekend cottage adjoining us, ourselves and our guests. Soon we were made to understand that the courtyard belonged exclusively to Cliffe House, they paid the rates for it and no one else had the right to park there. So began a period when I rushed out of the house the moment I heard a car coming up the road and beckoned it into the area in front of our house if the passengers were visitors for us. The moment anyone spoke outside all four dogs barked continuously. I can well imagine that these dog loving people must have resented the noise made by the children during that year – although we took them out so much and they were always in bed early. It must have been late August or early September when I came up the hill on the Lambretta to find a car parked on the sacred land. I immediately made the usual enquiry of the driver and at that moment the owner of Cliffe House appeared and I endured a vocal character assassination of considerable magnitude.

Ray happened to be staying overnight in a marquee at one of the Derbyshire shows, where he displayed and sold items made by handicapped people the following day. When he arrived back I told him that I could no longer bear to live in such an unfriendly atmosphere. If he wished to remain in Matlock we would have to move. To my surprise he seemed not to mind where we lived. By then Clive was seven and it seemed reasonable for me to resume full time teaching – I had done some supply work in Matlock. For one thing I realised that unless I went back to teaching full time, the pension I would receive for 21 years' service from 1942-63 would not be very much: I couldn't envisage Ray receiving much pension either. The thought of old age with only a minimal income was not attractive. We both fancied going to live in Hampshire – I'd always loved Hampshire, and especially the presence of Edgar and May in Lymington made it attractive. I made one or two applications in that area, but nobody wanted me, and by the end of September when the news came about the boys' reunion with mother, it became necessary seriously to get a teaching job – somewhere. And the house had to be sold.

The boys departed quite happily and we were able to dispose of unwanted furniture – among other things a three-piece suite that had belonged to Aunt Mary, some of the beds and bedding - to their new home in Chesterfield. I remember going to visit them soon after their departure, and then realised what they had missed during their time with us. Simultaneously, the radio, television and the whole family shouting at each other created a cacophony of noise that was unbearable to me. But they liked it. I had given them plenty of utensils for kitchen use, but not a kettle; and water for tea was boiled in a saucepan. I visited them once again to see particularly how Nigel was getting on, for I sensed that he needed affection more than the others.   Years later, I had a letter from the mother thanking me for what I had done for them. I have often wondered what happened to these children and if the year's stay they had with us had any benefit at all.

Meanwhile house selling and job getting were the serious issues. Several applications had a negative response and we realised that our dreams of a home in the south of the country were unlikely to be realised. I suppose I could have applied to Newcastle-under-Lyme but it was obvious that Ray did not wish to return to North Staffs. Eventually, I was offered an interview at a girls' school in Wilmslow to teach Geography. I remembered Ron Rigby, who had become a District Inspector in Manchester, and phoned to ask if we could call to see them on the day of the interview. He immediately asked why I hadn't approached him if I wanted a job in Manchester. I said that I didn't particularly want a job in Manchester, I would go wherever I could get a job. I was unsuccessful at Wilmslow, which was disappointing to me for I loved teaching Geography, but I had an interview at Ellesmere Port and at the same time Ron had engineered a job in Wythenshawe at Poundswick School which had recently become comprehensive. I was accepted at Ellesmere Port, but refused the job because the headmistress had not even the grace to see the applicants and also I began to think that it might be better to be in Manchester where at least I knew Ron and Flo.

They were also very good at finding possible houses for us to move to and we finally selected a very good Wimpey semi in Cheadle Hulme. But selling the house at Matlock was not easy. All the dreams of making a fortune after converting a cottage faded fast. We had only one applicant. While negotiations were underway there was a severe snowfall and we prayed that it would be gone before our vendee came to see the house. It was; but the price we were forced to agree to, £4,800, meant that over seven years we had made just £300. The cottage had cost £2,000. We had spent £1,500 on the first stage of refurbishment, another £500 later and at least £500 for the new Rayburn, storage heaters and decorating. Thus we were obliged to exchange that spacious house for a three bedroomed semi – for which we needed a £2,000 mortgage.

We left Matlock on a mild day in December. Pickfords brought their van up the hill and by the afternoon had loaded it and departed. Clive watched it go down the hill and announced that it had turned towards Derby at the bottom, which seemed strange to us. Any remaining goods were loaded into the Landrover and caravan and Ray and Clive departed for Cheadle Hulme. I followed on the Lambretta. We had imagined that Pickfords would have arrived before us, but by 6pm there was no sign of the van. On phoning up we were told that they could not possibly be there before the next day as there was only the driver to unload and suggested that we stay at a hotel. This would not have mattered but for the fact that on board they had our 22 cu. ft. freezer with a vast supply of meat supplied by our Matlock butcher as well as other items of frozen food. Eventually we persuaded to driver to appear, having appealed to Ron and Flo Rigby to help us unload. The huge freezer had to be installed in the garden shed which fortunately had its own electrical supply. We all pitched in to the unloading and sometime before midnight the job was done, Ron and Flo departed and the beds were erected. We did receive some compensation but decided never to employ Pickfords again.

It was good to be living in a community again, but there were some happy memories of Matlock. We used to bring old friends over from N. Staffs and when Clive was very small Nellie Brough used to love to come and became very attached to him – until he could talk, and she, being profoundly deaf, could not hear him. Fanny Madeley also came for a holiday. Mrs. Ford came for a visit, as did Poppy from Onneley; Nellie Mould brought over a bus load of WEA members for a day's outing and we provided the refreshments. Peter Shore, his wife and child came as did Alice Hackett and Lynda; Anne Phillips brought Ros and Roger. Harold and Betty Clark came on a three-wheeler and petrified us with their driving. Our previous neighbours, Mr. & Mrs. Cope came. Many of the people for whom we provided accommodation have remained firm friends and still write and phone. I had enjoyed looking after people and feeding them; and when Easter 1972 approached, it did feel strange not to be preparing the house for visitors. But by then, we had other worries.

22: MANCHESTER – PART ONE – CHEADLE HULME
(1971-74)

Christmas 1971 was soon over. I remember the Rogersons visiting us when the famous Morecambe and Wise show that included André Previn was on the TV, and how we enjoyed it. The new school term began on 4th January. Wythenshawe was not on any bus route we knew of; because it was winter, a covered vehicle seemed more sensible than a scooter (though in the event it was such a mild winter it wouldn't have mattered); the Land Rover was no longer necessary, so both our vehicles were traded for a smaller second-hand red car which was most unreliable. It was the worst car we ever purchased. However, it took me to Poundswick School, Wythenshawe, a three storeyed building with a 10-stream entry of pupils, beginning with P and ending with K. Although I was given some 'O' level English work with some of the P, O, or U children, I seemed to spend an undue amount of time with the Ks who appeared to be totally uninterested in anything related to learning. When I asked where I was supposed to begin with them I was told to tell them to copy anything I wrote on the board! I found that they had been in the habit of printing capital letters instead of joined writing and no one had thought to correct this; the work books were in a ragged dilapidated state and discipline was in short supply. The class for which I was class teacher – was it a 'w'? – contained one vociferous girl who refused to shut up or move – thus provoking a confrontation I had not experienced before. I forget now how I resolved it. There was no sign of any school work up on the walls; apparently it would have been pulled down had anyone been stupid enough to show it; teachers carried a bunch of keys around at all times and were required to unlock toilets to admit pupils and then lock them again; nothing could be left anywhere – not even in the staff room – at anytime or it would be stolen. This meant that everything needed for the day might have to be carried up or down three flights of stairs. Fires in desks; furniture thrown from 3rd floor windows and teachers being knifed all happened during my brief spell there. Truancy was rife; a favourite occupation of the truants was throwing stones at vehicles from the bridge over the M56. The headmaster, who was also a magistrate, was heard to comment that we would have something to complain about if we had to deal with the young offenders with whom he was familiar.

There were no celebrations for my 50th birthday which happened to be a Thursday. Ray gave me a little radio which has survived over 30 years.

The 'O' Level students were, by contrast, a pleasure to teach. The set books were Arthur Miller's *'The Crucible'*, and George Orwell's *'1984'* with both of which I needed to become familiar. I found myself sitting up till after 2am preparing work, and I was awake again by 5am, worrying about how and what I was to teach the W I C Ks. Ray did not find a job with the local council as he thought he might and was unemployed for some time, but at least he was able to look after the house and prepare meals. The Junior School to which Clive went was almost visible from the house and he did not need to be accompanied. He was not very happy there because in Matlock he had been introduced to linked writing and here they made him print again; there he had felt a 'big' boy for infants and juniors were in the same building and he was now a junior – but in Cheadle Hulme he was in the lowest class of juniors. And I think that my obvious strain and unhappiness affected him. For I was undergoing the same sort of stress that I had endured when I began teaching in Chase Terrace.

I may have survived to half term by which time Ray had got a temporary job working for National Westminster Bank in the printing department and cycled to work each day. Feb. 24th was our 10th wedding anniversary but neither of us remembered it until the post came with a card from Sylvia Parsons, whom I had taught at Glass Street. Then one morning I woke up in bed sobbing. I had reached the end of my tether. Ray immediately hauled me off to the doctor who prescribed "Mogadon" and said I was not to return to work for a month. Ray then drove into the country and stopping at a country inn bought me a large sherry and I was asleep before we returned home. The "Mogadon" tablets ensured sleep at night. I feel sure that the headmaster and staff thought that I was malingering, but I was living through a nightmare made worse by the fact that we now had a £2,000 mortgage that had to be paid and I was the only one who could earn enough money to pay it.

I did return to Poundswick for the last month of the term, each day determined that I would survive and do my best to teach. I remember finishing off *'1984'* with my class and observing that if they looked about the school they would see that 1984 was apparently not far off. I discovered that there was a 50% turnover of teachers each year; it was no wonder that the children were so difficult – they lacked continuity, and turning a Grammar School Comprehensive had not improved the standard of education.

I told Ron Rigby that I could not guarantee retaining my sanity if I were obliged to go on teaching at Poundswick, and he suggested a move to an ESN (Educationally Sub Normal – modern term Special Needs) school in Bradford, Manchester near Grey Mare Lane, which needed someone to teach reading to individual children. The summer term saw me established there, and I was installed in a small room, receiving non-readers one by one. Now I had never been taught to teach reading – in 1940 it was assumed that reading was taught in the Infants department and that by the time a child reached the Junior School he/she could read. So this was a new experience and I used every device I could think of to stimulate and encourage these children to read. One day an advertisement appeared in the Guardian; Manchester University were offering a two-year part time course leading to a Teaching Certificate for the teaching of handicapped children. I applied and in September joined a group of others in a room off Fennel Street twice a week. The course was invaluable. I learned much about disability and in particular, how to teach reading.

Meanwhile Ray was quite happy with NatWest and would have liked to have been given a permanent appointment there, but there was a rule that temporary jobs could not be made permanent. Thus he applied to

Manchester Council for a job driving the elderly and disabled in Manchester. He was not happy, for he seemed to spend much of his time waiting. I thought afterwards that as his knowledge of Manchester was almost non-existent, and his sense of direction severely limited he really was not the best possible person for the job. What he really wanted to do was to run a home for the elderly, and in June an advertisement appeared asking for people to be trained as Deputy Wardens in Lancashire. He sent for an application form. It so happened that the arrival of the form and the Wimbledon tennis fortnight coincided. For the first time the men's final was played on a Sunday and the participants were Stan Smith (USA) and Ilie Nastase (Romania). I shall never forget the excitement of that final or the memory of trying to fill in the application form while watching.

We went to Preston for the interview and were delighted when Ray was accepted. He was to go to Broadway House in Chadderton for six weeks training and provided that that was successful he could then be sent anywhere in Lancashire for weekends or longer periods to relieve wardens who were ill or on holiday. Even now when I turn left off the A62 towards Chadderton, I remember the first time we drove there, never having been there before. Mrs. Mellor was the Officer in Charge of Broadway House, a 50 bedded Home for the Elderly. Ray took to the job like a duck to water and she and her husband were so delighted with him that after the six weeks training they went on holiday, leaving him in charge. They told him that they were going to retire at the end of 1973 and would recommend that he should be appointed then. At that time Chadderton was in Lancashire, but was shortly to become part of Oldham Metropolitan Borough as a result of boundary changes.

It was fortunate that Clive was such a sensible child as when the new term began in September Ray was in Chadderton and I had to leave home before 8.30 each morning to get to Bradford, not to return till after 4pm. And twice a week in the evenings I was involved in the teaching of handicapped children course in Manchester. I would prepare lunch for him and set the electric cooker to have it heated for lunchtime when

Clive would come home, eat his lunch and lock up again before returning to school. I was unhappy about leaving him in the evenings, but he was perfectly capable of getting himself off to bed and was always asleep when I returned home.

Christmas 1972 found Ray at a Home in Kirkby, Liverpool, though they brought him over for Christmas Day which we all enjoyed. During 1973 Clive and I would go each weekend to which ever Home Ray was looking after. Some had purpose-built bungalows for the Officer in Charge – Southport and Kirkby were in this category, others like Lancaster, Walkden and Worsley had accommodation within the Home – as did Broadway House. One of the nicest was near Padiham where the Warden's quarters were a lodge, once belonging to a big estate. Ray really fancied this.

Just before Easter Ray was made Deputy Warden at Chorley. To begin with his accommodation was within the Home, but soon there were two new semi-detached houses – one for the Warden and one for the Deputy. It was a real joy to go to Chorley for the weekends. From our bedroom window we could see Blackpool Tower. It was only 22 miles to Southport with its miles of sandy beaches and here, later, when only 13, Clive learned to drive the car. But as the summer wore on, Ray became more and more dissatisfied with the way the Home was being run and longed for the opportunity to run his own Home. There was a vacancy at Lancaster during the summer holidays. We took the caravan with us so that we could combine the interview with holiday. On the way a huge vehicle passed us, causing the caravan to sway from side to side, frightening us all. Ray determined that this would be its last trip and the only time it emerged again was when being taken to Chadderton. We even looked round Morecambe for a possible home – and found one of the nicest bungalows I have ever seen; unfortunately, immediately in front of the lounge window was a massive gas holder. Imagine having to look at that every time you looked out of the window! Secretly I hoped that Ray would not be appointed, for I dreaded the thought of another move and the necessity for me to find another job in a totally unknown area. Meanwhile we enjoyed our holiday, explored Arnside and saw the sudden onrush of the tide. I was much relieved when Lancaster didn't want Ray – it was a small home and the salary depended on the size of the home -. In the autumn we learned that the Mellors were retiring, and true to their promise, they recommended that Ray should become Officer in Charge at Broadway House, and the New Year of 1974 saw him installed there.

23: MANCHESTER PART TWO – CHADDERTON (1974-82)

In all I spent eight terms teaching in Bradford. They were not particularly enjoyable. Several of the children I tried to teach had serious mental problems and with few exceptions the staff were not on my wavelength. Pleasant memories include shopping during lunchtime at Grey Mare Lane Market where I was able to buy clothes for Clive quite cheaply; trips to the swimming baths; Monday mornings spent at Parrs Wood School where a group of our children were taught gardening – potting plants, sowing peas and beans – by an excellent teacher, and one wonderful day when I was sent off to a local SSN school and the children were taken to the canal – or was it a river? - beyond Hazel Grove. Peace reigned as the boat slowly proceeded and then returned. It was there that I saw the little girl, mentioned earlier, who was almost a mirror image of Kathleen Jones – and learnt that she suffered from hydrocephalus. There was also an occasion when I accompanied a group of children to the Free Trade Hall for a most excellent and informative concert. One happy memory was during a period when we visited some of the children in their homes. One little boy told me with great joy that his mum and dad had had a celebration meal "and there was a candle on the table". Inside another typical terraced house a younger brother of the child I had come to visit insisted on singing the Christmas song, "*Little Donkey*". It was beautifully done and as I looked around I remembered the house I was born in and thought how familiar it was. Obviously the actual teaching was not high on my list of happy memories. I particularly hated Wednesday afternoons when I was left in charge of a class of boys while their male teacher took some of them elsewhere.

Then one day, while I was about halfway through the course for teaching handicapped children, I saw a job advertisement for a teacher for reading, (Grade 2), at an ESN school in Chadderton. Ray had begun his job at Broadway House in January 1974 and during that year we realised that it would be sensible to move from Cheadle Hulme to

Chadderton, 15 miles to the other side of Manchester. As it was, we only had the weekends at home. Meanwhile we were concerned about moving Clive to another school. People in Chadderton recommended Yew Tree, which was a few minutes walk from Broadway House. Despite all our efforts Clive was not doing as well as we had hoped at the school in Cheadle Hulme. He was almost eight before he read with any pleasure and it was not until I learnt about cross lateralism that I realised why – he was left eye dominant and right arm and leg dominant. I saw the Headmaster of Yew Tree School to ask if he would admit Clive and suggested that he be put in a 'B' stream. Clive was always unhappy if placed with children whom he regarded as cleverer than him. This ruse succeeded; Clive was amazed to find so many children well below his intellectual capacity and from then on never looked back. For his final year in the Junior School he did well in the 'A' stream.

Also during 1974 we endured the saga of selling 1, Waverley Drive, Cheadle Hulme. We unfortunately employed a far from honest estate agent to begin with, who had promised an almost instantaneous sale with a huge profit. Weeks became months, the house remained unsold, but we hadn't found a suitable property in Chadderton. We had decided that it would be better to be in North Chadderton as we were told that the school there was good; and we thought that 2 miles was far enough to be away from Broadway House. One day, one of the District Nurses, who lived in a bungaloid estate in North Chadderton, told us that one of her neighbours was leaving and selling her bungalow. We went to see it and decided that it would do. It was a semi-detached bungalow with a good garden facing the south-west at the back. The kitchen was square and a reasonable size, but there were only 2 smallish bedrooms, lounge and bathroom. Fortunately it was possible to have a dormer built on, giving two more bedrooms.

We changed the Estate Agent and within a fortnight had sold the house in Waverley Drive for a good profit, enabling us easily to buy the bungalow and afford to have the dormer attached. We had already brought over to Broadway House the old kitchen cupboard that my father had made in 1895, and since I was unhappy about a wall and the back door blocking the view to the hills, decided to have the kitchen extended; the back door being replaced by a large window giving an excellent view of the garden and hills. The extension made it possible for a back door which opened on to the drive and there was room for the old cupboard and the kitchen table we had brought from Matlock. Later we bought kitchen units; the 22 cu. ft. freezer fitted along the interior wall.

It was convenient to be living at Broadway House during 1974. We had two bedrooms, a living room, bathroom and kitchen and it meant that Clive would not be left on his own while I attended the course begun the previous September. Moreover I did not have to get meals – though Ray stopped the care assistants cleaning our quarters – and thus had time to write essays and prepare work. Ray was also engaged on a course, and I did quite a lot of the written work for him. Looking back, I find it difficult to remember even the journeys to Bradford Grange School, let alone what happened there. I can remember only one day when I was feeling particularly afflicted by the sheer tedium of my job and returned to be accosted by demented ladies. There really was very little intellectual stimulation. We brought the old caravan over and Ray placed it behind the bungalow garage. He then fixed an electric cable so that when we moved I could use it for work connected with the course – which finished in July 1975. I had learned much about the teaching of reading, the various types of handicap that prevailed and some of their causes.

I applied for the job at Chadderton and if ever prayers were offered it was then – the thought of Bradford Grange to the end of my teaching career was unbearable. I was interviewed by the headmaster, John Callaghan and possibly another person. Perhaps the course I was doing was in my favour; I was appointed and I remember us driving John Callaghan back to Rochdale.

I also remember cycling from Broadway House to Ferneyfields School to begin the new term in January 1975 and the feeling of enormous relief that I was no longer at travelling to Bradford Grange. Meanwhile later that year the builders transformed and enlarged the bungalow, but it was not really habitable till the following year. Clive, having begun the Autumn term of 1975 at North Chadderton School – which had gone comprehensive at the same time – was obliged to stay for school dinners for the whole of that term because the bungalow was uninhabitable. All my hopes that he would continue to have school dinners once we were living there were soon dashed. Once we were in residence in Trent Avenue he came home each day for dinner as long as he was at school. When he was 13 he joyfully became a deliverer of newspapers which involved early rising. He saved his earnings and eventually donated them to the purchase of golf clubs and a camera, saving all the payslips. 'O' Levels at 16 were most encouraging. He particularly excelled in Geography, but the projects for this subject had been so time consuming that I feared they might occupy an even more large proportion of the study required for 'A' levels. So he opted for stratospheric Maths, Further Maths & Economics. Alas, the Maths teacher developed hepatitis and was missing for six months. No one passed in maths. And Clive achieved only one 'A' Level which was insufficient for a university. He applied to Plymouth and pursued a course on Business Studies.

Our new next door neighbours did the removal in their van - no more Pickfords, so it was cheap and comfortable. Clive had one of the new upstairs rooms, the other one with two single beds and the old chest of drawers being the spare room. It was just possible to get between the beds. Our bedroom was so small that one could draw the curtains back without getting out of bed. Ray retiled the bathroom and because I'd fancied a plum coloured bathroom suite, it was installed. The two old easy chairs which had been in the house at West Brampton were sold and we bought a new gold, dralon three-piece suite. Ferneyfield School was only about half a mile away; Broadway House 2 miles.

To begin with I used to sit in the staffroom with individual pupils and soon became very interested in each child and its particular difficulties. A wooden two storeyed building was being constructed and eventually I taught upstairs there. I became very familiar with the Pirate books – the Red Pirate (Roderick), the Green Pirate (Gregory) and the Blue Pirate (Benjamin). I devised a phonic reading programme which was surprisingly successful. On one large piece of cardboard I stuck pictures illustrating each letter of the alphabet. They had to be phonic: thus A for apple, B for bed, C for cat. The initial letter, in three sizes, (because to these children even the size of the letter made it look different) appeared on cards matching the size of the pictures. To begin with the cards were in alphabetical order and the child was asked to make the sound of the letter followed by the name of the picture – thus A for apple – and place the letter card on top of the picture. Once all the pictures were covered up the child was asked if he/she could remember any of the pictures underneath. They usually could and the cards were removed as they were remembered. Later the cards were presented in any order and the child had to find the right picture. I was surprised to find that if I turned the picture sheet over so that no pictures could be seen, the child remembered the exact position of the pictures and could place the letter card in the correct place.

I decided to use the same method for teaching blends. Thus BL could be for blue, BR for bridge etc. There were 31 of these and although the children found this more difficult it was surprisingly successful with these ESN children. Finally there were 22 digraphs. These, naturally proved most difficult: AI for chain; AR for car; OI for oil. But when tried out on a normal child who had reading difficulties, the whole method was most successful. And it could be played as a game in groups, with the letter cards shared out. In addition there was the invaluable list of 200 basic words which could be taught on flash cards. I maintain that any normal child can be taught to read quite quickly just using these methods, followed by learning the use of the 'magic e' and then being given passages including such homonyms such as 'there. their; as, has, where, were, is, his – for these parts of speech were useful – and encouraging the child to select the correct word. Sentence construction is vital and each new word learned should be placed in a sentence and spoken.

During the 1970s the government was determined to eradicate illiteracy. We were told that there were 2,000,000 illiterates in the country and various schemes were introduced, books published and local authorities given money to set up suitable learning facilities. In Oldham advertisements appeared for four coordinators whose job would be to visit people seeking help, provide a course of lectures for volunteers willing to teach people who applied for help and match teacher to pupil. The headmaster suggested that I apply. I was accepted. So began one of the most rewarding parts of my teaching career. I visited people in all walks of life who had difficulty reading and met some wonderful people who were willing to devote their time to teaching them. There were usually a set of five lectures, each one to do with one aspect of teaching people to read: I gave the one on phonics. I also began to teach at evening classes; on Mondays at Crompton House and on Wednesdays at Royton, and some of the people I interviewed came to these classes. I remember one man, a builder who had transformed his house into a mini palace, yet could not read. He began to attend the classes at Crompton House and became a competent reader. Another was a plumber: I can't remember what in particular I did for him, but thereafter I had to force money on him for any work he did for me. There was one girl who could not be relied on to spell 'the' yet progressed to college education. There were failures, of course. Young men who had been persistent truants at school thought that a magic wand could be waved and that they would be able to read overnight. I remember one, through whose window could be seen in huge letters, 'OLDHAM BREWERY'. He had lived there for years and had never thought to enquire what it said. One young man who applied for help was a Moslem Fundamentalist who made more of an attempt to convert me than to learn reading skills. During this period many expelled Ugandan Asians came for help. Their spoken English was good, but their written work betrayed their lack of grammatical skills.

We began to have holidays in Cornwall and booked a holiday from a brochure but found many of the claims untrue and disconsolately walked along the coastal road towards Porthleven. It was a very hot day and I needed a short sleeved blouse. Finding a shop that sold ladies garments, we bought a suntop and a blouse; then told the proprietor our disappointments. She immediately offered to rent us a flat on the sea front – would we like to see it? It was all that we could wish for: one large bedroom with a double and single bed; a large lounge and a fitted kitchen. There was also a covered balcony where games could be played on wet days. We booked it for the next year and enjoyed several holidays there, visiting Kynance Cove and the Minack open air theatre further along the coast at Porthcurno. One year we took the ferry to the Scilly Isles, but the sea was so rough that Clive and I were sick and Ray felt so ill that his appreciation of the Scilly Isles was severely limited. He insisted on queuing up early for the return journey so that seats were available.

One year he decided to have an expensive holiday in Scotland, visiting Mallaig, staying in a seafront hotel in Oban, visiting Iona and also the place where his Aunt Maggie had lived before her departure to Birmingham. It was undoubtedly an enjoyable holiday – Ray and Clive were able to play golf at Oban, but it was obtained on credit and this always worried me. In retrospect perhaps I worried too much and we should have splashed out more. I would have loved to go abroad but Ray was terrified of flying; so we were restricted to mainland Britain.

In 1977, Cousin Mary Hall living in Canada, wrote to say that she was proposing to visit us. Her husband had recently died so she was free to come. She came laden with gifts – embarrassingly so, for I felt I could never compete with her enormous generosity. I had asked her if she would like to visit the war graves in France where her father and our Uncle Arthur were buried. She liked the idea and was willing for me to drive her in France. Fortunately I had saved the letters that Edwin and Arthur had sent to my mother during the 1914-18 war and thus could obtain from the War Graves Commission the location of their graves. We crossed to France by the Hovercraft and picked up a hired car by which we travelled to Bethune where Edwin was buried. It was a comparatively small cemetery and we were soon able to find the grave; after which we made our way to a hotel and having practised, 'Une chambre avec deux lits,' we were shown to a room with two double beds which we later discovered was infested with mosquitoes. Next day we set out for Amiens and really enjoyed the French countryside, travelling on country roads and avoiding all towns. This cemetery was enormous. There was a sort of lodge by the entrance gate where the names of the identified dead were written in a book – Arthur's among them. We found the grave, beautifully tended, and as we stood there I remembered that it was August 15th – my mother's birthday – and thought how appropriate it was to visit this grave on this anniversary, for Arthur was like a son to my mother. The drive back to the coast was rather more fraught. The various car indicators were in unfamiliar places and I trained Mary to help by holding up an appropriate arm! But the experience of finding these graves was well worth the effort of the journey and quite unforgettable for both of us.

Cousin Mary Hall from Canada

While Mary was with us we tried to visit as many relations as possible. She was most anxious to visit Meaford where she had stayed as a child with her mother during the 1914-18 war. She said she remembered golden roses climbing up the wall. There were still roses on that wall, but no longer the golden ones that Mary remembered. Arthur and Jen welcomed her very warmly and Jen took us to visit an old lady in a Home who remembered her mother and we visited Moddershall where her mother had lived.

We also visited Cousins Marjorie and Harold in Yorkshire, and Cousin Marion in London. Marion had recently lost her husband and both Mary and I sometimes found her behaviour a bit odd. But she brought her brother, William, to meet Mary. By the time Mary returned to Canada we had visited as much as possible of the family and seen a fair bit of England.

From the start, Ray set to work to improve the running of Broadway House. He discovered that it was run on the theory that the bulk of the work should be done on Mondays, less on Tuesdays, and so on so that by the end of the week there was very little to do and the Mellors departed on Friday evening for their seaside bungalow, returning Sunday night or Monday morning. One soon understood the need to get away, but every weekend the place was left in charge of a care assistant who slept in. Fortunately no major disaster ever took place. The convenience of the staff took precedence over the needs of the residents. Thus, with one night care assistant to look after 50 people and ensure that they all arrived down for breakfast each morning, the job of getting them up, washed and dressed, began at 2am in the middle of the night. This inevitably meant that the process of getting them off to bed also began as early as 6pm, though there would be two care assistants to cope with that and the job would all be done by 10pm when the night care assistant arrived. Thus between 10pm and 2am was a fairly peaceful period and it had been known for a care assistant to make phone calls to a boyfriend in Turkey. Ray perceived that there was no social life for the residents, some of whom would be falling asleep in the afternoon. Breakfast over, the staff made beds, did the washing, cleaned the Home while the residents just sat.

Ray decided to make the time of reveille later by 15 minutes each week so that it would be assimilated almost unnoticed. By the time a more reasonable hour was reached, he applied for another night care assistant so that all could be down for breakfast by 8.30. Every morning when Ray was on duty he was up between 7 and 7.30, making a tour of the Home to see how things had gone in the night. Sometimes there would have been a death and the care assistant would lay out the corpse, having washed the hair. When we went to live in the bungalow, the room in Broadway House we had used as a lounge became the sleeping in room and Ray became convinced that a benign spirit was present. When a death was imminent, it was as if he were woken up and 'told'; and sure enough within minutes a care assistant would appear with the news. I never experienced this strange phenomenon, but on occasion Ray would have the dog with him and recalled how it would cower and its hair stand up on end when these 'messages' came. He would always go to the bedside if the person were still alive, sit with them, hold their hand and even tell little stories to make them smile. During one March the Angel of Death was particularly busy; One of the best care assistants, Emma, was on duty one night when five of the residents died. She said she just had time to prepare one before the next one expired.

Ray was keen to bring a little social life into the Home and now that bedtime did not begin at 6pm arranged little outings, perhaps to a local pub, or a day trip to Blackpool. Ever since he had seen Garden Parties in the Homes in Derbyshire, he was keen to arrange them. There as a huge lawn at the back of the Home which lent itself to this. Colourful bunting decorated the area, food was prepared, alcoholic drinks were ordered and music which could be heard up and down Broadway was performed. There was one famous occasion when I was dragged in to tell fortunes by palmistry! The amazing thing was that I was complimented on the truth of my assertions!

All this had required hard work, and must have made life less somnolent for the residents but there was one fly in the ointment: Ray had trained with Lancashire Social Services and liked that methods he had been taught. In 1974, Chadderton ceased to be part of Lancashire and was joined to Oldham. One of his superiors, a Mr. McCorquodale, was very good to Ray and even took him to Southport on one occasion to watch one of the Open Golf tournaments. Ray never forgot this and developed an interest in the game, went, with Clive, to various venues and we all were present at Lytham St. Anne's when Ballesteros won in 1979. But other officials seemed to be forever changing their minds about how Homes should be run. There was the brilliant idea that residents should be allowed to lie in bed till they felt like getting up; it didn't matter what time of day the beds were made. The fact that there might be an organisational difficulty never seemed to occur.

I shall never know how far the interference he suffered affected him, or whether the fact that I was working full time plus two evenings at night school caused him to feel neglected. I really think that this is unlikely, for there was always a meal for him to come home to – often he wouldn't eat it, having fed at the Home. He would sometimes amuse us with extraordinary stories about events at the Home and then the television would take over and there was little more conversation. There were 27 staff in all at Broadway House, all of whom were female and I think he was a good boss. He certainly made them laugh. During 1978, his behaviour became more erratic; I learned that he had reverted to drinking at lunch time; he would disappear without explanation and be impossible to contact. He took to sleeping upstairs in the spare room. On one occasion he said he was leaving me, and took himself off to a hotel in Oldham- the B&B charge being then £25. This annoyed me, for he was far from generous with housekeeping money and I even had to write letters to him to explain what money was required to pay bills – all of which I paid. It was impossible to have a rational conversation without him flying into a temper. The relief I felt after he had gone was very great: a burden had slipped away. But next morning a tearful Ray was on the phone begging to be allowed back home! I could never have shut the door on him. For where would he go? What would happen to him?

It was toward Christmas 1978 that light began to dawn. He took to taking one of his care assistants to visit her husband who was in hospital having had an operation and then taking her back home to Greenfield. This became an almost daily occurrence. By now I had had rumours from the Home that the lady involved had managed to secure for herself an Officer-in-Charge job at one of the smaller Homes in Werneth through Ray's influence – and that was presumably where he was when missing. I decided that the time had come to see this lady and since one of the hospital visiting days was Sunday, suggested that she and her three sons could come for tea after visiting. It was a most interesting situation. After tea I produced games like Monopoly, Cluedo, and even Snakes and Ladders only to find that these boys had never been introduced to such games and also showed no signs of civilised behaviour. I had heard that one of them was having problems reading and even offered my help! It took Ray a long time to take them all home. The following weekend it so happened that an Adult Literacy Course was being held in St. Anne's on Sea, to which I was going. Leaving Clive, aged 14, in charge, I invited mother and sons again, and heard a full report from Clive on my return. Because of snow, there was only one lane open on the motorways; even the sea was slightly frozen. Ray took me; but he certainly did not fetch me back – one of the people on the course did that and Ray did not even bother to return home till late and then drunk.

The matter was never discussed and a deep silence descended. Ray came home as little as possible – bringing his washing with him, and I thought it wise to let matters take their course. We were due to travel to Cornwall during the February half term and I remember thinking that if he wanted to spend the half term with his amour he was welcome. Ever since we were married it had been my aim to give him some happiness;

if that could not be done and he could find some happiness with someone else, better that than nothing at all. I was not bothered about adultery; that was a physical matter; it was the sheer neglect, lack of cooperation and gross unkindness that hurt.

We went to Cornwall taking one of Clive's friends with us; by the time we got to Exeter the weather was several degrees warmer and I remember sitting outside without a coat. Of the rest of the holiday I have no recollection. That was the last holiday we had with Clive in Cornwall - he elected to holiday with his friend's family that summer. Sometime between March and August, I think, Ray decided to abandon the romance. I shall never know what happened. We had not arranged a summer holiday, but Jean and Malcolm Marsland (second cousins) had a small chalet in Colwyn Bay and offered it to us for a week at the end of July. The holiday coincided with the death of Lord Mountbatten and we watched the funeral while on holiday. It was a good holiday. We visited various National Trust properties and enjoyed the Colwyn Bay promenade. One day we decided to see Plas Newydd in Anglesey and afterwards drove on until we came to Aberffraw where we were delighted to find acres of sand dunes. Ray had acquired a dog, Brandy, because the owner was moving away, presumably to a place where dogs were not permitted. He was part Labrador and needed a lot of exercise. We let him loose on the sand dunes and five hours later he returned, exhausted. This, we decided, was the place for a holiday with a dog. We enquired at the Post Office and discovered the Bodorgan Estate which let cottages out from Easter until October. And so began our love affair with Anglesey. We booked a holiday for the following Easter, and from then on until the end of 1982 we went several times a year, staying in different cottages.

Brandy: 1978-1989

24: EARLY RETIREMENT (1980-95)

Nineteen Eighty was the year of my 58th birthday. It was also the year of my retirement from full time teaching. Early that year John Callaghan told me that if I wished I could finish at the end of the school year. If I wished! Certainly teaching at Ferneyfield had been less distasteful than some. During the previous year I had volunteered to teach Domestic Science as the teacher concerned was attending a year's course. I really enjoyed this though I had no qualifications. Each week I would decide what to make; decided what it would cost; the children brought the estimated money and took home with them the result of their labours. At the end of the year the fund was slightly in profit. My disaster was rice pudding; it had not occurred to me that there would be a problem transporting it by bus to their homes, but in the event there was rice pudding everywhere except in the dishes. My great success was Seville orange marmalade. On the first day a class would cut up the orange peel and put the peeled orange into a muslin bag, add the water and leave for the next day when the marmalade was made. That class then cut up orange peel for the next day. By the end of the week there was a fair supply of marmalade in jars supplied by the pupils, each of whom took home a sample. After this I became a class teacher and taught most subjects. We began to have after school 'meetings' with 'advisers'. We were introduced to the new system of putting ticks in columns to indicate a pupil's progress, e.g. See how many instructions a child can remember (1) Pick up your pen (tick when done) (2) write your name (3) put your pen down. When all three instructions were obeyed without pausing between them, three ticks would be applied. This tedious way of recording progress did not appeal to me. I could see the way things were moving in education and was delighted to write out my resignation and then cross off the days that remained one by one. I remembered the early, wretched days of my career and my mother telling me that I was 'wishing my life away'. Well, I had survived thirty years of gainful employment. Wouldn't it be wonderful if I could have another thirty years without having to go out to work? I intended to continue to teach at night school, for this I enjoyed, and my adult pupils voted with their feet for me to continue – which I did till 1987.

I came home from school on that final Friday and, though champagne would have been appropriate, I contented Clive and myself with a bottle of Pomagne while watching Sebastian Coe win the 1,500 metres race at the Moscow Olympics. I had finished my race too. Next day I walked Brandy in Tandle Hill Park and almost hugged the ground with joy. I had waited a long time for this exquisite happiness.

There was plenty of painting and decorating waiting to be done at home – Ray did the painting and I the papering. The garden too occupied us both and each day the dog had to be walked. Often I would go back with Ray part of the way to Broadway House and then walk the dog back home across the fields. A new housing estate was being built and I watched it grow. I doubt if there are many fields there now. I found that I was devoting a lot of time to a young illiterate Irish woman who lived near us. I wrote her story down as she told it to me, believing that this would encourage her to read it. It seems she had married, emigrated to Australia and had two children. Her husband had treated her badly, they returned to England and were divorced. At present there was a court case to decide who had the care of the children. I swallowed all this, feeling very aggrieved for her. She had since met someone else who I eventually met – a very caring, compassionate man. She lost the court case; the husband was given custody of the children. She left the area and the last I heard of her was that her lover had left her and she was mentally unstable. You can't win them all!

During 1980 the Oberammergau Passion Play was performed and having heard so much about it while at school learning German, I resolved to go. Clive was willing to go with me. Unfortunately the plan became known at Broadway House and two of the care assistants asked if they could come. They were very pleasant ladies, but I really did not want any extra company. However, one could not refuse their request and on 12th August we departed. We stayed at Mondsee at first and enjoyed coach trips in the area. It was 21st August before we left for Oberammergau, where we enjoyed swimming in an open air pool, surrounded by hills. The whole of the next day was fully occupied watching the truly impressive play. We returned on the 23rd.

Betty at the top of Dachstein, Austria

In 1981 I flew to Toronto and stayed with Cousin Mary for a week before flying to Denver, boarding a Greyhound bus and thus visiting Salt Lake City, Sacramento, Yosemite, San Francisco, Los Angeles, Flagstaff and the Grand Canyon. It was a wonderful trip. To economise I spent two nights travelling by coach and one in a bed. At one breakfast stop, a group of girls joined me and we discussed worldwide travel – which I encouraged them to do while they were young. I had had to wait until I was retired. They looked amazed and one said that I looked no older than her mother who was 43! Much encouraged I began to feel like 43 until I asked a tram guard in San Francisco the price of a ticket. "Senior citizens a quarter," was the reply. Perhaps they have younger senior citizens there?

Betty at the Grand Canyon 1981

During the summer of 1982 we stayed for a fortnight at one of the nicest Bodorgan cottages, only a short footpath's walk on to the Rhosneigr beach where we walked Brandy each day. We met an elderly man, also with a dog, who said he had been Mayor of Colchester. He and his wife had a bungalow in Rhosneigr and would we like to visit them for coffee? It was a beautiful bungalow; completely compact and having a shower, toilet, bedroom and a balcony upstairs as well as two bedrooms and all facilities downstairs. To our amazement they asked if we would like to rent this bungalow instead of, and for the same price as the Bodorgan cottages. It seemed too good to be true, but the following February and again in May we were able to have a holiday in this delightful bungalow. It was a relief for Ray to be able to have a break from Broadway House during February instead of having to wait till Easter.

We went again in the September. The family must have spent the August holiday there and left it for us to clean up – which we did. But while there one day when there was a very low tide, I walked Brandy along the sands skirting the Valley air field and saw in the distance a caravan site. Ray had been watching us through binoculars and also noticed it. Next day we drove to Rhoscolyn, found the caravan site and put a deposit of £50 on a new caravan with the intention of getting a loan from the bank to pay for it. I was a little worried – I always was when we had to borrow money – but it proved to be one of the best investments we ever made. The site was open all the year and made it possible for Ray to have a break whenever he could – thus, I am sure, prolonging his life.

For Ray had been afflicted with various ailments almost all our married life. He had gall bladder trouble – a non-fat diet – lumbago, stomach problems (all his teeth were extracted) and chest infections at Matlock, gout and further chest problems in Chadderton. During the November of 1983 it seemed that nothing that I prepared for him to eat was acceptable and I bought a microwave in desperation so that he could get something he fancied out of the freezer, defrost and eat it. I shall never forget the weekend of December 17th-18th when we heard the sad news of Arthur Shelley's death from cancer of the liver. Ray went to work at 5pm on the Saturday, and having noticed the advertisement of a carol concert in Manchester Cathedral when visiting the dentist, I determined, most unusually, to go there and even treated myself to a meal at a café nearby. Thus, by having a dentist in Manchester, was my future mapped out for me. I enjoyed the concert enormously and felt thoroughly at home in the Cathedral.

Meanwhile Ray had arranged a party at Broadway House for the Monday evening. He was not well but went to work at 2pm. I joined him during the evening. The party was a great success, but Ray was obviously ill, yet he refused to give in and stayed the night as planned. He returned next day and went straight to bed but refused to let me send for the doctor till the Thursday. It was a virus pneumonia. Having had scarcely any sleep for two nights lying beside Ray, I finally went upstairs and immediately fell asleep, but during that night Ray thought he was dying and I felt very guilty the next day. He was ill all over Christmas, though he did sit out of bed on Christmas Day. I felt that I couldn't leave him to attend Arthur's funeral and it was well into January 1984 before Ray recovered.

Outside our bedroom was a sunless patio adjoining our neighbour's patio. Our original neighbours had left years before and were replaced by a couple who were not merely unfriendly, but positively hostile and seemed to be permanently engaged in hammering. Indeed we had even given some thought to moving ourselves for it is unpleasant living in close proximity to unfriendly people. Ray's illness made me decide to have an extension to the bedroom built over the patio so that if he were ill again I could sleep on a bed settee in the extension and be at hand if he needed me. I knew a good builder, a Mr. McGinty, an architect drew up the plans and we submitted them to the local council. There was quite a delay and we discovered that our neighbours had placed an objection, but eventually, in June, work began and within a fortnight was completed – from footings to electricity. This gave us a room 12 feet square and was one of the best organised jobs I ever remember. I had intended that I could sit in it while Ray watched TV in the lounge, but soon found that Ray liked being in it, so we found ourselves with TVs in kitchen, lounge and extension. But it was never used for the purpose I intended; Ray's health problems now concerned his heart.

By 1984 Clive had finished the course in Business Management at Plymouth and selected the fast food industry for his career with a firm called Huckleberrys, who trained him. Unfortunately they sold out to Wimpy with whom Clive was never very happy, but he got jobs at Southampton, Portsmouth, became Assistant Manager at Reading and came home periodically.

One day I found an advertisement in a newspaper – can't remember which one – announcing that Manchester University was offering part time courses for mature students to gain a BA degree. Was it possible, I wondered, that at last I might gain a degree? There were seven subjects to choose from. I immediately dismissed History of Art, or Nursing, English Literature, (too many books to read) and History because I'd done so much of that at school. Then there was Theology. Well, now, I'd always had an interest in religion – Scripture had been one of my few successes at school – so why not apply for that course? It was so long since I had done any profound study or written essays such as I had learned to do at school that I felt far from confident, but in September a Study Skills Course was offered by way of preparation for the degree course. I joined it, found it most enlightening and realised that most of the participants were way behind me when it came to essay writing. So in October 1985 I enrolled at Manchester University for a BA Theology Course. This involved ten modules: some people were able to do three or four a year, but I thought I might manage two. I was still involved with night school. We began with the Early History of Christianity and the lecturer was Ben Drewery, who had returned from retirement to help out. Of all the lecturers we had, Ben was the most memorable – and most generous with his marks. There were also lectures on Ethics with Tony Dyson and later John Elford. There were also a few lectures from Graham Slater. I managed to pass the exams the following June. Two down and eight to go.

From childhood, religion had fascinated me but there were always more questions than answers. The Theology Course shed light on many aspects of Christianity; the people who had influenced its development and the continuing arguments about the faith. But the more I studied, the more questions there seemed to be. The books of New Testament had been put together to serve the communities which were being formed during the first century AD. Were the stories in them true or were they there to illustrate the amazing message that Jesus was both man and God? What about other faiths? One could no longer assume that Christianity alone was the valid faith. Interfaith relationships were surely now of prime importance. So all that I could honestly believe was that there is a loving Creator and that love, agape, was the most important thing in life. I had also discovered that for me, it was the hardest.

I now forget how I became involved with the Oldham Conservative Party, but it was through the Chairman at that time that I got such an excellent builder for the extension. One day I remember going to a luncheon party where one of the ladies mentioned that she was joining a cruise in the Mediterranean just before Christmas – a celebration of 75 years of Girl Guiding. It sounded wonderful and incredibly cheap so I asked if I could join and promptly handed over £5 as a deposit. We left by coach for Gatwick on 15th December from where we flew to Athens, saw the Acropolis, embarked on what proved to be an Irish Ferry at the Pireas and set sail for Port Said where it had rained and we saw a car half submerged on the side of the road. It was a long bus trip to Cairo but were shown the Mosque of Mohammed Ali and the museum containing the Tutenkhamen exhibits which were most impressive. We then proceeded to the pyramids where we encountered an Arab camel driver arrayed in gorgeous garments who wanted paying to have his photo taken. We found the Egyptians very keen on pound notes. I even encountered one who wanted to sell me his horse! I did have a very brief ride on a camel and bought some postcards.

Betty and Camel - Egypt – 1982

We returned very wearily to the ship – the coach journey seemed to last for ever and having been cajoled into buying odd bits of cheap jewellery, we were glad to get a good night's rest. Next morning we disembarked at Ashdod in Israel. Immediately we noticed the striking contrast with Egypt. There was no sign of desert – every inch of ground seemed to be under cultivation. We were taken to Jerusalem, and saw both the 'Garden Tomb', the Church of the Sepulchre and Old Jerusalem before being driven down the long road to Jericho – and one could so well imagine the story of the Good Samaritan. We did not see Jericho, but were taken to the Dead Sea via the caves where the Dead Sea Scrolls were found. It actually rained while we bravely entered the Dead Sea. I say bravely because the water was opaque and it was impossible to see the nasty sharp stones the feet encountered. It was also a long walk to where one could actually float and prove that it was impossible to drown. We returned to see Bethlehem and the Church of the Nativity where we did a little shopping before being taken back to our ship.

Our next stop was Cyprus where we saw the Kolossi Castle, Apollo Temple a Roman Villa and Amphitheatre and I resolved that when it was possible I would like to spend some time there. We then sailed on to Turkey, docked at Kusadosi, were taken to Ephesus – never to be forgotten, especially the House of Ill Repute; were taken up a long hill to see Mary's House - allegedly the home of the Virgin Mary while under St. John's care. It remained me vividly of our house in Matlock – up a hill and surrounded by trees, but I rather think this suggestion was regarded as verging on the blasphemous. I found the Turks less offensive than the Egyptians when bargaining and was persuaded into buying a small Muslim prayer mat.

We then sailed on to Crete and were shown round Knossos. We boarded a Tri-Star plane that flew to Gatwick where the coach was waiting. I phoned Ray at the Hilton Service Station. He met me in Manchester and we sat up talking until Christmas Eve arrived.

It was clearly impossible to prepare for a Christmas Dinner at home, so we had decided to book one at the Beach Hotel in Anglesey. This was one of our very best ideas. We left for the caravan in Anglesey during the morning of Christmas Eve, taking cards and presents with us, and on Christmas Day, having rejoiced in our presents we set out for the Beach Hotel, and were shown into a dining room where the portrait of Disraeli graced one side of the fireplace, and that of Gladstone the other. The meal was superb. Each table enjoyed a whole turkey and we were able to take home with us whatever remained. We drank Barsac, wore paper hats and rejoiced exceedingly. It was the best Christmas ever.

1986 was not such a good year. Ray had increasingly frequent bouts of illness and during the year both angina and emphysema were diagnosed so early retirement was suggested. He had a wonderful party at Broadway House on 27th November when many nice things were said about him. Earlier in the year Clive had come home from Reading and announced that he had given his notice in as he could stand it no longer. Ray was most upset by this and continued to worry about it for the next six months, But Clive had his mind set on running his own business and spent much time in Manchester doing market research on various cafes and restaurants. He wanted his own fast food outlet and believed that a certain Joe with whom he had worked in Portsmouth would join him in the venture. Unfortunately, he was unable to get a bank loan because he had no collateral and we were quite unable to help him. Joe did come over once or twice but it was obvious to us that he was not serious. In the meantime Barry Coop, who had long since sold the newspaper shop, had established himself with Volvo up in Oldham and remembering Clive's diligence as a newspaper boy, asked him to go and work for him. Clive was reluctant to do this as he had set his mind on the fast food business, but Barry frequently sent Clive to pick up or deposit cars all over the country, which was beneficial to both. Toward the end of September, Ray could stand it no longer and told Clive firmly that he must go and ask Barry to employ him – as he obviously wanted to. So Clive went up to Oldham and began to sell Volvos.

In 1987 we were both 65 and various endowment and insurance policies were due, also Ray got a lump sum. We went to an exhibition at G Mex to do with investment and invested some money in what was then called MLA The Manchester Evening News advertised a holiday in Vienna, a place that Ray had had romantic ideas about – he loved the Strauss Waltzes – but there was one snag; we would have to fly to Munich and Ray had not hitherto been prepared to fly anywhere. The lure of Vienna won and we flew from Manchester Airport.

There were several never to be forgotten moments such as the champagne on the Johann Strauss boat on the Danube, the glory of the Melk Monastery which we visited as we sailed down the Danube; the visit to the Opera House – not that we saw an opera, but we were taken all over the building and saw the vast expanse behind the stage. We were taken to the Vienna Woods and shown the hunting lodge where Prince Rudolf committed suicide. Salzburg and various lakeside resorts were visited and we had a day at Heilbronn and Berchtesgarten, though we didn't go up as far as the Eagle's Nest. We had a walk round the lake below and I took a nice photo of Ray eating a very expensive ice cream – which he enjoyed.

But the whole trip was almost ruined by the courier, a very worthy woman who could not stop talking. For everywhere we went she had massive amounts of information which was poured out well in advance; on the return journey we were told in detail what was to happen next day but when the next day came the schedule had been altered. When things went wrong, which they generally did, she worked herself up into a frantic state. One evening we were told not to have coffee after the meal as we would be having it at the top of the Donau Turm. Still digesting the meal we were taken to the Donau Turm only to find that it was fully booked (she hadn't thought to book it). We were then transported to an English Pub where we dallied until it was time to board the Johann Strauss Boat. She had the unfortunate habit of dumping us for as long as five hours without any guidance. All might have been forgiven, but she actually asked for a tip for her and the driver and when we were asked to fill in a form to say what we thought and I commented that it had been an expensive trip, she immediately contradicted, saying that it had been a cheap trip. It was a pity that Ray's first excursion by air had been so spoiled.

During the year we went to the caravan as often as we could and also to Wimbledon for the final weekend. We saw some play on court one, but not the central court where Pat Cash beat Lendl in the final. We stayed at the Heathrow Park Hotel, adjacent to the airport, and Ray was fascinated by the arrival and departure of planes. Towards the end of July I took Brandy with me to Bridgend where I stayed to look after Muriel Howell's dogs while she was supervising a holiday course at the University. We had some splendid walks.

For many years I had corresponded with my old history teacher, Miss Cowe – whom I had adored when young. She had been a most excellent teacher. I had visited her when she lived in Norwich. She then moved to Budleigh Salterton and then to Sidford, so I had promised to visit her after leaving Bridgend. She had booked me a room at a local hotel. She had engaged in long telephone conversations during the early part of the year about the people next door using her electricity, but I was unprepared for the dementia which involved her belief that her neighbours were listening to our conversation. I heard her attempts to defeat the electricity piracy by having a big square torch switched on on the landing all night. This was obviously expensive, and when I arrived she asked me to take her to Sidmouth to buy two oil lamps. I offered to fix them for her but was refused and when I called next morning found she had cut all but an inch off the lamp wicks – which then could not be lit. She was probably angry with herself, but turned on me so violently that there was no point in staying and Brandy and I walked to Sidmouth. I did return later, by which time she had calmed down somewhat, but the whole episode was so upsetting that when I awoke at 4am next morning, I lost no time in returning home and was back in Chadderton by 10am. A week later on the Sunday evening, I had a call from the Sidmouth police. She had been found dead in bed and I had been the last person to see her.

Later in the year we had a most beautiful day in Durham and bought a limited-edition St. Cuthbert plate for £48 — only 500 have been made. There was also a trip to Windsor by coach and one with the Friends of Manchester Cathedral to Cartmel Priory in the Lake District.

I had not been able to pursue my degree course at the University 1986-7 because of Ray being so frequently ill and, of course, Clive coming home complicated life somewhat, but I now saw no reason why I could not attempt one module during the 1987-8 and I registered to do Biblical Studies. This involved only a Tuesday morning, but there would be, of course, essays to be written. Evening classes petered out, for which I was not sorry. On Christmas Day we went to Audley to stay with Tony (son of Don) and Janet Rogerson and family. It was a splendid Christmas and a good end to the year.

Having decided that flying is not necessarily a dangerous pursuit, Ray was quite happy to have a holiday in Tenerife in January 1988. We had a very nice apartment in one of the quieter areas and got about mostly by bus. Having explored the south of the island we decided one day to go north. Unfortunately it poured with rain and the sight of us both in garments intended for the sun must have looked odd — and it was cold.

I had decided to visit Canada again and asked Ray if he would like to accompany me, but he declined — which was just as well for the humid heat in Toronto would have been too much for him. Having spent a week with Mary I flew to Calgary where I had arranged to hire a car at the airport. It was a little automatic Chevrolet Sprint; I was nervous to begin with, but once I had mastered left hand turns I was extremely happy with an automatic and indeed found it difficult to use gears when I returned home. I stayed one night in the Youth Hostel in Calgary and then motored to Banff where there was an excellent Youth Hostel for eight dollars a night. From there I drove to Moraine Lake, the Ten Peaks and so to Lake Louise which was very touristy, though beautiful. Then I made for Whiskey Jack, a remote hostel up the Yoho Valley and not far from the Takallaw Falls. On the way I gave a lift to two young Brits whose father had a caravan at Silver Bay, and they then stuck with me for almost the rest of the trip, which took us up to Jasper, where we had a merciful shower for a dollar in town and stayed at a Youth Hostel for two dollars a night. We had to draw all our water from the stream and boil it for drinking. We visited the Maligne Canyon which is very picturesque. I then returned to Banff where I had time to visit the Sulphur Springs where I bathed and then took the Gondola to the Sulphur Mountain at the top of which I had a meal and surveyed mountain goats. I was unwise enough to walk along the Fenlands in the evening where I was bitten unmercifully by mosquitoes before returning to the Youth Hostel. It was time to return to Toronto and as the plane from Calgary was due to depart very early in the morning, it seemed sensible to stay as near as possible to the airport, especially as the car had to be returned there. A phone call to the Airport Hotel secured a bed for the Friday night. I had been extremely economical with overnight accommodation so it was a delight to be given a room with a 5' bed, table, chairs, settee, coffee table, television and desk, bathroom and shower fully equipped with everything that could be desired for the purpose of total cleanliness. The cost for all this magnificence was $93. The beer was $3.50 a bottle. I had a leisurely swim in the pool followed by a salad lunch and an exploration of the airport. Then began the torment of the mosquito bites acquired in Banff. They were everywhere that had been exposed. So I swam again, had a jacuzzi and sauna followed by a shower and hair wash. Having managed to watch a Clint Eastwood movie, I prepared for bed. Alas, there was very little sleep because of my tormentors and at intervals I had baths and even got into bed with wet legs to ease the fury of these wretched bites. I had a continental breakfast at 5.45, was at the airport at 6.55 ready for departure at 7.25, arriving Toronto 12.45.   It had been quite an adventure.

During this year I seemed to be increasingly involved with Manchester Cathedral. I had been drawn into the Friends of the Cathedral, who had an annual outing to another Cathedral and an Autumn or Christmas Fair. During 1988 I decided to use up my considerable collection of old Christmas cards to make new ones with a printed message and sell them, so I became very familiar with the Cathedral while doing this. I also joined the Manchester/Toulouse Association which had been formed in 1969.   It was an ecumenical group – R.C.s French Protestants, and Anglicans – who met to strengthen their commitment to each other and to learn more about developments which it was hoped would lead to greater unity. Every year there was either a visit to France or the French people came here, and over the years some very close friendships had been made, especially with people who were bilingual.

Although we did not attend the Cathedral every Sunday – sometimes we were in Anglesey, or Ray was not well enough – we became a taxi service to a lady who lived in Crumpsall, Beatrice Hornby. It was easy enough to bring her back from the Cathedral as it was on our way home. We discovered that she had had an elder sister who had looked after her and a husband who "carried her about", both of whom had died within a short time of each other, leaving her bereft, apart from the kind services of a friend, Mary Lever, who lived within easy walking distance. Gradually it became apparent that dementia was setting in. She would appear for the 10.30 service at 9am; wake up in the middle of the night and phone Mary. I once asked her home for a meal one Sunday, but she had no idea when it was time to go – and Ray never asked her again. We did take her with us to the Friends' visit to Cartmel Priory and I remember her eating separately each vegetable on the plate instead of a mixture. I began to take her to the 1.10pm Eucharist either on Mondays, Wednesdays or Fridays. Once she dipped her finger in the wine; I also had to take her to the toilet, pull her pants down and up again. These visits had to be discontinued when she refused to sit but began to wander all over the cathedral. Mary Lever and her daughter finally arranged for her to enter a Home in Blackley which had been a private house, and periodically she would be admitted to the psychiatric ward at North Manchester Hospital where Mary and I would visit her. Here she had room to walk up and down all the time, whereas in the Home she took to walking up and down the stairs all the time. Mary died early in 1990 and Beattie was transferred to a home in Chadderton where I continued to visit her, usually at meal times when the actual feeding of her was the only possible way of communication.

By 1988, we had already started to convey May Woodburn to and from the Cathedral. She lived in a block of flats in Higher Blackley, the occupants of which had deteriorated in quality – not a Christian comment! – since she had moved there in 1970 and never a week went by but we heard of lifts that didn't work or were urinated in, fires, noise, flats being vacated and every piece of equipment being removed. She was devoted to the Cathedral; was on the rota for making coffee on Sunday mornings; made altar cloths, goods for the Christmas Fair and even gave sweets to all the choirboys each Christmas. Her father had died when he was 25; her mother remarried and had more children, but May never liked her stepfather. She had worked in a mill since she was 14 and now had chest problems resulting from the fluff created there. She had never married. One proposal was refused because the young man, although eligible and acceptable, was a Roman Catholic. She had very definite ideas about what was right and wrong.

Towards the end of September I decided to try for another module at the University and signed up for Renaissance, Reform and Renewal with Dr. Ian Sellers. Ray and I had a day trip by public transport to Wigan Pier – a most interesting day and the cost of transport was only 12p each. We also motored to Ryton, near Coventry and visited organic gardens there. En route we went through Rugeley, Hednesford and Chase Terrace that I had hardly visited since I left in 1944. The house I had lodged in was vastly improved; there was a built in garage and a room above. On the way back we called to see Alice Hackett, Ray's cousin, in Birmingham.

During November, Mary Lever's daughter, Maralyn (spelt like that) and I went to Amsterdam via the Hull Ferry, enjoyed a trip round a cheese making factory and an interesting trip on the canal.

But in December I embarked on a coach trip to the Hartz Mountains in Germany which was to include Berlin. The Hartz Mountains were like a winter wonderland; all the fir trees were tipped with snow. We visited a Christmas Market at Goslar, and stopped for a meal where a "witch" appeared and I remembered *Walpurgis Nacht* from schooldays. I bought a circular cloth and some long socks for Ray in one of the villages – my German just adequate – and was rewarded by a delightful mending set of cottons, needles etc. But the main attraction was the trip to Berlin. As we approached the East German Frontier we saw nine lanes in each direction, each with 3 carriageways and double strip lighting. We stopped and a guard embarked, compared each passport photo with the face of the owner, examined the toilet for evaders and departed. We had been warned not even to show a camera or it would have been confiscated, and we proceeded through Luneberg Heath at no more than 50 mph – because, we were told, that was as fast as Ladas could go! We were also told the story of a coach whose driver tried to take a short cut to a hotel only to be met with a tank and forced to reverse all the way back.

In Berlin we were driven to the Brandenburg Gate where we took photos of the Wall. We saw the Reichstag and the Russian War Memorial guarded by a soldier and a dog. It would have been unwise to approach it. We were taken to Checkpoint Charlie and given time to shop before returning. The examination at the frontier took three quarters of an hour. We learned that British passports fetched a high price and clung on to ours with determination. It had been an intimidating experience and when unification was achieved the following year, I was doubly glad that I'd seen Berlin while the Wall was up.

Berlin Wall & Checkpoint Charlie 1988

Soon Christmas approached and again we planned to go to the caravan and have our Christmas dinner at the Beach Hotel. Ray and I went on the 23rd and Clive followed on Christmas Eve. We went to the little church of St. Ffraid which is adjacent to the Beach Hotel before the meal which was much as we remembered it in 1985. This time there was a Scottish lady playing bagpipes. We returned to the caravan to open presents. Clive departed Boxing Day and we stayed till New Year's Day.

The next two years were very eventful. Although I was no longer engaged in Adult Literacy, I was frequently very tired and had arthritic pains in arms and legs. I was increasingly involved at the Cathedral and in visiting Beatrice and other people. There were trips to Newcastle-u-Lyme and London for school friends' reunions. While down south I visited Dorothy Tittensor, now a very old lady in Orpington. We had our fair share of visitors too. Visible from our back door, on Oakbank Avenue, lived an elderly couple, Mr. and Mrs. Turner. Mrs. T. had looked after her husband too devotedly so that he could do nothing for himself and when she became ill he could do nothing for her. When she fell, he would phone Ray to go and pick her up. We found ourselves increasingly going to their aid with meals and one day social services were called; the doctor (whom Ray knew) found that they had been taking each other's tablets. He suggested that Ray be in charge of the tablets and each day he went round seeing to it that they had the correct medication. Then Ray fell ill and I carried on the good work. Apparently there was a niece but we only saw her once. The couple had been great travellers and had showed us some excellent photos of Turkey, among other places. We tried not to smile as we were introduced to the "Pinnarets". Mrs. T. eventually went into hospital and Mr. T. was looked after by a home help. The bed was downstairs in the front room. Ray got into the habit of standing at the back door and looking over the fence at the Turners' house to see if anything was amiss. One day he observed smoke coming out of the kitchen area and told me to phone 999 while he went round to see what he could do. Fortunately, Mr. T. had forgotten to lock the front door and Ray got in, wrapped him up so that when the ambulance people came they were able to take him to hospital. The doors to the living room and kitchen had been closed so no smoke had escaped into the front room. I found myself making coffee for people from two ambulances and two fire engines. Apparently the lady who was looking after Mr. T. had gone out leaving a pan of oil on the cooker. Mr. Turner died the next year and Mrs. Turner made a wonderful recovery but was put in a Home on the other side of Oldham where I once took some neighbours to visit her.

GREATER MANCHESTER
COUNTY FIRE SERVICE.

A.J. Parry M.I.Fire E, County Fire Officer

Divisional Commander 'C' Division

Your Reference

Our Reference   HW/HB/35.8

Contact Senior Divisional Officer
          H. Woods

Date   22nd August, 1989.

Mr. J.R. Smith,
28 Trent Avenue,
CHADDERTON,
Oldham.

Dear Mr. Smith,

The action that you took at the fire which occurred at 126 Oakbank Avenue,
Chadderton, on Tuesday, 8th August, 1989, has been brought to my attention
by the officer in charge of the appliances that attended the fire.

The Officer reports that you observed smoke issuing from the rear of the
premises and knowing the occupant, Mr. Harold Turner, to be severely disabled
you instructed your wife to call the Fire Service and then went to the house
to see if you could be of any assistance. You entered the premises and saw
Mr. Turner, who was partially clothed about to enter the kitchen which was on
fire. You stopped him from doing so and then closed the doors between the fire
and yourself, took Mr. Turner into the front room, dressed him and then assisted
him from the premises.

Your actions at this incident not only reduced the amount of fire damage to the
premises but also obviously saved Mr. Turner from further distress and injury.

I would like to take this opportunity to commend you for your actions, especially
in this day and age where persons tend to ignore other peoples distress. Such
actions are therefore highly commendable and should not go unnoticed.

Yours sincerely,

H. WOODS
DIVISIONAL COMMANDER

'C' Divisional Headquarters: Maclure Road, Rochdale OL11 1DN. Telephone: Rochdale 341221 Telex: 668105.

Ray was frequently far from well, but the trips to the caravan kept him
going. In April we had a holiday in the Algarve. It was an offer – free
accommodation but meals to be paid for. The hotel itself was
sumptuous, the food lavish and varied and the twin-bedded room and

balcony all that one could desire, but the weather was appalling. During the entire week there was only one half day when the rain abated and the sun shone. There was a splendid swimming pool but it was too cold to swim in it. So we spent the time doing little excursions in a hired car. We went to Cape St. Vincent – not that there was anything to see, and it was a desolate drive. *(The sea battle just off the coast here in 1797 was where Admiral Jervis, born at Meaford Hall, commanded the British fleet and defeated the Spanish, leading to him being awarded his title, Lord St. Vincent.)* We stopped in Lagos and Armacao on the way back. We visited Silves, an old Moorish city and visited castle and Cathedral. We were invited to view Timeshare property, and one particular apartment was very attractive, but for us, it was easier to get to Anglesey. We returned home on Saturday, 15th April to news of the Hillsborough disaster and a week later, with the Cathedral Friends visited Liverpool and its Cathedrals. We attended Evensong at the Anglican Cathedral and signed the Book of Condolence. All flags were at half-mast.

Some of the most memorable events of 1989 were the four weddings we attended. There was also at least one funeral – that of Eveline's husband, Albert Shore, who died on 30th August. By sheer coincidence we were over in Newcastle the previous day to tidy up the grave in St. George's Churchyard and there saw Ernie Key, Kath's husband, who told us that Albert was ill. Had he lived another week they would have celebrated their golden wedding and had intended to go to Venice. But when we saw Albert it was obvious that there could be no Venice and next day the news came that he had died. It must have been a terrible blow for Eveline - to be preparing to celebrate 50 years of marriage only to suddenly lose her husband.

The weddings were very joyous affairs. The first was in Bardsey, Yorkshire where Frances Hampton, Laura Hampton's (nee Ford) daughter married Tony White on 20th May. Not only was it a splendid occasion but it was good to renew the acquaintance of so many members of the Ford family, some of whom had travelled from Vancouver. The following Saturday, 27th May, we went to

Loughborough for the wedding of Jane Bell and Raymond Bacon; another delightful occasion. On August 19th Jane's brother Andrew was married to Joanne Vesey in Cardiff. I shall always remember the Welsh harpist sitting at the corner of the swimming pool of the hotel as she played. Then on 2nd September we went to Chaddesley Corbett for the wedding of Ray's niece, Kate Smith to Richard Spoehrer. The first three of these weddings have been successful and fruitful but Kate's was disastrous. The husband was less than pleased when she became pregnant and left her before the baby was born the following 29th September.

During May also we had our annual old schoolgirls' reunion in London and in June I visited Esther Murch (nee Boulton) who, with her husband had retired to the Isle of Man. I had arranged to go with Connie Dyson from St. Luke's, Chadderton, to Toulouse on 11th July. This would have been the first occasion that I had joined the Manchester/Toulouse Association for one of their meetings abroad and I had made all the arrangements, currency etc. for Connie and me. But on 26th June Ray decided to lay paving stones at the bottom of the garden and refused to stop for food until he had finished. The next morning he woke with sharp pains across the chest. Having called the doctor an ambulance was sent and Ray was admitted to the Royal Oldham Hospital having had a heart attack. It so happened that I was expecting Marion Morris (Eveline's daughter) and son to visit us that day, and somehow they had lunch. But the hospital phoned with news that Ray had had another attack, and again I went there immediately. Fortunately Ray did recover and was able to come home on 5th July having been diagnosed with diabetes as well; so it was a case of small meals every three hours and no sugar. Connie was not best pleased to hear that I was unable to accompany her to Toulouse, but I did take her at 6am to catch the coach for Gatwick. Ray gradually improved, but Brandy began to bleed from the mouth and cancer was diagnosed. The vet though he might survive for three months. It was an accurate estimate; he had his last walk in Chadderton Park on the afternoon of Monday, 2nd October where I sat with him as he lay on the grass. The following day he had his final injection. He had suffered enough.

We missed him and it seemed strange to have no dog to walk. Ray felt his loss very keenly and we did consider getting another dog, but as things turned out it was as well that we did not. Towards the end of October we had a delightful coach trip, visiting Cirencester, Winchester and the New Forest. We went to the caravan for Christmas and I remember how delighted Ray was with all his little presents and how much we enjoyed our Christmas Dinner at the Beach Hotel – and even booked for Christmas 1990 – We stayed with the Rogersons at Audley for the New Year celebrations which included a firework display at midnight. It had been a truly wonderful end to 1989.

So 1990 began with great hopes. Clive had been looking for a house ever since he left Reading and we had surveyed more properties that we could count, but at last he had settled on a little end terraced house in Shaw and we devoted our energies to getting it habitable for him. He had some structural alterations done first and there were improvements to be made to the central heating system. Eventually Ray did the necessary painting and I papered all the rooms. The ceilings were so high that we had to hire a suitable ladder for the upstairs rooms. I remember during that hot August, when we could see the Gulf War looming on the horizon, I was scrubbing the wooden bedroom floors which required a fresh bucket of water for each patch. I wondered if they had ever been scrubbed before. There was a fish and chip shop just round the corner and Ray and I would sit in the lounge window consuming their products for our lunch. Then we brought floor coverings quite cheaply – a vinyl for the kitchen and carpets for the other rooms. The front bedroom was 14ft by 10ft, quite a big room and two single beds fitted easily. For some time our garage had housed two of Broadway House's cast-off wardrobes and chests of drawers. All of which came in very handy. Clive elected to sleep in the back bedroom.

With the aid of frequent visits to the doctor and changes of tablets, Ray survived that winter well. In February we had booked a holiday to coincide with our wedding anniversary at one of the Greenwood Grange houses in Dorset close to Thomas Hardy's cottage. On Saturday. 24th February, we first of all travelled to Alsager to join over twenty other people in celebrating Nelly Mould's 90th birthday.   It was a most splendid affair; everything that one could wish for and it was so good to see Nelly achieve such a prestigious birthday. We set off at 3.30 for Dorchester and arrived 9pm; the accommodation was excellent; we had several walks in the area and even visited John and Marjorie Brooks in Devon. And we booked a bungalow for the following February.

After visiting the caravan in March, we joined Don Rogerson, his family and the choir at Llandudno where a most enjoyable and friendly week end was spent. The choir entertained us and we saw the ski slope on the Great Orme. I even considered the idea of joining OAPs for ski ing lessons! And in April, when we were again in Anglesey, we were both impressed by a new caravan that had recently arrived. It was superior in every way with a fully fitted kitchen, a better water heater and bathroom, three bedrooms, two with twin beds instead of bunk beds and a 4/6" instead of a 4ft. bed in the main bedroom. We bought it and Ray fitted up an extra light in the kitchen while I made curtains for the lounge doors and kitchen entrance.   We bought net for window curtains from Longsight Market when on our way to Poppy Morton's funeral in Madeley on 18th April.

For some time I had been taking Mary Lever to visit Beatrice almost every Wednesday afternoon. I liked her and on 16th May had had lunch in Manchester with her before going to see The School for Scandal at the Royal Exchange Theatre. So it was a shock when, at the end of May, her daughter phoned to say that her mother had had a brain haemorrhage. I began to visit her in Crumpsall Hospital, though trips to the caravan, Cambridge, Ipswich, and Carlisle on the Settle-Carlisle railway intervened. The latter was particularly pleasant, for Ray had been with the Cathedral Friends the previous year and thoroughly enjoyed showing me the sights that he had been shown. He found the walk to the castle too much for him – though he would have enjoyed a military event that was being staged. Mary died on 21st July. aged only 67. Now I visited Beatrice alone.

August was fully occupied at Shaw. On 2nd September we all went to Oulton Park where Clive was to drive a racing car round the circuit – a prize for some promotion. He did 10 circuits – one and a half minutes each. It was a most lovely day; it was the last outing we were all to have together.

We were invited to another wedding at Bardsey on 29th September – Frances's sister Alice was getting married. Valerie Hargrave had asked if she could stay with us over the Saturday night as she was showing beagles at Heaton Park, so it looked like being a busy weekend. 28th September was Ray's 68th birthday and in the afternoon he insisted on polishing the car so that it would be resplendent for the wedding. At about 10.30 that evening he developed a pain in the chest; and having phoned the doctor an ambulance came and took him to hospital. Clive and I returned home at 3am. having been told that it was angina and diabetes. Apologies were phoned to Bardsey in the morning and Valerie arrived in the evening after I had visited Ray. Her beagles won two first prizes, so she was well satisfied and returned home on the Sunday.

It was curious that Ray seemed to make a good recovery and no one seemed very alarmed whereas the previous July he had been banned from driving for two months. I fetched him from the hospital the following Thursday and on the Saturday I was fully occupied with the Autumn Fair at the Cathedral for which I had earlier that year made quantities of marmalade. Mary Preston was in the habit of buying about 40lbs of Seville oranges from Smithfield market and we shared them. We also gave each other garden produce such as runner beans and blackcurrants.

I had made arrangements to go to the Conservative Party Conference in Bournemouth in October and as Ray seemed to have made a good recovery he encouraged me to go. It was to be the last conference dominated by Mrs. Thatcher and I found it interesting at the fringe meetings to notice the obvious disquiet of people like Ken Clarke and Chris Patten. On the Thursday there was a great array of eastern European heads of state on the platform – Mrs. Thatcher obviously delighted to show them off.

We were at the caravan from the 16th –25th October and on the 28th I joined a coach for another short trip to Germany; but it was most forgettable in contrast to the wonderful trip the previous year – and with hindsight I wish I had not arranged to go.

During November Ray arranged for roof repairs to be done and the huge sycamore tree at the bottom of the garden to be removed. Clive was preparing to go to live in Shaw and we bought various oddments for him from Oldham Market. He finally departed on 11th November having removed in small stages – the last article being the bed. From 13th November, when Geoffrey Howe finally rebelled, anyone interested in politics could not help but be fascinated with the activities of the Conservative Party and having gone to the caravan again on the 21st we were out buying newspapers next day as Mrs. Thatcher's resignation was announced. We stayed till the Sunday, the gas cylinder having become empty on the Saturday; Ray's final action being to turn off the electricity.

Looking back it seems strange that I should have mentioned to Ray some new rented accommodation being built in Llandudno – but I always felt that he liked the idea of change. He would have moved to Anglesey years before had it been practicable. And he was certainly far from well. The same firm had already built similar accommodation in Warrington, and on the way back, having had a good meal at a Little Chef, he drove to Warrington to view it. His comment was, "Its nothing but a glorified [retirement] Home." So we arrived back and he sat for ages by the kitchen window. Later that afternoon I got a meal and Clive joined us, complaining that his upstairs telephone did not work. Ray rolled up our extension wires and said he would fix it next day. During that evening we watched snooker on TV.

Next morning (Monday 26th November 1990) I was up first and made tea. Ray woke with a severe pain across his chest. I called an ambulance and he was in Royal Oldham Hospital by 8am. Having phoned Clive who came, I stayed until mid-day and in the afternoon went to get Ray's pension, returning to the hospital at 5pm to find Ray in a critical condition. His blood pressure had plummeted and he was wearing a catheter. Clive came from work. We briefly spoke to him before he was taken by ambulance to the intensive care unit; we waited in an adjacent room and were told that the next two hours were critical. Just after 10pm we were informed that he had expired. He lay on the bed with huge beads of sweat covering his face. I think he must have suffered greatly.

The funeral on 4th December was in Manchester Cathedral; David and Joan came. John Atherton took the service and the Prestons came to the buffet lunch at Blackley. Eveline and family, John and Margaret Bell, Peter Harvey and Jen and many others were a great support. Looking back, I think that Ray knew that he had not long to live, for he saw to it that various jobs were completed, but nothing was ever said. The ball of extension wires remained on the table for several days.

Clive stayed with me for a time, for, almost within a year, the dog, Clive and now Ray were gone. And I had to learn once more to live alone. There was no shortage of work. The boiler developed a leak and a new boiler was installed; I spent about three months sorting out possessions and deciding what to throw out and what to retain. I decided to have a new kitchen fitted – a job I couldn't have faced had Ray been alive, and as the units were installed so I wall papered it and Clive came each evening to move furniture.

In September 1991 I decided to resume my attempts to gain a BA in Theology and committed myself to two modules.   But I was also determined to go to South America which I had dreamed of ever since the age of twelve. I joined a group with "Explore Worldwide" for a three week visit to Peru which was to take place over Christmas and the New Year – 1991-2. I kept a comprehensive diary of this fascinating journey which covered Lima, the desert, a plane trip over the Nazca lines, Christmas Day in Arequiba, a visit to an island in Lake Titicaca, where there was a storm of biblical proportions, a train journey to Cusco and from there to Machu Pichu, and Ollontatambo where we witnessed a strange Epiphany procession. We climbed Inca ruins and marvelled at the ingenuity of the builders and visited markets walking precariously on cobble stones. The New Year saw us in the equatorial forest beside a tributary of the Amazon and we finally arrived back in Lima. Despite all water drinking precautions, several of us suffered almost continuous diarrhoea and some were much reduced in weight. Much to my chagrin, in three weeks I lost only 10lbs. Mercifully Clive met me at Gatwick and I slept nearly all the way home. Then on 13th January we gave a party for my 70th birthday.

Top- Betty signing book on Island of Taquile – 500 steps at 3950 metres high. (Two weeks before her 70th birthday in sandals!)

Bottom – Betty at Machu Picchu

Although there was no hope of dislodging the Labour M.P. Michael Meacher from his Oldham seat, the local Conservative Association provided a good candidate, one Jonathan Gillen who was quite a live wire and introduced some novel ideas for canvassing. I found myself very much involved with the campaign and because Jonathan had no immediate local base during the last week, I offered him my bungalow where his wife, children and mother stayed. I went to sleep at Clive's house in Shaw. We fully expected the Labour party to win the election and were delighted when John Major won – albeit with a very small majority. Mrs. Gillen Snr. continued to keep in touch with me. Jonathan was not a candidate in the 1997 election.

I continued with my two modules for the BA degree, and became more and more friendly with Mary Preston who had taken to sitting with me in the Cathedral where she poured out her troubles, which were many. The Prestons had a severely mentally disabled son whom they visited each week at Calderstones and Mary was generally unhappy with the treatment he was receiving. She worked hard to raise funds to enable parents to visit their children by special bus and provide extra facilities. Sometimes I had lunch with the Prestons and I remember doing so before one of the exams. I did pass these modules: I felt fairly confident about the first, but the questions in the second one I found difficult. During the year Ronald and Mary needed a new car – a Volvo – and Clive was able to supply them with one.

I still felt that I did not want to visit places where Ray and I had been, apart from the caravan, and even there it was an effort to visit even the Penrhos Nature Park. So I decided to visit the North York Moors – an area unknown to me. One reason was the desire to see Middleham where Richard III had lived, for his story fascinated me; was he a villain or not? I found an excellent B&B place at East Witton, visited the castle at Middleham and next day went round Mount Grace Priory and considered how monks had lived there in their own individual cells. At least it must have been a peaceful existence. Riveaulx Abbey was magnificent in its ruin and I spent the night at Helmsley having had an excellent meal of roast duckling at The Feathers. Little could I have guessed how familiar the area would become in a few years' time. Castle Howard was visited on the way back home.

Early in August I visited David and Elsie Smith at Kinver and saw their grandson, Tristan. Later I enjoyed a more extensive tour visiting friends en route to the Abergavenny and Ebbw Vale Garden Festival. It was good to see Alice Hackett in Birmingham and take her out to lunch. The Garden Festival was fascinating and from there I motored on to Bridgend to stay with Muriel Howells. The next stop was in Sidford, Devon where I stayed the night before visiting John and Marjorie Brooks for lunch. It was an easy journey to Yeovil for a visit to Tom and Edith Dudson at East Coker where they had previously shown me the memorial to T.S. Eliot. Next day I went on to Lymington to see Edgar and May with whom I had so frequently stayed. But May was now 95, Edgar 87, so I stayed at a B&B place. But it was good to see them. It was to be my last visit for they both went into a Home, May having become demented and Edgar clearly not able to cope. She lived to be 100. Tom Dudson died in 1997 and Edith too went into a Home.

I visited my sister-in-law, Anne Phillips, in Southsea and from there went to Reading and visited Gordon Campbell whose wife – and friend of mine – had died the previous year. He too died in 2002, but I kept in touch with his daughter, Jean Schultz, who was my only God child. I had intended further visits but my guts began to plague me, as had frequently happened after the Peru experience, so it was time to go home.

I had already done seven modules towards the BA degree and it had taken seven years to gain them – with gaps of two years when I couldn't have coped. The prospect of having to get through another three was not encouraging. Then one day George Brooke phoned to say I now only needed two more and could do them together, thus the final exam would be in June 1993. I was overjoyed and gladly registered for courses on the Evangelical Revival with Henry Rack.

I noticed early in 1993 that my right leg was becoming increasingly painful and sciatica was diagnosed. It seemed to last for months and was followed by arthritis in the hip. But despite this I pressed on with the BA Course, went to Toulouse with the Manchester/Toulouse Association in April and to London in May for the annual reunion of school friends. The moment of truth arrived in June when I took the final two exams. On 2nd July Elaine Graham phoned to say I had passed albeit only a 2.2 though I learned later that it was a borderline 2.1. I phoned Clive and Prestons with the news and was distressed to hear that their garage had been forced open and the car vandalised.

The degree ceremony was held on 5th July and Clive, with his friend, Mark, drove me to the University. I was the penultimate candidate to shake the hand of the Vice-Chancellor and I was near to tears as I realised an ambition I'd had for 50 years. There was a photo taken of all the new Theology graduates on the steps of the Arts Building followed by light refreshments. By sheer coincidence the Hallé was celebrating a Sir John Barbirolli anniversary in the Town Hall with a magnificent dinner after which there was a speech by Lady Barbirolli. I persuaded Clive to go with me for it seemed a wonderful way of celebrating my graduation. I remember telling Brian Redhead who would have been Chancellor of the University had he lived. He suggested that I should now embark on a PhD!

Earlier in the year I had been attracted to a modest cruise around Italy which had the advantage of visiting several beautiful places without having to move from hotel to hotel transporting luggage. However, Thomas Cook informed me that it had been cancelled and would I instead like to spend a fortnight cruising in the Caribbean. I required no persuading and so the first fortnight in August was spent at sea visiting 13 or 14 islands and enjoying far too much of the ever present food. I kept a diary of this celebratory event and determined that I would revisit at least one of the islands one day. I even won several small prizes for my appearance on the stage as a cowboy – my stick as the horse – but my hip was becoming increasingly painful.

In October I attended part of the Conservative Party Conference in Blackpool, but again my guts caused a premature return home. In

November Clive and I were invited to the wedding of Philip and Julie Hargrave in Frome - a most enjoyable occasion and on the way we again visited David Smith, Clive's uncle. He was suffering from prostate cancer and it was to be the last time we saw him. Another one I should never see again was Isaac Todd who died on 22nd November and to whose funeral I went. I certainly had much practice at weeping with those who wept and rejoicing with those who rejoiced.

During 1994 I began to visit sick people who had been in the Cathedral congregation; Nellie Mould died; Alice Hackett had her 80th birthday in Birmingham to which I went; May Woodburn removed from her appalling Crumpsall flat to a warden controlled one on Holland Road and I helped her move. But the biggest shock occurred on 6th June. I had gone with a Cathedral group to York on the Saturday and developed severe diarrhoea so that I spent Sunday in bed and remained there on Monday. The previous Wednesday I had been to visit Mary Preston who had had a lump removed from her neck - the stitches still being there. To my complete disbelief Ronald phoned on the Monday morning to say that Mary had died. I phoned the Cathedral to confirm this dreadful news. It was true. She had suffered an embolism as a result of this fairly straightforward operation. Ronald was totally distraught for he had relied on her totally for all domestic arrangements and his domestic skills were almost entirely limited to making tea and coffee.

The christening of Ronald's second grandson, William Cunliffe, took place at St. Anselm Hall later that month. Ronald was concerned lest he break down and had John Elford at hand; but all was well. Early in July a group of people from Toulouse arrived and I had Monique Destours staying with me. There were talks in French (translated) and in English (translated) – all of which made the proceedings rather lengthy. There was an outing to York, prior to which I had a nasty fall in Shude Hill which really was the start of all my hip problems. But the trip to York included a visit to Bishopsthorpe where we were shown round by The Rt. Revd. John Habgood, Archbishop of York. I had been impressed by him when watching his enthronement on TV, but my enthusiasm was increased by the tactful way he showed this ecumenical group round his home. He is a very great man.

In mid July Anne Phillips celebrated her 80th birthday in Southsea to which Clive and I were invited. We stayed at a hotel in Southsea and I was, perhaps, so uninterested that we arrived for the feast two hours late, but were just in time for the conclusion. While down there we were able to visit Jane and Ray Bacon, and also pay Edgar and May a final (though we did not know that) visit at Lymington. Anne's birthday was somewhat overshadowed by the news that her brother, David Smith, was dying: in fact his funeral at Kinver took place on 22nd July. I motored to Birmingham and took Alice there.

During August the pain in my right leg was getting progressively worse: I remember vividly walking to Total Care to visit Beatrice and being obliged to get a bus back. I saw a physiotherapist in Royton who discovered that it was not sciatica: an X-Ray on 31st August confirmed that I needed a hip replacement.

The rest of the year was occupied with much Cathedral activity; May was taken to church each Sunday; I helped at the Cathedral Shop on Mondays; there were Tuesday evening talks in Advent. In December I took advantage of a coach trip to Cologne and walked round that wonderful Cathedral where exquisite nativity scenes were depicted and I attended a service there.

I noted in my diary that on 30th December I visited Ronald Preston for lunch and on 1st January 1995 he sat with me in the Cathedral.

25: Manchester Part Three – Fallowfield (1995 – 2001)

I see that on 17th January 1995 I was up at 6am. and motored over to Fallowfield to pick up Ronald and so proceed to Smithfield Market where I bought 40lbs. Seville oranges and some lemons ready for the marmalade making sessions. We had breakfast and then went to visit Gwilym Morgan for empty jars before I returned home. All the marmalade was made by the end of the month.

In February the doctor at last suggested that I see a specialist about the hip – much to my relief for there were few days when I did not need to rest in the afternoon. A physiotherapist visited me and supplied me with a trolley and arm crutches.

News came that Beatrice Hornby had died and I went to her funeral at the Cathedral.

In the same month my battle with the Income Tax concluded with a cheque for £1,126 being sent to me. Having ignored me since everything to do with Ray was completed, they suddenly began to demand more money from me for the caravan lettings, which we had always disclosed. Huge sheets arrived for completion and despite all my efforts to explain what proportion of the year I had been there and what proportion it was let, they were not satisfied. In desperation I sought an interview at Oldham Tax Offices and was fortunate to have the services of a Mrs. Newton who discovered that too much tax had been taken from Building Society interest and that no extra money had been allowed to me since I was 70. Later that year I bought a Parker Knoll reclining chair and bed settee with the money. It was money well spent for these had firm seats and I was increasingly unable to get up from a low seat.

As one does after a bereavement, I had offered to help Ronald Preston and from time to time I either accompanied him or took him to Calderstones to visit Mark who had had a fall shortly after his mother's death and could no longer walk. The routine was a lunch in the canteen, followed by meeting other parents Then Mark would be heaved into the back seat of the car with Ronald beside him and we set out on a 20 mile trip round the countryside. Thus I saw some of the loveliest of Lancashire villages, but when I looked through the mirror father and son were generally asleep. Two or three years later it was decided that it was no longer possible to get Mark into the car and we would push him round the grounds in a wheel chair, which was really a much better idea for they both stayed awake! In April I pruned his roses and realised even then how limited was his sight.

Towards the end of May the Manchester/Toulouse Association had arranged for a meeting at the Benedictine Monastery at Bec in Normandy and I had offered to take Ronald, Rita and Des Jones in the car.   We crossed the Channel all sharing a cabin, and having disembarked, despite the sun in my eyes I managed to get my passengers safely to Bec.   It was a very enjoyable interlude. The accommodation and the food were good and much of interest was learned.   The day after we arrived back home a beautiful bouquet arrived from Ronald by way of thanks.

Also during May I saw the consultant about the right hip and he was confident that it would not be long before I could have the operation. The call came in August and I had the hip replacement on 14th. At first all went well though the necessity of walking to the toilet day and night every two hours became a strain, especially as it was so difficult to move my foot. Ronald came to visit me every Saturday on his way to see Mark and I made him laugh as I quoted Psalm 121, 'He will not suffer thy foot to be moved.' By the end of the following week I was judged fit to go home, but on the day before, having just lunched, I stretched up to grasp the triangular hold – before getting out of bed – when the hip dislocated. The pain was excruciating and nothing could be done for hours because no anaesthetic could be given on a full stomach. During the evening the hip was relocated and eventually I slept. Because of this I spent nearly five weeks in hospital, three of them on traction. I was measured for a brace which I had to wear for three months. I was never to walk normally again. During the entire period Clive came every evening to visit me and after the dislocation, when I was in a separate ward, he brought the TV from home so I was never short of entertainment.

I finally returned home on 15th September to be greeted by Clive who produced fish and chips. He had put the bed in the lounge so that I could watch the TV. A District Nurse came to bath me at first but Clive had to do it later. There was also a physiotherapist and a Home Help who were very good – and neighbours and friends kept calling. It was not until October that I was able to go out in the car and I remember Clive taking me on a trip to Keighley and the Ogden Reservoir which was wonderful after being so long confined to four walls. Towards the end of November Clive took me to the caravan for the day. He tidied it up after all the summer visitors and we returned the same day. My first drive in my car was on 1st. December when I bought the chair and bed settee already mentioned from Stocktons. After that I was more independent. On Christmas Day I took May to the Cathedral for the morning service and Clive and I had lunch together after which he produced a video - 'Forest Gump'- which we both hugely enjoyed.

I continued to have a Home Help until February 1996 but by that time I was fairly mobile though unable to walk properly. Visits to the hospital confirmed that one leg was shorter than the other and one shoe had to have an extra piece on the heel and sole. Fortunately this did not affect my driving and during the year I was able to make good use of the car.

Almost every Sunday I took May Woodburn to the Cathedral where I was increasingly involved, not only with the marmalade making for the Autumn Fair, but with visiting the sick. I liked doing this and enjoyed the company of several elderly ladies in hospital or in sheltered accommodation. One was Mrs. Pike who had only one leg yet insisted on getting me tea and a biscuit; there was Edith Gregory who Vannie Atherton had taken to the Cathedral Sunday by Sunday until she could go no more; there was Doris Dunham who had been one of the most staunch members of the congregation and always wore a magnificent hat with a wide brim; there was Helen Burley whose funeral I later attended and was struck with the kindness of her family to one who had known her very little.

I was asked if I would edit the Cathedral Newsletter and I plunged into this with great fervour, trying to gather pieces of interest by members of the congregation. Some did not like the 'editing', process for I would go through each script making slight emendations where I thought necessary.

Age Concern had arranged a trip to Tunisia for a fortnight in March and although my capacity for walking was much restricted I decided to go. While there we were taken to a thriving Medina, to the village of Herglia where there was a market and to Monastir where we were taken round on a 'Noddy' train. It was a good holiday.

In May I enjoyed visiting friends and relations who lived on the east side of the country. The first stop was Matlock where I visited the Wardmans who had been my neighbours during our period there. They now lived in a pleasant bungalow, perched on a hillside in Hackney and still kept chickens. Then I visited Greta Summerfield whose husband had died so tragically while helping a motorist in the snow. She was a great one for entertaining and produced wonderful meals. I remember her trifles having whole cherries, not the halves that my mother had been content with. From there I went to Loughborough to stay the night with Margaret and John Bell – second cousins – in their splendid and hospitable home. From there I drove to Market Harborough and visited Jean and Dick Swingler whose friendship went back to the war years. Dick and his first wife Dorothy had divorced. I remember visiting them when divergence was at its height and, separately, I was the recipient of the misdoings of the other. It was not pleasant. He had married Jean and had a son who was about 15 months older than Clive. They visited us once at Matlock and I was appalled by their prudishness and over protectiveness of the child. It did not surprise me that he left home and was seldom heard from. They were great gardeners and Dick helped at a greengrocery stall in Market Harborough market. Later he suffered from MS and died in 1998.

His first wife, Dorothy, still lived in the house they had acquired about 1950 when houses were hard to come by. She married twice after the divorce, each time to a husband who was competent at DIY and the house was like a miniature palace. They both died and she finally lived with a man younger than herself who fulfilled the same requirements. Alas, he died too, and her final years alone were sad indeed. The last irony was that after her death no will could be found and the magnificent house passed to cousins who had scarcely kept in touch with her. However, she was always very kind to me and I enjoyed my visit in 1996.

My cousins, Peter and Sybil Jones, were surprised to receive a phone call from me when I arrived in St. Ives and it gave me great pleasure to take them out for lunch and stay the night. My next port of call was Northampton where I stayed with Judith Dunmore who with her late husband and family had stayed at Matlock. She had had two hip replacements and had recovered well. In Stanford- le-Hope I stayed with Hilda Cogger who with her late husband and family had also stayed with me in Matlock and had kept in touch ever since. From there I travelled to Colchester and visited Alan and Freda Adams. Her mother, who had been my next door neighbour when we lived in Cross Heath, Newcastle, was still alive and it was good to see them all. My final calling place was Ipswich where I stayed with Eva Martin, one of my old school friends, whose scholastic achievements were much superior to mine. She had taught German for years in Bristol. We visited Aldeburgh while there.

Meanwhile preparations went ahead for a new bathroom. My friend and plumber, Peter Smithies, had been approached and during June and early July and he had suggested that I visit showrooms to decide what I wanted. It was a tiny bathroom but I had seen a semi-circular bath in a similar bungalow and felt that such a bath would give me room to turn around. There was no way I could get out of a conventional bath. It was also possible to align the toilet and wash basin together with a cupboard under the basin and shelves at the end of the bath. The whole bathroom was gutted; it was then fully tiled and the new bathroom suite was fixed, together with a shower, a big mirror and two corner cabinets. It was a delight to bath in. When all was finished, Peter gave me a list of all the items which had been bought and refused to claim a penny for his work. It was altogether too generous and at Christmas I saw to it that he was recompensed.

The lounge and hall badly needed decorating and once this was done I bought new carpet for the hall and also had the bedroom and extension carpeted. I put new wallpaper in these rooms and when all was done felt that the house was as I wanted it – and wallowed in the pleasure it gave me. I should have thought back to the transformation I achieved at Whitehouse Road where within three years I had left for Matlock.

But for the moment my thoughts were filled with a surprise experience. Sir John Ford, who had completed his diplomatic career as High Commissioner for Canada, invited me to join him at a Buckingham Palace Garden Party. I motored down to Guildford where he lived and having spent the night there was taken to the Palace next day. When I saw the enormous queue waiting to go in my heart dropped, for standing was not my strong point. However, John drove straight up to an entrance where he dropped me off and went to park the car in Waterloo Barracks. So we entered the Palace and were soon in the gardens at the back. The weather was perfect. I noted all the high-rise buildings surrounding the Palace and realised that despite all the security there was little real privacy. The Queen and Duke of Edinburgh greeted people presented to them and this was followed by tea. Promptly at

4pm it was time to go. On the way back, John kindly stopped to visit my cousin Marion in Fulham.

Next day I travelled to Aldershot for the christening of Peter and Sybil Jones's grandson, Joshua, another memorable occasion which Clive also attended. We stayed in Alton and after the christening and the most generous provision of food by Joshua's paternal grandmother, Clive took me towards the Portsmouth area and we had an excellent meal in Soberton.

The Manchester/ Toulouse Association had arranged a visit to Toulouse in September and this time I stayed with a very hospitable lady who unfortunately had no English, so conversation was well nigh impossible. Moreover her loo was outside which was inconvenient during the night. There was, however, a bidet. Our French friends were always most hospitable and we were wined and dined in various places. Most of the days were spent hearing talks in French and English (translations from each included). We had a coach trip to Montsegur in the Pyrenees and learnt much about the Cathars. They appealed to me. I have much sympathy for heretics.

I notice from my diary that I was taking Ronald Preston to Calderstones every other Saturday and often shopping for him. When there were special lectures at the University he asked me to go with him. Sometimes I cooked lunch for him. He phoned me most days and by October it occurred to me that I was being courted! At the end of November he took me to a ballet at the Palace Theatre – *Alice in Wonderland*. It was quite delightful and we had pancakes at the Pancake House afterwards. I learned later that Ronald had had ballet lessons during his childhood and could still pirouette!

December came and with it a fortnight's holiday in Cyprus, again with Age Concern. Again I had a double room all to myself and during the fortnight was able to tour much of the island including the Troodos Mountains, Nicosia, Limasol. Paphos and Lefkara where I bought a neck chain and ear rings purporting to be of gold, silver and platinum. Alas, constant wear eventually removed the glistening surface. I even hired a car and drove three others to the Baths of Aphrodite and the surrounding district.

And so Christmas and the New Year came around again. Certainly I had given no thought to what the New Year would bring. I reckoned that 1996 had been a pretty good year; I had had good holidays, done a lot of visiting and had acquired a new bathroom and some days I could walk reasonably well.

Looking back on 1997 I now wonder how I survived. I seemed to be increasingly involved with the Cathedral, what with the Manchester/Toulouse Association, lectures there, editing the Newsletter, reading poems for Albert Radcliffe and visiting sick people as well as taking May Woodburn there each Sunday. There were the marmalade making sessions in January ready for the Autumn Fair later in the year. I had also joined a group of volunteers taking sick children to hospitals and would be called upon once or twice a week - with waiting at the hospitals this could take several hours. Increasingly I was taking Ronald to Calderstones to visit Mark and became useful to him typing articles.

Every other Wednesday afternoon I took old ladies to play whist at the Baptist Church Hall. There were rarely more than seven and the rules were much relaxed so that if one made a mistake she was allowed to retrieve her card and replace it. There was usually tea and cake or biscuits and a very small prize. We all enjoyed it.

Early in February Ronald and Ben Drewery motored to Caistor to buy pork from an excellent butcher known to Ben, who had lived in the area. Ronald had lived there from the ages of 7 to 12. Ronald's pork was to go to his daughters, Ann and Lindsay. I stored it in my freezer ready for them and entertained them when they fetched it. The pork was so good that I suggested to Ronald that we could both go to Caistor for further provisions for my benefit. On 15th March, a lovely day, we set out for Caistor and while there I was shown the house where he had lived as a child, Caistor Grammar School which he attended and where his father taught Chemistry, the church where they worshipped and his mother's grave, adorned with a marble angel. She had died when he was only ten.

To my amazement he offered to go with me to the caravan at the end of March and while there we visited people with whom he and his family had stayed many years ago. And as we sat in the two armchairs, we found ourselves discussing marriage, for it was clear that we were much in sympathy with each other. If we were to marry I felt that it would be better before the winter set in, for the journey from Chadderton to Fallowfield, thence to Calderstones, back to Fallowfield and so to Chadderton was increasingly laborious during dark winter days.

I gave the idea of marriage long and careful thought. There was no doubt that I could supply Ronald with companionship, act as his secretary, his chauffeuse, his housekeeper, shopper and entertainer of his guests. And at last I would have an intellectual companion with whom I could share ideas. But the thought of having to leave my newly refurbished home and relinquishing my independence was not an easy one. Moreover Clive was appalled at the idea. " You need someone to look after you, not to spend the rest of your life looking after someone else," he reasonably argued. And Ronald saw the point. He was 84 and I was 75.

One day Ronald produced his old academic gown which dated back to 1935 when he graduated at LSE. It was in a sad and sorry state. The gathers were all apart, the back of the neck was torn, there were places of wear which needed darning and the remains of long forgotten meals decorated it. It was far too fragile to be sent to a cleaner. I took it home with me to mend and as I spread it before me with needle and cotton I realised that I loved this man whose love for me had rejuvenated him after Mary's loss. The darning done and the gathers restored it had to be washed. Fortunately it was a dry, breezy day. I gently lowered it into a bath of warm, foaming water and proceeded to stroke away the debris, probably, of 60 years. The water became totally black. After many rinses I hung the gown outside to dry and proudly presented it to its owner next day – almost as good as new.

Ronald and Betty

His daughters, their husbands and children had lunched at my home at Easter and towards the end of May, Ann, the elder daughter, asked us to have lunch with them. The weather was glorious and we thoroughly enjoyed a barbeque meal outside. I had arranged to do what I had come to regard as my annual visitation to friends and relatives and having dropped Ronald off at home, set forth on my travels.

It was an exceptionally wonderful trip. I drove through the Welsh countryside along almost deserted roads with deep appreciation of the glories of the landscape and enjoying to the full the exquisite liberty that I was soon to relinquish. I visited Muriel Howells in Bridgend, Bernard and Valerie Hargrave in Wolverton, John and Marjorie Brooks in Sidmouth. John and Margaret Bell were on holiday in Devon with their grandchildren and had asked me to join them. The revelation of my marriage plans resulted in a great celebration with champagne at the Deer Park Hotel and the children made congratulatory cards.

Next day I arrived at East Coker to visit Tom and Edith Dudson and from there paid my last visit to Edgar and May Hopkinson, now in a pleasantly appointed Home. May, now white haired, had some dementia which was a great trial to Edgar who had been her prop for many years. She had always refused to admit to ageing and would lean on him rather than use a walking stick. I should never see them again for May, having achieved her 100th birthday, died and within 18 months Edgar followed her. I did visit Tom and Edith once more only to discover that Edith had dementia and felt obliged to beat a hasty retreat. Tom died soon after this and Edith went into a Home.

My last visit was to Aldershot to visit Helen Jones and Paul King. Paul's mother gave me a great welcome and produced a lunch of similar proportions to the one that graced Joshua's christening and having stayed at the same hotel I set out for home next day and spent the evening with Ronald.

August 14th was the date we had fixed for the wedding; Ronald discovered that his parents had married on that day – mine had married on August 16th – so we appeared to be in good company. But before that there was the enormous job of deciding what was to be retained and what discarded. Mary's clothes were just as she had left them three years before and all had to be removed. Age Concern was a grateful recipient of the clothes and other articles. I seemed to be dashing backwards and forwards from Chadderton, sorting out goods, preparing meals and on one occasion serving lunch to Ronald and the Bishop. In July some of the Toulouse members visited Manchester and we had the usual talks, services and a day trip to Holywell. Our visitors commented on the great improvement in Ronald's spirits. Indeed he was very happy. We found we were being invited out to lunch quite frequently and I began to get to know some of Ronald's vast number of friends.

The wedding dress was made by a couturiers at Delph from a piece of golden material I had acquired long before. It was superb. The banns were called at the Cathedral and Canon Paul Denby made history by suggesting that anyone who knew of any "just cause or impediment" against the marriage should form an orderly queue at the back of the Cathedral! We had made arrangements for the wedding breakfast to be held at the Midland Hotel. I would very much have liked to spend the first night after our wedding there and Ann and Ian offered to pay for it but Ronald simply said that there was nothing on in Manchester in August and wanted to go straight to Yorkshire (his choice) for the honeymoon. I now think that I should have been more insistent, for the idea of driving to East Witton after the wedding did not appeal and really Ronald should have realised this. The only other way round the problem was for me to take the car to East Witton the day before. Heather Mulverhill kindly offered to drive her car there and bring me back.

The Cathedral did us proud. There was wine and cake for all who attended. John Elford presided; Albert Radcliffe preached; Gwilym Morgan read one lesson and Lindsay Owens the other. Gordon Stewart played the organ and refused to be paid for his services. Mark was brought from Calderstones by his kindly carers, one of whom made a video of the ceremony. There were about twenty people at the wedding breakfast – of whom four only were my guests – Clive, Jen, Margaret and John Bell. It had been supposed to be a family only affair but first one and then another of Ronald's old friends decided to come – mostly old ladies – and included were also John and Anne Elford and Albert and Trena Radcliffe. When the festivities were over, Clive drove us to East Witton for the first night of our honeymoon.

Marriage of Ronald and Betty

The Guest House was the one at which I had stayed during my earlier tour of Yorkshire when I had been the first guest. The proprietor produced champagne at breakfast and the meal was substantial. I would have been quite happy to remain there but Ronald had booked three nights at The Pheasant in Harome. The hotel was excellent though the late meals and hot weather were not conducive to much sleep. We visited Scarborough next day and went to the theatre to see, *'Lucky Sods'*. Sunday saw us at church in the village, the service being taken by the Revd. Bob Shaw. He looked oddly at Ronald as we walked out and to our amazement we received a letter from him later, saying that he had studied for his BD with Ronald but couldn't believe that Ronald would be in such a small village.

Ronald's great friends, the Flintofts, lived next door to Rievaulx Abbey and after a pleasant drive visiting various villages known to Ronald, we were given a great welcome from Frank and Joan before returning home to Manchester on the Monday. John Coleman was due to return on the Tuesday; he needed to be met, given overnight accommodation and returned to the airport next day. And so life with Ronald began. I gained some amusement from the thought that my name would now join his in Who's Who and The International Who's Who. Who would ever have thought it?

Days were spent reorganising furniture, going over to Chadderton for the fruit and vegetables I had planted in the Spring and freezing them. I continued to help at Age Concern in Oldham and sometimes stayed the night in Chadderton and had my hair done on the Saturday morning. Ronald did not enjoy my absences, but Chadderton had been my home for over 20 years and it was necessary to decide which of my possessions I needed in Fallowfield. Although I had given the bungalow to Clive, it was March 1998 before he moved in there and I could not help still regarding it as home. Sundays saw us attending the Cathedral before speeding off to Calderstones for lunch and then taking Mark out. Sometimes we called on Ann and Ian in Bury before returning home. It was necessary to go to the caravan at the end of the season to tidy up. But Ronald never again went with me – he apparently didn't care for it - and resented any time I spent there.

It soon became clear to me that an essential part of Ronald's life was visiting the sick – but now I was required to take him – for his eyesight had deteriorated so much that he could no longer safely drive. Clive was able to sell his car and we had a new garage to replace the dilapidated one that had housed it. Sometimes we had elderly neighbours in for tea; we had several visitors, some of whom came for lunch and others stayed the night.

For the past year or so, Ronald had been engaged in helping a young Latvian student, Normunds Kamergraus, now resident in Sweden, who was studying for a PhD on Ronald's work on Social and Pastoral Theology and Economics. Periodically he came over here and had been staying in Gorton. Soon I was ferrying him there and back and also both of them to the University. I suggested that it would be easier if he stayed here. It was no trouble to feed him and both men spent long hours in consultation.

At the beginning of November a party was held in Prestbury to celebrate Gwilym Morgan's 80th birthday. It was a splendid affair and it was a joy to meet so many of Ronald's old friends. But the following night Gwilym suffered a stroke, which, although it appeared to be less than severe, robbed him of any independence and despite valiant attempts to regain his strength, there was a slow decline. He died three years later. During that time Ronald visited him almost every Wednesday afternoon, with increasing sorrow, as Gwilym's memory deteriorated.

With the approach of Christmas came the realisation that Ronald was in the habit of sending 250 cards or letters to his multitude of friends, all of whose names and addresses were carefully kept in his card index, with details of significant events concerning them. I sent about 150. An annual letter had to be typed for him but he was still able to address the envelopes. It was a major operation – added to which presents for the family needed to be bought and the Christmas Dinner prepared. His daughter, Lindsay Cunliffe, her husband Peter and son William joined us on Christmas Day as well as Clive.

If 1997 had been a busy year, 1998 was feverish with activity and looking back it was no wonder that I frequently suffered acute arthritic pain – my right leg 'giving way' on two occasions. My remaining four teeth were extracted because of ulcers and I had bouts of neuralgia. At the end of the day the word 'exhausted' frequently features in the diary. But first, in February, we were to have a real holiday in St. Lucia. Since my Caribbean Cruise I had often thought how much I would like to revisit those islands. The choice of St. Lucia was because it was the nearest island to St. Vincent where lived one, Sehon Goodrich, the Bishop of the Windward Islands whom Ronald had met in 1978 when lecturing in the Caribbean. Unfortunately, the proximity was no great help as it was necessary to fly to Barbados in order to get to St. Vincent.

The hotel was superb. Meals were cafeteria type with plenty of choice and there was a large swimming pool with sensible brick steps and a handrail into the water – a great advantage for the arthritic. Ronald enjoyed being covered in protective sun tan cream after a good swim, but realised that he could no longer read very much - the light was never right. This was a great blow to him for he had been in the habit of taking a huge tome with him on holiday. His daughters recalled "War and Peace". And he deplored the fact that there was no culture. Moreover the other people on holiday were Europeans. After a few days we departed for St. Vincent where we were met at the airport by a lady on behalf of the Bishop and conveyed to his home. That evening we attended a lecture in Georgetown, the subject being the history of St. Vincent. With questions, it lasted from 7.30 – 10.30. The humid heat did not help. But Ronald was highly delighted to find some culture at last and to be able to indulge in intellectual conversation. The Bishop and his wife were most kind, though they were so busy it was obvious that our visit was less than convenient. We were taken to Young Island next day where we had a wonderful buffet lunch and the use of a hut for changing into swimming gear for a pleasant swim. In the evening Sehon took us to see bananas being selected and boarded on a ship – a fascinating experience which has encouraged me to buy Windward Islands bananas ever since. Sehon called it, Preston's Day. Next day we were taken to Fort Charlotte where there were spectacular views and before we left the following day, Janet took us to the Bishop's Office, to the Cathedral which had a massive pulpit, and finally gave us a tour of the island with its winding, hilly roads, bananas and coconuts and black sand.

There were still several days to enjoy St. Lucia. At 7am on the Sunday we went by taxi to Holy Trinity Church in Castries and found the 6am service still in progress. The 7.30 service lasted till 9.15. The church was full of enthusiastic worshippers all of whom joined in reading the first lesson. I found it fascinating to realise how Anglican liturgy had been exported to this island and with what devotion the people attended church. It was impossible not to think of the huge contrast with English churchgoing.

We had been invited by Archdeacon Randolph Evelyn to join him for a trip round the island on the Wednesday. So once more we taxied to Castries where we were invited into a huge Ford automatic and driven first to the college complex where William Arthur Lewis, Nobel Prize Winner, lies entombed. This was a special moment for Ronald whose friend he had been. He remembered their first encounter at LSE; Lewis was sitting miserably isolated in a corner, streaming with cold, and Ronald, compassionate as ever, went to talk to him. We saw the extraordinary Pitons and were driven to a generous lunch from where they could be seen, after which we were driven through a volcano where sulphur rock was lying about. This tour of the island by a man who had met us only briefly on St. Vincent lives in my memory; he would not let us contribute in any way; he was gracious, generous and displayed his deeply ingrained Christianity with warmth and sincerity. He gave us a wonderful and memorable day out.

We returned home on 12th March, Ronald's 85th birthday, to face the second event of note that year. On 23rd March began the total refurbishment of the kitchen. I had often wondered how Mary had put up with it, for although it was not small, there was only one wall available for a unit, above which were two electric sockets for six appliances, so one had great fun removing and replacing these for toaster, microwave, TV, coffee maker, iron and radio. The door at the back led in to narrow passage where saucepans were deposited on a high shelf; Ronald's shoes and cleaning materials lodged underneath (after his death I counted 15 brushes). Adjacent to the back door of the house which had bolts bottom and top, the latter being very difficult for me to reach, and facing this collection, was an enclosed stillage where wine and marmalade were stored. Beyond this an extremely cold area, eminently suitable for the fridge freezer, opposite which was the washing machine whose tubes were attached to the taps above a small sink. And beyond was an old bookcase where Mark's chocolates were stored having been bought in bulk from a cash and carry store. Dinner crockery was in a cupboard adjacent to it. I decided that Mary must have loved walking, for even the cooking utensils were arranged above this little sink and in the kitchen the tea cloth and towel were placed at the furthest point from the sink. She had clearly not been an advocate of time and motion.

The inconvenience caused by the refurbishment was really not very great, for there were plenty of electric sockets in the lounge to which the fridge freezer, kettle, toaster, microwave and radio could be attached. Clive and his friend Mark had cleared all the other transportable stuff into the garage. But the beginning of the operation seemed to go very slowly as men appeared late and departed early while the demolition took place; the new ceiling was placed too low and had to be raised and soon after the new utility room and shower had been fitted with units and plastered I came downstairs one morning to find the place full of steam. One of the joints in a hot water pipe above the utility room has come loose and the new plaster was saturated with water. A dehumidifier worked for two months and the units had to be replaced. It was towards the end of July that the work was completed and it was not until November that the central heating system was reliable. But the new kitchen was a great improvement. There were plenty of cupboards for storage; the fridge freezer was included; there was a dishwasher; there were lots of sockets and the floor covering was simple to clean. Ronald had suggested a step-in shower where the crockery cupboards had been. This has been of great benefit to me. And in the utility room the washing machine was properly plumbed in with a sink adjacent and cupboards above and below. There were also radiators in both places.

Despite the state we were in, we continued to have visitors. Normunds appeared; in June we had a visit from some of Ronald's Canadian friends and there were sometimes people for lunch or tea. But at the end of August my cousins from Canada, Edwin and Etta Hall, came to stay for a few nights and we had much pleasure in driving them to Loughborough and to Stone to see relatives. Barely had they gone than a couple of Ronald's friends from Seattle came to stay. They went with us to Calderstones and I took them into Derbyshire where we visited Haddon Hall and Eyam. They pressed us to visit them and on 30th September we set out for the long journey to Seattle where they met us and during our stay with them were indefatigable in showing us round the city, including several churches, and even drove us to Vancouver where we met various professors from the University who knew Ronald and we were all invited to a most excellent dinner. The conversation was witty and varied.

On leaving Seattle we flew to Toronto where we stayed part of the time with the people who had visited us in June and part with Edwin and Etta Hall, who had gathered most of the tribe together to welcome us both. We travelled to Kingston and stayed in a cottage on Howe Island, owned by John and Marie-Jeanne Coleman. He had stayed with us immediately after our honeymoon and was a considerable mathematician who had worked with Einstein's assistant. They both gave us a great welcome and I felt a great bond of friendship with them. We also had lunch with Gretta Riddell-Dixon, a delightful octogenarian and long established friend of Ronald.

But it was an exhausting tour and I was glad to be able to go to the caravan for two days to relax. At the end of October we had a very significant visit from our Toulousian friends, including the Archbishop of Toulouse, who dedicated the St. Denys Window in the Cathedral. Ronald, decked in his DD robes, preached on this occasion. Prior to that, we had been invited to Bishopscourt where Caroline Mayfield presented us with an excellent lunch and next evening we dined with the RC Bishop of Salford and the Archbishop of Toulouse at Wardley Hall. It was a very splendid weekend. As I watched and listened to Ronald that Sunday I wondered how many more such sermons there would be from him. He was often asked to take services in the absence of a priest and on 8th November we went to Sacred Trinity, Salford where he took the service. It was to be the last one he took, for increasingly, the light was never right for him to read.

During the year we had made our weekly journeys to Calderstones, though sometimes Ronald had gone by bus. We had known for some time that Mark was going to be moved to a purpose built bungalow at Baguley and had been taken to see a similar one at Newton Heath. At the end of November he was brought here by his faithful carers, chief of whom was Neil Rawlinson and we all had lunch before being taken to see the new bungalow which Mark was to share with three others. The staff there were to be responsible for all the care needed and we were appalled to discover how little they were paid. It must indeed have been a labour of love. The four men were in residence there just before Christmas and Ronald and I were invited to join them for a Christmas Dinner. Unfortunately Ronald developed a nasty cold and was unable to go, but I remember how much I enjoyed the meal and the great kindness that was displayed. Another benefit of the move was that it was only a five mile journey instead of 35 miles.

Throughout 1998 Ronald, and Charles Birch, formally Challis Professor of Biology at Sydney University in Australia, were jointly producing Facts and Fables in Ecology and the Integrity of Creation. Faxes hurtled backwards and forwards. Ronald would write, I would type and off to the University we went to send faxes. Other documents required to be typed including a short biography of Stanley Booth-Clibborn who had been Bishop of Manchester; this was for The National Biography. So far Ronald had managed to write and read – even his own writing which often defeated me, but at the beginning of 1999 I noticed that the glossy paper of the Economist defeated him and from then on I would read him the articles he marked. I always enjoyed Bagehot but the views he expressed did not always go down well with Ronald. But the documents continued to flow. He wrote some vignettes, a sort of mini autobiography, chiefly, I think, for his daughters who visited us periodically with their families. In September 1999, Tony Dyson, who had succeeded Ronald in the Samuel Ferguson Chair of Social and Pastoral Theology, died and Ronald wrote an obituary. He was often called upon to write book reviews, but by the end of the year he could no longer see to read the books and I found myself reading, while he took notes. I think the first book was one by Michael Banner and I remember us both feeling considerable disagreement with the conclusions arrived at.

We were both delighted to see Mark so well settled in his new home and to begin with all seemed well. It was certainly easier to visit him; the carers took the four men out regularly on shopping expeditions or to some event and Mark responded well. But in January 1999 he seemed to be afflicted with more fits and the carers noticed that he had difficulty swallowing, thus the medication to prevent the fits was not getting into the stomach. The next five months were punctuated with periods in Wythenshawe Hospital, which was near. By the end of April he was in hospital being fed through a tube straight into the stomach. When he seemed stabilised he would be returned to the bungalow, but it seemed that once there, complications such as diarrhoea or an abscess would appear and he was taken back to the hospital. He had his 49th birthday there and his sisters and families visited him. Neil Rawlinson was indefatigable in taking us to visit Mark and would even push me in a wheel chair to the ward, which was some distance from the entrance. But Neil was overdue for a holiday and the hospital wanted Mark's bed; a conference was called for 22nd June which Ronald attended. The decision was made to keep Mark in there until Neil returned. Next day, we were to attend a sort of celebration at the Bridgewater Hall for SELHEL which was responsible for the purpose built bungalows. Ronald made an excellent speech thanking all concerned and then told me that he had heard that Mark was deteriorating. Having grabbed a sandwich we motored to Wythenshawe, only to find that Mark had died earlier that morning, Had we been at home, we would have been told. Ronald mourned the loss of his son. Both he and Mary had devoted much time and energy to caring for Mark, and Mary had raised £80,000 to benefit Calderstones and the parents who visited their children there. But, ultimately, relief took the place of mourning, for one of Ronald's worries was he would die before Mark. He was spared that.

We had two holidays as well as the annual August trip to the Yorkshire Moors. In April we were able to fulfil one of Ronald's desires by sailing with the Norwegian Coastal Express through the Norwegian fiords up to the North Cape and much enjoyed the scenery, the visits to Cathedrals and museums and some of the history of Norway. We were intrigued by the use of skis, especially at the North Cape, where we saw a motor bike equipped with skis. The varied bright colours of the houses made us realise how bleak and dark the winter days must be. And of course, fish seemed to be loaded or unloaded at every port.

In September we drove to Holyhead and took the ferry to Dublin where we were met by John Marsden, a very particular friend of Ronald, who guided us out of the city towards his home. We stayed with him for two nights and then, headed for Westport, where John had arranged for us to stay at the Old Railway Inn. We were fed extremely well there and next day departed for Connemara. We visited Kyle Abbey and Clifden having passed through a gloomy valley where The Hungry had passed 150 years ago. I could scarcely believe the transformation that had taken place in Ireland since my first visit on a bicycle over 50 years ago, largely, I believe as a result of joining the Common Market. Not only was there no sign of any 'hungry' but hovels I had witnessed with chickens running out of them were either gone or in ruins and the roadsides were lined with impressive gates leading presumably to fine houses in ample grounds. The roads themselves were well kept, road markings and signs were clear – indeed they were a great improvement on many in England. And the petrol was cheaper. Next day we visited Argyll Island – a delightful place – and the following day returned to Newbridge. After another night with John we returned home.

Ronald had been a Trustee of St. Deiniol's Library, Hawarden, for many years and each year in July he continued to be invited to the Founders' Day Celebration there. 1998 was the anniversary of Gladstone's death and a very special celebration was arranged at which the Rt. Revd. John Habgood was to speak during the church service, followed by lunch in a huge marquee in the grounds. I wanted to allow at least an hour and a half for the journey but was assured by Ronald that it would take only 45 minutes. Nevertheless, we did allow an hour and a quarter, but as we neared Frodsham all traffic slowed and stopped; thus the church service was missed. Despite ignoring speed limits and travelling when the M56 had little traffic, I have never arrived at Hawarden in under 50 minutes, and it certainly takes an hour travelling within the speed limits. In 2000, Ronald was made a Fellow of St. Deiniol's – and we did get there on time.

Ronald was a great believer in fitness and each morning did a variety of exercises. These had probably kept him fit during a necessarily sedentary academic life – though he and Mary had been great walkers. It was one of my sorrows that now that I had a husband who was keen on walking, I could no longer do so. But increasing age brought its problems. His prostrate troubled him during the night but visits to Manchester Royal Infirmary (MRI) confirmed that it was not cancerous; his hearing became less acute and a he was given a hearing aid which he was quite unable to insert and I was given the job. He had most of his own teeth, unlike me, and I took him to the dentist quite frequently. He had had a duodenal ulcer 40 years before and from time to time took medication that had been prescribed then. But in November 1999, there was a period of 10 days when nothing relieved the pain; no, he would not go the doctor, he knew what to do – which was to live on bread and milk and be up half the night. I finally took him to the doctor; she prescribed some new tablets to be taken an hour before food. Medication had moved on in 40 years. From taking the first tablet he never had another twinge. Success. But there could be no success with his eyesight which increasingly troubled him and may have contributed to his irritability. With a magnifier he could only manage a line at a time; Social Services provided a telephone with large numbers and with two telephones we could record 26 numbers, but if an unfamiliar number was required I had to dial it. He continued to go the University on Monday mornings, but had relinquished his office there. He enjoyed having lunch with Gillian Shepherd who had been his secretary.

Christmas approached once more and with it the stupendous task of letter, card writing and envelope addressing. But this time Clive and I had address labels prepared which somewhat diminished the time required, though Ronald couldn't see well enough to fix the labels, let alone the stamps. We had Christmas Dinner with Ann and family and Clive who drove us there and back. We spent the 'Phoney Millennium' as Ronald called it, quietly at home, listening to the radio and watching TV. At midnight we toasted the New Year with a Swedish liqueur given to us by Normunds on one of his visits. I couldn't get the cork off the champagne.

The year 2000 didn't seem much different from its predecessor. It began with several deaths and more were to occur before its end. George Howson had died just after Christmas. He was a Jewish refugee who had built up a successful business here. His Jewish wife, only two years older than me, described the horror of life in Austria under the Nazis and how she had escaped. What had appalled her was that playmates at school could develop into Nazi thugs. There followed two deaths of Cathedral people and then Elfreda Johnson, one of our neighbours who had been ill for a long time and whose husband was worn out looking after her. She had been a Matron and he was a man of letters. After her death we found that each room in the house was filled with black bags – halfway up the walls – containing purchases she had made from Charity Shops. We gave a little birthday party for her husband's 80th birthday in March. He survived her by 18 months, and was found dead one morning by a neighbour, having had a heart attack. During that time each alternate Friday that I went to the Age Concern shop in Oldham we filled the car with as many bags as could be squeezed into it. Some of the goods were quite valuable and the shop undoubtedly benefited. George sorted out the goods and wrapped them up carefully – crockery, jewellery, pictures – so that by the time he died it was possible to see space in the house. Ronald gave the address at his funeral in October 2001. Cousin Marjorie in Easingwold died at the end of January aged 93 and I went to the funeral. She had had a tough life, but had remained kindly and hospitable to the end. Her daughter, Angela, was indeed well named, for she cared for her mother with great devotion and missed her greatly.

There were several pleasant and delightful treats. We attended the Peter Donohoe piano recitals at RMCM where he played all Beethoven's sonatas to my great joy and later we were exhilarated by a performance of *The Magic Flute* there which was as superb as it could be; Simon Walsh took us to see a ballet at the Lowry and in July we were able to go to see the *York Mystery Plays* staged in York Minster – a truly unforgettable experience. We also went to Congleton, where some of Ronald's friends took us to see *Cosi fan Tutti*, another wonderful evening out. People feasted during the interval.

There were other outings. In May we combined Birmingham and London; Michael Taylor invited us to Birmingham to hear Hans Küng lecture at Selly Oaks; I stayed the night with Paddy McWhirter, a delightful friend of Ronald whose husband had recently died. Next day I went on to London to have lunch with school friends while Ronald, having returned to Manchester, travelled to London for John Bowden's retirement party. We met at Euston and had a wonderful evening amongst Ronald's many friends, arriving back at 1.15am.

In June we flew to Paris where we stayed at a convent north of the city with other members of the Manchester/Toulouse Association. While there we were taken to Senlis and Chantilly and were suitably impressed with both. On the Saturday afternoon we were taken into Paris to see a most excellent mimed performance of *l'Ressurection* which was deeply moving. Unfortunately, during the second half, Ronald was aware of uncontrollable diarrhoea. On returning he went to bed, having stripped off the soiled garments which I washed and dried. Both diarrhoea and blood were uncontrollable all night and because we were in separate single rooms I kept going to him and changing pants – it was a good thing I had taken plenty of my own(!) – and giving him water to drink. Each time I washed the soiled ones and hung them to dry by the open window. By mid-day he was much better but decided to return home as soon as possible. He had intended to take me round Paris before returning home, but that idea was abandoned. I stripped the bed and was horrified to find blood even on the mattress cover. Cold water removed all the stains and the dirty linen was put in the receptacle supplied for it. We were relieved to get seats on a plane that day, and even more relieved to arrive home. Next day the doctor assured him that it was probably a 'one off' incident – which was a great relief.

He was well enough to go with me to Kathryn Shelley's wedding in Stone on the Friday of that week – a very enjoyable occasion in glorious weather where he was made a great fuss of. The Annual St. Anselm Hall Reunion took place next evening and Ronald had arranged for former members of the Association who had been in residence during his time as Warden to gather here for coffee on the lawn on the Sunday morning. The weather was almost unbearably hot on the Saturday, and the door into the lounge from the patio needed to be opened – which was quite an operation with several keys. Many years of dirt needed to be removed and in addition it occurred to me that coffee might be less attractive than ice cold drinks, so to Sainsbury I went for a variety of suitable beverages. The dinner at night was, as ever, a huge success and we returned home late. Next morning Ronald was taken to preside at a Eucharist there and brought back, followed at intervals by middle aged men and their wives who had all enjoyed a huge breakfast at the Hall. Simon Walsh helped enormously with the refreshments and all departed about 1pm except a Dutch gentleman whose plane did not go till 5pm. So I provided a light lunch and entertained him during that roasting afternoon. I was aware that my legs and back were protesting loudly but managed to survive until he went. I prepared a meal for Ronald and Clive, who came at 6pm and then I collapsed into bed. The pain was so acute that I really wondered if some serious damage had been done. Next morning the doctor came and arranged for me to have an X-Ray. It revealed nothing untoward at all, and after a few days normality was restored. A subsequent X-Ray revealed gross degenerative changes in the lumbar and lower thoracic spine.

We had our usual quota of guests during the year. Jen Shelley stayed for a few days in January, Alan Williams in February, Normunds in May, John Coleman in July, and Jeremy Gaskell in August. There were frequent visitors for coffee and lunches, including two ladies from Stoke-on Trent whom I had taught during the 1950s. They took a taxi from the bus station and after lunch I took them for a trip to Daisy Nook where we had tea. Ann, Ronald's daughter, had asked if we could get some plates for her and Sylvia Parsons (nee Birnie) and Christine (nee Jones), having pottery connections, offered to oblige. Considering all the entertaining that I was called upon to do, I was amazed at Ronald's comment after lunch that day. "They're not going till 6 o'clock." Secondary Modern Schools had been unlikely to produce academics.

One great event in September was the book launch in Liverpool of *The Middle Way*, a collection of Ronald's articles on Theology, Politics and Economics edited by John Elford and Ian Markham. We were driven there and back and prestigious speakers such as John Habgood (who had written the Preface) and Michael Taylor, vied with each other in their praise. Indeed, most people are lucky if they get such a eulogy at their funeral. It was all well deserved and most enjoyable.

We had our annual trip to Yorkshire, calling on Robert Waddington, Kitty Brett, Frank and Joan Flintoft and Bob Shaw at Sproxton. All made us very welcome. On the return journey we visited Wakefield and its Cathedral. I remembered a Communion book written by Walsham Howe, a C19 Bishop of Wakefield, given to my mother at her Confirmation and still in my possession. At the end of October we went by train to Torquay for a Saga Music Holiday, which was excellently presented by Fred Edwards who introduced us to much delightful music. There was also a trip to Dartmouth Naval College. One of the reasons why Ronald was so keen on this venue was that living in Torquay were Carol and Philip Kinder, who had been in residence at St. Anselm Hall when he was Warden. They were a delightful couple who took great pleasure in entertaining us. Sadly, Carol had terminal cancer and could scarcely eat. A year later, she succumbed after a most gallant fight and Philip mourned the loss of his beloved wife.

Unfortunately, the return journey was disrupted by floods. No trains were running from Torquay and even though we could have been taken by bus part of the way, there was no guarantee that trains would be running from any station prior to Birmingham. Into the breach stepped Fred Edwards who offered to drive us as far as Birmingham and a much relieved Ronald accepted gratefully. We were even more grateful when this generous man bypassed Birmingham and drove us all the way home, before going home himself to Chinley. I shall always remember his kindness.

It was as well that we had much to distract us during the year, for Ronald's sight continued to degenerate. He was forever trying to find the right light to read by and seldom succeeding. One day we visited a friend at Wilmslow who had a special computer that could enlarge letters by turning various knobs. It was a wonderful device but I knew who would be turning the knobs, for Ronald had very little tactile ability. He couldn't distinguish coins and would empty his purse on the table for me to select the exact amount required to pay for the papers, which I then wrapped up in cling film for the newsagent. He continued to find it impossible to insert his hearing aid. So I was increasingly obliged to read to him while he made notes for reviews. He would write out articles for me to type and print. I doubt if he could see what he was writing. He was unable to exert pressure on his pen and required pens that would write without pressure, otherwise blanks occurred – though he remembered the words he had written and so 'read' them.

In June, our good neighbours, John and Ann Sutcliffe, informed us that they would be moving to Winchcombe, for they would both be retired by the autumn. We both were sad to hear the news for although we might go days without seeing them, we knew they were always there and John, being a United Reformed Minister, had much in common with Ronald. We were often invited for drinks and nibbles and we reciprocated. The effect of this news on Ronald was devastating for it was as if the rock to which he clung was being removed. Knowing how easily I could fall, or in the event of any other disaster, he had always known that Sutcliffes would come to the rescue. His first reaction was to suggest that we move into sheltered accommodation where a warden would be available, and we did make enquiries. But even the thought of the upheaval that this would involve frightened me; there were book shelves containing at least 1,200 theological books, apart from bookcases full of devotional books and English literature; it was a four bedroomed house with a large study and lounge, not to mention the newly extended kitchen.

Sutcliffes moved in November and for the best part of a fortnight Ronald slept neither by day or night and could not bear me to be out of his sight. A visit to the doctor became inevitable; sleeping tablets were prescribed. These were only partially effective. He would sleep for one or two hours, then take tablet which worked for another two hours; so diazepam was prescribed. This did calm him down but from then on it was noticeable that he lacked the energy that had once characterised him. The dark nights of winter did not help. Gwilym Morgan died on 28th November after failing slowly for weeks. Ronald reluctantly agreed to give the address at the funeral. He made notes which he could not read so I decided to record his words and later made a transcript of this very moving tribute to Gwilym.

We spent Christmas Day with Clive at home, having somehow dispatched the usual avalanche of cards and letters. Just before dinner, Michael, Adele and Katie Taylor paid us a flying visit which cheered us up enormously and in the evening George Johnson came for an hour which, I think, pleased him very much.   We also had several visitors including Jack Keiser during the days following Christmas. All this made the time pass well for Ronald. I also finished reading to him God's Politicians, an account of the formidable characters who brought the Labour Party into being and sustained it. This was familiar ground to Ronald and he enjoyed reviewing the book.

Despite the anxiety and sleeplessness which continued during the winter months of 2001, there were plenty of outings and visitors to distract Ronald.   We went to see *Nutcracker* at the Opera House, *The Magistrate* at the Royal Exchange, *La Boheme* and *Cavaleria Rusticana* at the Palace and *Falstaff* at RNCM.   Jack Keiser came to read to him; we began to receive talking books from Calibre, and he would sit listening with his little recorder. Unfortunately it was not possible to get cassettes containing deep theological arguments but some novels he enjoyed. His daughter Ann subscribed to Talking Newspapers for him and these were acceptable and informative. We began to go to Henshaws in Trafford where we found people whose sight was much worse than his. He had a talking watch and Social services provided a talking clock as well as the telephone.

As the days grew longer we were able to discontinue the "diazepam", but an X ray in February revealed fluid on the lung and water tablets were prescribed. Meanwhile I succumbed to a viral infection of the eyes – they turned bright red and were painful. Nevertheless we were due to have a holiday in Cyprus at the end of March that had been booked with Oldham Age Concern a year ago. I had always been very happy with these holidays and it occurred to me that Ronald might enjoy visiting the magnificent Orthodox monasteries in Cyprus. But during the year his health had deteriorated; he really didn't want to go and hoped that the doctor would forbid it. He didn't. It was not a success for Ronald who nobly and stoically endured the ordeal. We were on the 5th floor of a very good hotel but Ronald either could not or would not operate the lift himself; the lighting was subdued so that he could see even less of what he was eating; we had only one excursion, to Nicosia, and found the

Cathedral closed during the lunch hour. Each Sunday we took a taxi to St. Barnabas Church in Limassol and enjoyed the service but unlike other places that we had visited, the priest did not know and had never heard of Ronald, which was a disappointment to him. Of course, unlike other places we had visited, no friend of Ronald was to be found in Cyprus. There was an excellent swimming pool at the hotel which I enjoyed every morning and afternoon but Ronald found that swimming was too much for him. Each lunchtime we enjoyed a simple meal at a nearby café; dinner and breakfast were at the hotel. It was not the most exciting of holidays and for the last two nights Ronald suffered from diarrhoea which involved much washing and drying of clothes. We were glad to get home.

Fortunately the spring and summer were to produce several pleasant occasions. There was a colloquium at the University and Ronald was delighted to renew his acquaintance with Alasdair MacIntyre; we enjoyed the Annual Reunion at St. Anselm Hall in June; Michael and Adele Taylor invited us to Birmingham for a weekend where we enjoyed a concert; we spent several days at Winchcombe as guests of the Sutcliffes who kindly invited to lunch each day people who were known to Ronald; there was the usual trip to Hawarden which this year included a dinner and overnight stay since Ronald had been made a Fellow; in July we had the usual pork trip to Caistor, staying the night with Rachel Ollard, which was most pleasurable; we had a visit from John Marsden who took us to lunch at Prestbury and we enjoyed David Pailin's retirement party. And, of course, in August we made our annual visit to Yorkshire. From Canada we had the pleasure of visits from Gretta Riddell-Dixon and John and Michael Coleman and we visited Stuart and Pam Dalziel in Calver. The event that gave Ronald the greatest pleasure was the celebration of the 60th anniversary of his priesting, on 21st September. St. Anselm Hall organised a luncheon party for close friends and relatives on this occasion and more celebrations occurred at the Cathedral the following Sunday.

The doctor arranged for him to see a consultant at MRI in August when he had a series of tests which revealed a constricted Aorta – Aorta Stenosis. From then on there were regular visits to the Anti-coagulant Clinic to receive Warfarin tablets. Another appointment was arranged in October when the consultant told us that the aorta valve was seriously damaged. An operation was possible, but in view of his age it would be a very risky procedure. Without it, he might survive for possibly two years. We were considerably subdued.

Throughout the year we knew that Normunds' dissertation was being concluded. We received frantic e-mails asking for the names of authors and publishers and finally, when all the references were completed, the book was published. Early in November we received two copies of The Persistence of Christian Realism: A Study of the Social Ethics of Ronald H. Preston. Normunds' disputation in Uppsala was to be on 30th November; Alan Suggate of Durham University was to interrogate him. In vain I offered to read the book to Ronald. He might require chapter 9 to be read but he knew what all the rest of the book was about. Then came a letter from Alan Suggate; each paragraph began, '*Normunds says . . . . but I think your position would be….*' So chapters 7,8 and 9 were required to be read.

Meanwhile we had received a warm invitation from Professor Carl-Henric Grenholm in Uppsala to be present at the disputation. We should depart for Stockholm on 29th November and stay till 2nd December. We booked a flight accordingly.

Sunday, 25th November had been Mary's birthday and Ronald always tried to have a family gathering on that day. We had lunch at Harry Ramsden's and all the family, apart from Ian, came here for games and tea. Ronald had lunch at the University next day and returned home furious that he had lost his French beret – it was still at the University. He insisted on going for a walk but returned shaking uncontrollably. We should have gone to a meeting at the Cathedral that evening, but I went alone having put a hot water bottle in bed for him and when I returned he was in bed. He had had to stop several times for lack of breath when going upstairs. Next morning he was most distressed. He had had a similar shaking fit during the night and had been incontinent. Having had a bath and clean pyjamas he settled in another bed and I called the doctor. Our usual doctor was away, but since it was a Group Practice another one called and having sounded him front and back announced that he was suffering from lack of blood sugar and should eat plenty of sweet things. I informed the doctor that we were due to fly to Sweden on the Thursday and the reply was that it would be perfectly all right to go. But that evening he was incontinent again and I decided to call an emergency doctor who advised hospital. We were there by ambulance soon after midnight. Tests were administered during the night; at 8.30 am a consultant informed us that he had had a heart attack and there was much fluid on the lungs which would have to be drained.

I dashed back home knowing that the Swedish trip would have to be cancelled and fortunately the Cathedral Secretary was able to do this for me. I gathered together toiletries etc. that would be necessary and phoned Ann who came over immediately. At 2.30 pm he was moved from a trolley to a ward and the Dean visited him. During the evening he was moved to a four bedded ward where he seemed very perky next morning when I visited him, the fluid having been drained. In the afternoon Canon Albert Radcliffe took me to visit him. Immediately Ronald asked him if he would do something for him. He had made notes on the William Temple book that I had read to him but had not been able to write the review. So, pen and paper in hand, Albert took down the words that flowed effortlessly from Ronald. There was a pause during which there was a discussion on Hegel and then the review was completed. Albert took it home, e-mailed it to me; I read it to Ronald next day; there was a small alteration which I phoned to Albert and the review was sent to the publisher.

The following day, after tests, we were told that he needed to have a valve replacement and a bypass and they were willing to operate.

Ronald willingly consented. But Saturday and Sunday are waiting days in hospitals and by the Monday he had a temperature which continued throughout Tuesday and Wednesday when they discovered that the infection was in the urine. John Elford took me to visit him on Wednesday evening and we were much relieved to be told by a smiling nurse that the infection was being cleared and the operation would go ahead. The three of us recited Evensong, Ronald said the prayers, John the Bible readings and I the intercessions. Next morning I came downstairs to find the answerphone on. Ronald had died at 5am that morning.

26: EPILOGUE (2003)

Ronald's death was merciful. One of his fears was that he might have a long degenerative illness, having seen how Gwilym's quality of life had deteriorated. Had he lived, had the valve replacement operation been totally successful, his inability to see to read and write would have continued to frustrate him, for his eyes had been the most important of his senses. There were excellent obituaries extolling his person and his work; all his theological books went to the library of Manchester University. The Scott Holland Lectures of 2002 were dedicated to him and in 2003 a Colloquium was held in his honour at the University. He was a great man, touched by genius.

Now I have time to reflect on my long life which began so inauspiciously in 1922. Gifted writers have devoted their efforts to the inter-war conditions in Britain between 1918 and 1939. There were the nouveau riche who were able to afford luxuries, but the vast majority of people had a struggle to make ends meet and within the working and lower middle classes were divisions – those who aspired through sheer hard work to 'better' themselves and those who were content to live from hand to mouth. I think that fear was a predominant emotion amongst the former group – fear that they would be 'looked down on', fear of illegitimate births, fear of what other people thought of them, fear of looking poor even though they were poor. Certainly my mother had all these fears. She must have wondered why it was that, as she once told a friend, 'Betty doesn't know what fear is'.

But I did have fears in my youth. I was terrified of failing them; of failing to live up to the high hopes they had of me; of them ceasing to love me because I had failed them. I believed that I had to earn love. And it had taken me a lifetime to discover that love can be unconditional. During my youth I thirsted for love which I believed would come from a devoted husband for whom, I think, I would have been prepared to be a door mat. Fortunately, no sensible man would want a door mat for a wife. I could not understand why the available men I met were inevitably unacceptable to me and why the ones I fell for either didn't want me or were married.

I realise now that I lived in cloud cuckoo land, for marriage for me has consisted of hard work and deferring to the wishes of the partner in an attempt to make him happy. Alas, one may give pleasure, but not necessarily happiness. There was seldom real companionship. The only time Ray revealed himself to me was when he was slightly drunk. His emotional life prior to marriage was never revealed and because of this I was unable to reveal mine. He was a closed book. Time after time it seemed that he wanted to defeat me, to create circumstances that I could not withstand. Yet he was essentially a kind man; he cooperated in the house; he disliked pretentiousness; he could be jovial. But he had no real friends, only acquaintances. Until our marriage his life had been in the army or the Military Police where one talked to men in bars and formed no lasting friendships. So as he moved from Birmingham to Newcastle, from Newcastle to Matlock, from Matlock to Cheadle Hulme and from there to Chadderton, he had no friends to leave. Yet for years I longed to return to Newcastle-under-Lyme where my friends were. Instead I travelled with him. His only real friend was the TV set which would occupy him every evening, irrespective of what was portrayed and towards the end of his life the afternoon was included as well. Conversation and companionship could not compete with television.

By contrast, Ronald had a great gift for friendship and retained his friends; some dated from LSE (London School of Economics) days; many from his time with the SCM (Student Christian Movement) – he called them his SCM Mafia. Many were clergy, some of whom he had taught; still more were the men who had been at St. Anselm Hall from 1948-63. No wonder his Christmas correspondence was so great. It is not unusual for me to meet clergy who had been his students and still revered him. Unlike Ray, he was able to reveal himself both physically and mentally. I think he would have been quite happy to wander about naked if convention had not made this impossible. He wore only the tops of pyjamas. This capacity for openness was a great delight to me and I was able to reveal myself.

Of course, I could never have hoped to be able to engage in serious theological arguments and discussions, nor did he expect me to. But we were on the same theological wavelength. We agreed on the subjects of women priests, homosexuality and common Christian values. But politically we were far apart and it was impossible to discuss politics or even read aloud to him any comments with a right-wing tinge. He dismissed Matthew Parris as a good journalist, but that was all he was. As a good Socialist he was all for taxation, but took steps to secure his estate against inheritance tax. He believed in equal opportunities in education but made sure that his elder daughter went to the best school he could find. At least there was conversation between us, and much humour. He used to love reciting limericks which I now regret I didn't write down.

He had a tendency towards anxiety which became more pronounced during the last year of his life. He'd certainly had enough to be anxious about, having had a son who had severe learning difficulties and one daughter with slight learning problems. And as macular degeneration developed he became increasingly frustrated and impatient with his inability to read. He was not a tactful man and I sometimes wondered if I ever did anything right, for criticism sprang easily to his lips. Yet on one occasion he remarked that after his death there would be a queue forming to marry me. Mercifully it hasn't happened. But he was totally unaware that he might be giving offence – indeed, his concentration was such that he could be unaware of my presence. Sometimes, cooking in the kitchen, I would be listening to a radio concert, blissfully bathed in classical music. He would appear and immediately begin a conversation, unaware of my preoccupation. I became adept with the 'off' and 'mute' buttons. But on one occasion he really was proud of me. I was asked to read "And death shall have no dominion" by Dylan Thomas at a service on 18th September 2001 in the Cathedral. It was an expression of solidarity with the American people after 9/11. Several people thanked me and asked if I were a professional. "No," said Ronald, "she is my wife."

It is strange to feel liberated from all desire after spending the major part of my life torn between the physical and emotional longing for married love which I believed would satisfy me physically, emotionally and intellectually, and the desire for liberation. These are not compatible. Had I married young I would have been much diminished by the constraints inevitable in what was then, a male dominated world, and misery, and perhaps divorce might well have followed. I would have found this harder to bear than remaining single until I was 40.

Fortunately, I have been well blessed with a son whose love and care for me are beyond the bounds of anything for which I could ever have hoped. Perfect trust exists between us. I was delighted when he set up his own home for I did not want him to feel entrapped by elderly parents as I was, and he is free to move wherever he wishes. He has taught me to use a computer, he supplied me with an excellent car and sees to it that it is well serviced. I can rely on him in all emergencies. Yet he lives his own independent life for which, also, I am thankful.

Life is uncertain. Disability and death can suddenly change a well-ordered life. I remember the four lines of W.S. Landor from when I first enjoyed the *Golden Treasury* and they come to mind now:

> I strove with none, for none was worth my strife;
>
> Nature I loved, and next to Nature, Art;
>
> I warmed both hands before the fire of life
>
> It sinks, and I am ready to depart.

But not just yet!

Betty Preston – 2003.

Printed in Poland
by Amazon Fulfillment
Poland Sp. z o.o., Wrocław

54672063R00170